ED
HING

CfE HIGHER

GRAPHIC COMMUNICATION

COURSE BOOK

Peter Linton and Scott Hunter

CONTENTS

GUIDE TO BOOK CONTENTS - SECTION LOCATOR

WHY GRAPHIC COMMUNICATION?

PROGRESSION

The graphic communication course offers progression to Advanced Higher and, potentially, on to courses at university or college.

CAREER PATHS

Career routes can take students into: Architecture, Construction, Engineering, Industrial Design, Graphic Design, CAD Technician, Digital Design, Game Design, Urban Planning, Animation, Publishing, Printing and many more.

CREATIVITY

Graphic Communication is a creative process. It involves understanding your target audience and creating graphics which strike a chord with that audience.

PROBLEM SOLVING

Solving complex graphical problems, engineering tasks or construction projects equips GC students with transferable skills and builds the confidence to tackle ever more complex challenges.

RELEVANCE

Students will learn in a creative environment using state of the art 3D CAD software and industry standard DTP software. The resources used in schools can be the same or similar to those found in industry and at university. The relevant nature of this experience can provide a practical bridge to a career or further study.

SKILLS

The diverse range of skills students acquire can lead them from a school experience to working in an industrial environment. Skills such as manual sketching and illustration or complex CAD techniques will add to the skills set of our young people and help prepare them for life beyond school.

HOW TO USE THIS BOOK

IF YOU ARE A TEACHER .....

You have several options:

USE THE BOOK AS THE BASIS FOR YOUR COURSE

You may need a few introductory drawings to kick off the drawing skills sections but this book will cover the course comfortably and, once you have regulated the time spent on each project, the course can be tackled in the allotted time. The book will help you organise learning tasks and projects. Exam style questions are slotted into most sections and it makes the process of homework and exam preparation integral to the project tasks. You can download the course planner online - see inside back cover for information.

SLOT PROJECTS INTO YOUR EXISTING COURSE

The projects can be used flexibly, for example the Mini assignment project suggests that students identify a product or design their own and deconstruct it graphically. You may approach the same project but using a product that you have identified. It can be tailored to your needs or preferences.

USE THE BOOK AS A STUDY AND REVISION RESOURCE TO PREPARE STUDENTS FOR THE EXAM

All the examinable areas are covered and there are dozens of EXAM PREP questions that will help ensure your students are prepared for the course exam.

USE THE A3 DRAWING WORKSHEETS TO SPEED UP THE LEARNING PROCESS

Worksheets are available to download from our website.

The worksheets come in graded sets; some are quick and easy to use while others are more challenging and time consuming.

You can select the best option for your class.

IF YOU ARE A STUDENT .....

PRACTICAL SKILLS

This book will help to develop and refine your practical skills from freehand sketching and illustration to 3D CAD and DTP techniques. It will guide you through skills that you can practice and apply to your course work assessments.

PROBLEM SOLVING

The emphasis on problem solving tasks that you will meet in your 3D CAD work, your drawing board work and your creative project work, will help develop your problem solving skills and prepare you for course assessments as well as your life beyond school.

The project tasks step you through projects that will challenge you and help ensure you learn and demonstrate the skills needed to pass the course.

KNOWLEDGE

It will help prepare you for your prelim and course exams by presenting the knowledge you need to learn in an interesting and largely graphical way. The knowledge sections are backed by dozens of EXAM PREP questions that will test your knowledge in each area of the course.

EXAM PREPARATIONS

There are dozens of EXAM PREP questions that will help prepare you for the course exams. You should start them early in the course. Build your knowledge gradually and optimise your learning. The answers can be downloaded from our website.

LEARNING APPROACHES .....

CREATIVITY

This book adopts a creative approach to the project tasks. Whenever possible students are encouraged to tackle projects using a design approach. However, this book can be used just as successfully by replacing the design task with a product or method identified by your teacher, so don't worry if the approach you take in class differs a little from the approach this book takes, the outcomes will be similar.

TECHNICAL EXPERTISE

This book teaches the understanding of technical graphics by learning the principles of projection and technical drawing on the drawing board before applying this knowledge onto the computer.

Don't worry if your teacher takes a purely CAD approach. Your teacher will have an alternative method of teaching drawing principles and you can still learn the process of drawing by reading through the worked examples in this book.

SUPPORT AND EXPEDIENCE

The drawing topics covered in the book are supported by A3 worksheets which can be downloaded from our website. These worksheets are mostly 'graded' from 'quick and straight forward' to 'more challenging and complex'. The ones you tackle will depend on your teacher. However, you can download them yourself and work through the tasks at whatever level of challenge you are comfortable with.

A GUIDE TO DRAWING STANDARDS SECTIONS & ASSEMBLIES

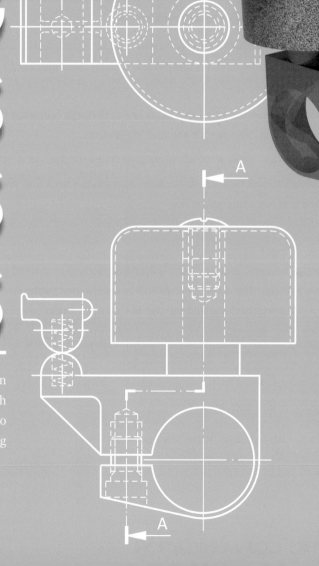

Drawing standards and conventions represent an international language that covers all forms of engineering and construction. In the UK standards have been described in a reference guide called BS: 8888. The abbreviation, BS, means British Standards. This text book summarises most of the commonly used standards, conventions and symbols.

Drawing standards are described in more detail in the schools and colleges version of BS8888 which is a reference document. You should refer to BS8888 when you are creating or interpreting drawings and you require clarification.

DRAWING STANDARDS & CONVENTIONS

Introduction to Drawing Standards

These standards can be applied to any drawing that is produced in Britain and can be understood anywhere in the world.

The advantages gained by using British drawing standards are important because:

- Standards used in the drawings are **consistent across Britain** and, increasingly, around the globe. They are **universally understood.**

- The common drawing symbols and conventions have been designed so that drawing features such as screw threads etc, is **simplified,** making them **quicker to draw** and **easier to understand.**

- Applying world-wide drawing standards helps **break through language barriers**; important in supporting cross border engineering projects.

- Drawing standards and conventions are **built into 3D CAD software** so that the drawings produced always conform to the same standards. Check that your software is set to BS8888 and not a foreign version.

Scales

Scaling is used in drawings because, at some point, a drawing needs to be printed on paper or viewed in its entirety on a screen. The choice of scale will be determined by the size of the object, the clarity of the detail required and and the size of the paper it is to be printed on.

A drawing scale is normally chosen from one of the following standard options:

Full size drawings: 1:1.

Enlargement scales: 2:1, 5:1, 10:1, 20:1, 50:1.

Reduction scales: 1:2, 1:5, 1:10, 1:20, 1:50, 1:100, 1: 500, 1:1000

The scale of a drawing should be recorded in the title block as: ORIGINAL SCALE 1:5

Abbreviations and symbols

Abbreviations are used extensively in production drawings often to clarify important details and also to save space. You will use them in this book and in your course assignment and you may also come across them in the course exam.

AC, AF	Across corners, Across flats		MAX	Maximum
ASSY	Assembly		MIN	Minimum
BS	British (Drawing) Standards		mm	Millimetres
CBORE	Counter bore		MTL	Material
CHAM	Chamfer		No.	Number
℄	Centre line		NTS	Not to scale
CRS	Centres		O/D	Outside diameter
CSK	Countersunk		PCD	Pitch circle diameter
CYL	Cylindrical		R	Radius
45°	Degree symbol		RD HD	Round headed screw
DIA	Diameter (in a note)		RH	Right Hand
Ø	Diameter symbol		SCR	Screw
DRG No	Drawing Number		SFACE	Spotface
EQUI SP	Equally spaced		SPH	Spherical
EXT	External		SR	Spherical radius
FIG	Figure		SØ	Spherical diameter
HEX	Hexagon		SQ	Square (in a note)
I/D	Inside diameter		▢	Square
INT	Internal		STD	Standard
LH	Left hand		⊽	Surface finish required
LG	Long		THD	Screw thread
M	Metric screw thread		THK	Thick (thickness)

DRAWING STANDARDS & CONVENTIONS

Note for teachers and students

Understanding the drawing standards and conventions used in engineering production drawings is an important feature of this course. You will need to apply these standards in your project work and you will be expected to demonstrate your understanding of them in the course exam.

Drawing Standards BS8888: This section summarises most of the commonly used standards, conventions and symbols. Drawing standards are described in more detail in the schools and colleges version of BS8888 which is a reference document. You should refer to BS8888 when you are creating or interpreting drawings and you require clarification.

Drawing tasks: The drawing tasks are supported by worksheets that can be downloaded from our website. Most drawing worksheets come in 2 or 3 levels of complexity, e.g. "worksheet section 1" comes in three levels 1a, 1b & 1c.
Drawing 1a requires the full drawing to be completed from scratch.
Drawing 1b provides a part-completed drawing as a starting point.
Drawing 1c requires only that cross-hatching is added to the sectional drawing. You don't need to complete all of the drawings in this book, but they will help develop your understanding and visualisation skills and the worksheets can save you time. Your teacher will advise you which ones to tackle.

Exam prep: These ask the type of questions you will face in the course exam. These are short written or sketched tasks that can be done quickly and are ideal exam preparations and revision tasks.

CAD approach: The same drawing tasks can be carried out using CAD. Each component can be created and the assembly built so that production drawings can be produced from the assembly. Your teacher will advise whether or not you should adopt this method.

Drawings of a bicycle bell are used here to explain drawing standards. It is important to understand how the components of the bell assemble and how they are held together to make a functioning product. Study the component drawings and the assembly drawings before you work through this section. There are a number of tasks to carry out. Some are drawing tasks while others require written answers.

Orthographic projection

Orthographic views are set out using the **third-angle projection** layout shown below. The third angle projection symbol should always accompany orthographic drawings in order to explain or confirm the layout.

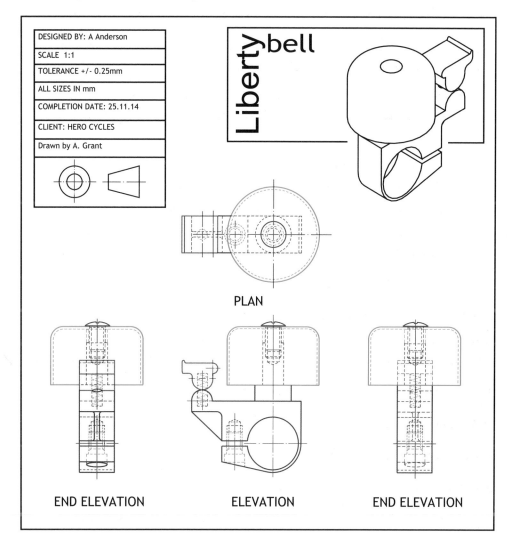

LINE TYPES

You will be familiar with many of the common line types from the N5 course. Get to know them again, they form part of the drawing standard that you will apply in your own drawings.

Continuous thick line

Application: Visible outlines and edges.

Dashed line

Application: Hidden edges and outlines.

Chain line thin with thick ends and changes of direction.

Application: Cutting planes (section lines).

Continuous thin irregular line

Application: Limits of partial or interrupted views and sections.

Long dash - dot chain line thin

Application: Centre lines, lines of centres of symmetry, pitch circles.

Continuous thin line with zig-zags

Application: **break lines** to show limits of partial or interrupted views and sections on non-cylindrical sections. It saves space by shortening long items.

Continuous thin line

Application: Dimension, projection and leader lines, cross-hatching, short centre lines, outlines of revolved sections

Double dashed chain line thin

Application: Outlines of extreme positions of moving parts or bend or fold lines on flat surface developments.

Flat Face

Application: To indicate a flat face has been created on a cylindrical bar.

Solid shaft

Hollow shaft

Continuous thin line with curves

Application: **Break lines** to show limits of partial or interrupted views and sections. Saves space by shortening long items.

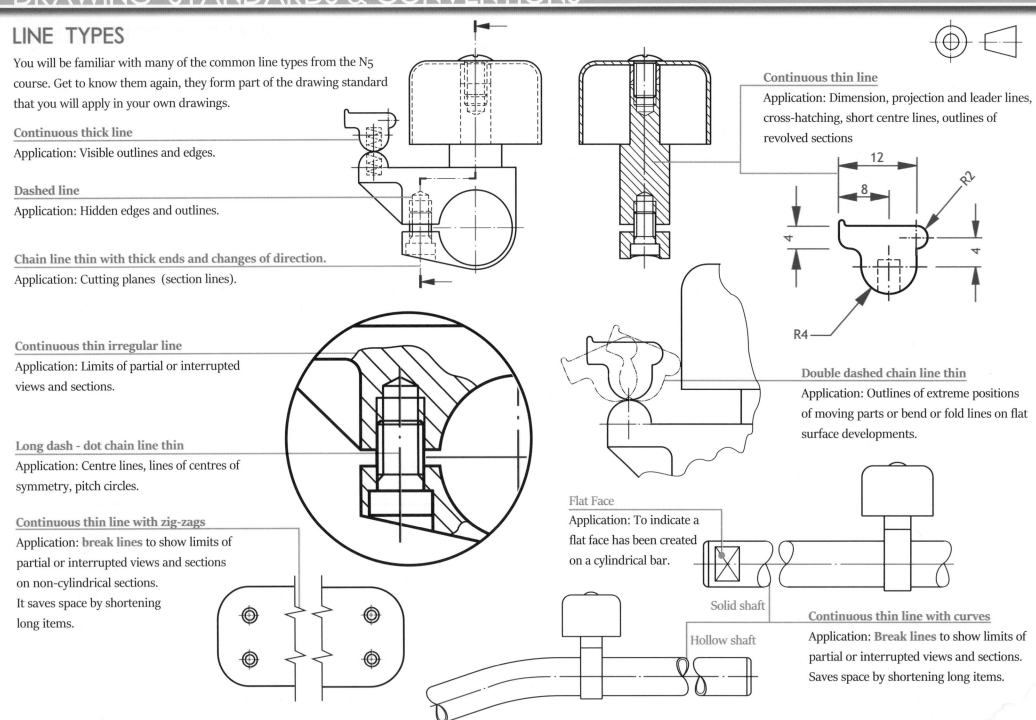

LINE TYPES & SCREW THREADS

Line types continued

Lines of symmetry and pitch circles can crop up in your course work.

A line of symmetry is a space saving option when symmetrical objects are drawn. The axis is a centre line which is extended well beyond the object. Two short parallel lines are added at each end. The line of symmetry indicates that the shape is mirrored across the axis.

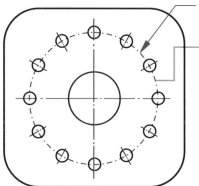

PCD 60

A pitch circle is used when a circular array of repeated features is required. The diameter of the pitch circle is know as the **Pitch Circle Diameter** or **PCD.**

Drawing repetitive features can be simplified by showing a single feature and the locations of the additional features.

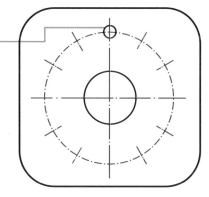

This applies to **repeated features** both circular and linear as is the case here.

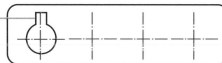

Screw threads

Screw threads are shown as conventions that have been simplified by using double lines instead of a helical thread. These are common features in production drawings used to show both internal and external threads. Screws and bolts are common standard components and it is likely that you will incorporate them into your course work and find them in questions in the exam paper.

External screw thread

A thread on the outside of a screw or bolt.

Broken inner circle   Screw thread

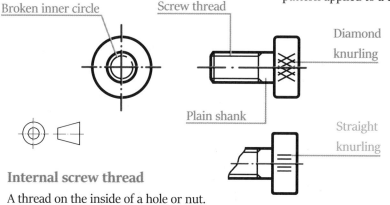

Plain shank

Knurling

These symbols represent a textured pattern applied to a cylindrical component

Diamond knurling

Straight knurling

Internal screw thread

A thread on the inside of a hole or nut.

Broken outer line

Internal and external screw threads assembled.

Internal thread

Bottom clearance in the blind hole

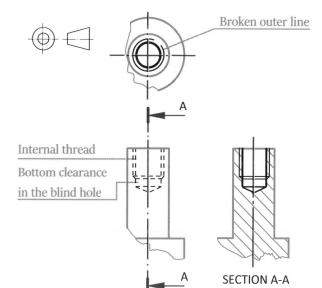

A

A

SECTION A-A

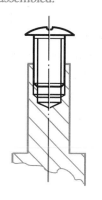

DIMENSIONING

Production drawings are created so that a products can be manufactured. Adding dimensions to these drawings gives the manufacturer the information needed to make the components that can be assembled into a product.

Generally, it is component drawings that are dimensioned, not assembly drawings.
Dimensions are applied to a drawing using British Drawing Standards and Conventions as described in BS 8888.

Linear Dimensioning

Dimensioning lengths, breadths and heights can take up a great deal of space on a drawing. They can also clutter and impede clarity on a drawing.
It is important to set out linear dimensions properly.

Basics

Learn to apply the basic dimensioning standards shown here. A range of methods are shown but the methods used should be consistent in any one drawing.

Extension lines have a gap at the drawing and extend past the arrow head.

Dimension lines have slim, closed arrow heads.

Dimensions are read from the bottom and the right hand side. Some **R** and **Ø** dimensions excepted.

Dimensions can be placed inside or outside the leader lines depending on the space available.

Centre lines are suitable datum points from which dimensions can be shown.

Dimensions should be placed **outside** the drawing whenever possible.

The radius (R) is always used to dimension an arc (not a full circle).

Annotations can provide clarity when a conventional dimension cannot.

Diameter Ø, is used to dimension a full circle.

Leader line

Parallel dimensioning
Each dimension starts from the same datum point or edge making it less likely to accumulate dimensioning errors during manufacture but it does take up a great deal of space.

Chain dimensioning
Dimensions run one after the other and in line. This method can lead to accumulated dimensioning errors during manufacture.
It takes up less space than parallel dimensioning.

Combined dimensioning
Uses both parallel and chain dimensioning. Useful when space is limited or when the drawing is complex.

Running dimensions
Similar to parallel dimensioning. All sizes are taken from the same origin (datum point). Uses less space on the drawing.

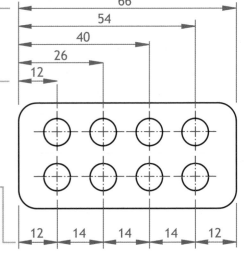

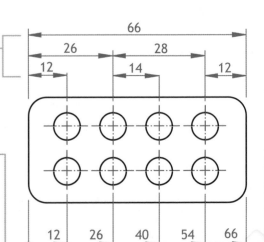

DIMENSIONING & DETAILING ORTHOGRAPHIC COMPONENT DRAWINGS

When and what to dimension

The dimensions that you apply in your coursework drawings will be applied to component drawings and generally to more than one orthographic view. How you set out the dimensions is important. They need to be clear, uncluttered and conform to British drawing standards.

Principles of Dimensioning

- Units should not be shown on the dimensions. The millimetre unit, mm, is recorded in the title block and applies to all dimensions with the exception of angles.

- The degree symbol is applied to angles.

- A drawing should not be over-dimensioned; only show each dimension once.

- Clarity is important; set out the dimensions so they are neat and clear.

- Don't cross extension lines over other extension lines unless it is unavoidable.

Enlarged partial views improve clarity and enable dimensioning of small features.

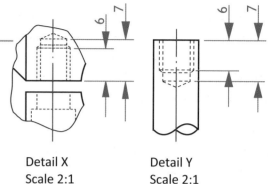

Detail X
Scale 2:1

Detail Y
Scale 2:1

Ø4   M6   Ø14   Ø8

14

WEB 2

M6

PLAN

Hidden detail should be included where it aids understanding without impeding clarity.

42,5

27,5   11

Numbers should be placed above, and centred, on the dimension line.

Longest dimensions are placed outside shorter dimensions.

Ø4 x 6 DEEP

R4

4

15

44°

38

16   22

A **title block** should include:
Your name, date, scale, units used, tolerance applied, drawing number and 3rd angle projection symbol.

3

2

6

R11

15

20

R10

Ø6 C'BORE Ø8

Angles are dimensioned so that the number can be read from the right or bottom of the drawing.

END ELEVATION

ELEVATION

A **view title** should be added under each view.

Use a **note** to describe features succinctly.

Drawn by: J Anderson
Date: 11.12.16
Scale: 1 : 1
All Sizes in mm
Tolerance: +/- 0.25
Drawing 1 of 6

DIMENSIONING ORTHOGRAPHIC COMPONENT DRAWINGS

Dimensioning circles and cylinders

There are several ways to apply dimensions to a feature.

Choose the method that is clearest and neatest. Options for dimensioning circles, holes and cylindrical features are shown.

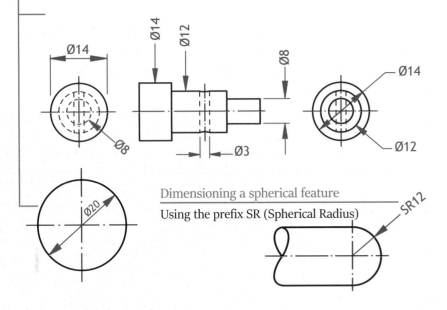

Dimensioning a spherical feature

Using the prefix SR (Spherical Radius)

SR12

Dimensioning radii

There are also several ways to dimension a radius. It is not always feasible to show the centre of a radius. Options are shown below.

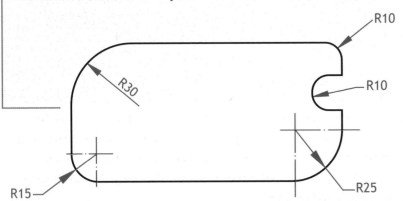

R10
R30
R10
R15
R25

Dimensioning special features

Special features such as screw threads, spheres, counter bores, countersunk holes, chamfers and arrayed holes require different treatment. A note is often used to clarify the dimension.

Dimensioning holes

Arrays of holes can be dimensioned as a group.

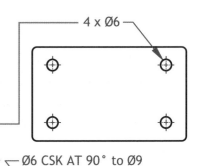

4 x Ø6

Ø6 CSK AT 90° to Ø9

Ø12 x 20 deep

Countersunk holes

CSK is the abbreviation for countersunk.

The depth of a blind hole may be shown as a note on the dimension. Countersinks are used to recess screw heads below or flush with a surface.

Chamfer

The length and angle of the chamfer should be shown in the note. Notice the use of a comma to separate the whole number from the decimal point. Using a decimal point is also acceptable.

2,5 x 45°

Dimensioning screw threads

A metric thread is denoted by the symbol M.

The number represents the external diameter of the thread.

External threads

Dimensioning options: The size and length of the thread should be shown. The second option combines both.

10   M6

M6 x 10

Internal threads

Dimensioning options.

M6 x 12 deep

M6 x 8 deep

M6

M6 x 12 deep

12

ASSEMBLIES, SECTIONS AND EXPLODED VIEWS

Assembly Drawings

Products that have more than one component need assembled, either by the assembly line in the factory or by the consumer at home. In both cases drawings that explain how the product is assembled are produced.

Assembly drawings fall into three categories:

<u>Assembly drawings</u>

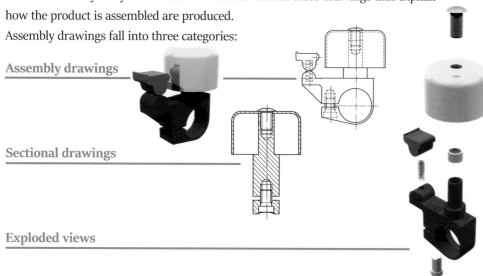

<u>Sectional drawings</u>

<u>Exploded views</u>

Assemblies

Assembly drawings give information to manufacturers about product assembly. They can also provide consumers with information about home assembly and are often used in instruction brochures and leaflets. Rendered assemblies are also used in promotional publications.

Sections

Slicing a product to show the inside of the assembly is another way to show how the components interact. Sectional views are generally used by manufacturers to describe how components interact together in an assembly. Sectional views can be technical in nature and are normally too complex for use in consumer instruction brochures.

Exploded views

Separating each component in an assembly along an axis so that it describes how the parts fit together is an important way to explain how a product assembles. Exploded views are used in manufacturing but also in promotional, instructional and assembly publications to aid home assembly and support the consumer.

Drawing assemblies and sections

You will draw assemblies and sections in your course assignment where they will gain you marks but you will also have to interpret complex assemblies and sections and answer questions about them in the course exam.

The best way to learn about assemblies and sections is to draw them on paper. This process will help you understand how these drawings are put together and will prepare you for questions in the final exam. An important part of your learning involves working out how components fit together to make a product.

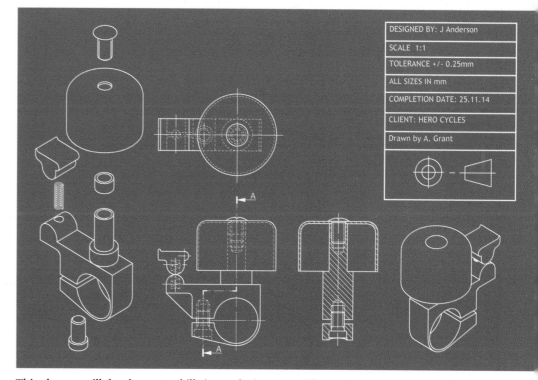

This chapter will develop your skills in producing assemblies and sections and it will help prepare you for the course exam paper. Drawing standards and conventions are covered in depth in the exam paper and you need to be ready to interpret technical drawings and answer questions about them. Visualisation is another examinable skill and this section will help develop your visual interpretation skills.

THROUGH SECTIONS AND PARTIAL VIEWS

Features of a sectional view

Learn the drawing conventions in this section, you will need this information in your exam.

Through section

A section that cuts straight through an object without changing direction is known as a **through section.**

Arrows indicate the direction the section is viewed from.

A **cutting plane** must be shown on an adjacent view. It is given letters to distinguish it from other cutting planes.

Cross-hatching of adjacent parts should change direction in order to distinguish each component clearly.

A

A

PLAN

X

Web

The function of a web is to increase the strength of the component. When a web is sectioned along its axis (along its length) it is not cross-hatched.

SECTION A-A

Features such as **spindles, axles, shafts, screws, nuts, bolts** and **fixings** should not be sectioned.

Cross-hatching
Hatching should always be at a **45°** angle.

Hidden detail is never shown on a sectional view.

The view title is labelled with letters corresponding to the cutting plane.

Features of partial views

A partial view shows a part of a component or assembly. The part view is generally enlarged to show a feature with greater clarity. An enlarged partial view is useful when a small detail needs to be shown more clearly. It normally involves scaling up a small part of a full view by 2:1, 4:1 or 5:1. The enlarged partial view is removed from the full view.

The new scale of the enlarged partial view must be shown.

In both examples shown, the enlarged partial views of the section reveal small details clearly.

DETAIL X SCALE 2:1

Cross-hatching screw threads
When there is no screw in the hole the cross-hatching finishes on the **inside of the screw thread.**
When there is a screw in the hole the cross-hatching stops at the **outside of the screw thread.**

Titles
Note the different ways to title an enlarged partial view.

Scale
The scale of the enlarged view should always be shown.

ENLARGED VIEW SCALE 2:1

STEPPED SECTION AND PART SECTION

STEPPED SECTION - SPECIAL FEATURES

Features of a Stepped Section

A stepped section is used when internal features cannot all be revealed by a through section.

In these bell drawings the holes with screw threads are staggered (in different planes or positions). The technician stepped the cutting plane so that it passes through the centres of both holes.

Stepped cutting plane

Where the cutting plane changes direction **thick lines** are used.

Stepped section

The change of direction on the stepped section is **not shown** as a line. The cross-hatching simply continues.

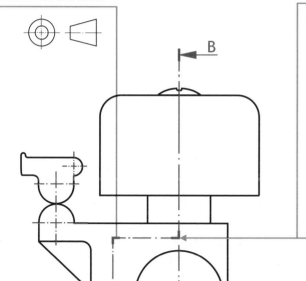

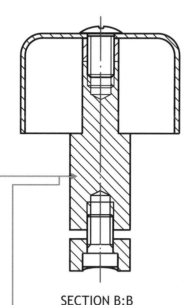

SECTION B:B

Stepped section - Cross-hatching

The cross-hatching should not change direction where the step occurs.

Draw the stepped section shown on this page. Download worksheet 'Stepped section 1' from our website to support you with this task.

EXAM PREP

PART SECTION - SPECIAL FEATURES

Features of a Part Section

A **part section** is also called a **partial section** or a **local section.**

When an internal detail needs to be shown in a small part of an assembly a **part section** is used. This eliminates the need to show a full section. A part section focuses on features that show important information. In this example, the clamping screw and the counter bore are revealed by the part section.

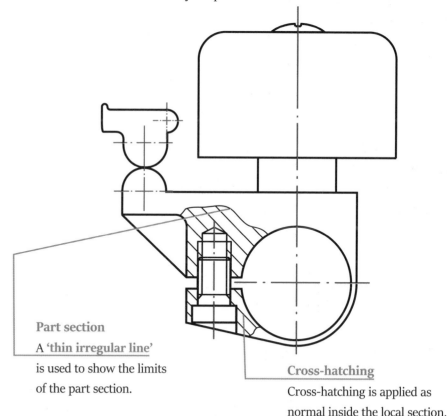

Part section

A **'thin irregular line'** is used to show the limits of the part section.

Cross-hatching

Cross-hatching is applied as normal inside the local section.

Worksheet alert

You can download the worksheets online to support you with this task - see inside back cover for more information and website details.

HIGHER GRAPHIC COMMUNICATION

HALF SECTION AND EXPLODED VIEW

Half-section - Special features

A half-section is used when there is a need to show both the inside and the outside of an assembly or component.

This type of section normally removes one quarter of the assembly or component but it is called a half-section because the sectional view shows half the external and half the internal view. It requires a **stepped cutting plane**. A worked example of this drawing is shown on page 23 and an A3 worksheet is available online.

Stepped cutting plane

The cutting plane slices through the centre of the object along a line of symmetry turning to create a right-angled step.

When an **edge** is created by the cutting-plane it is not shown on the half-section. Instead, a centre line is used.

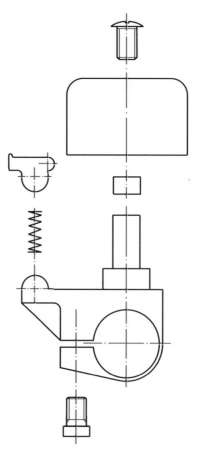

E

This quarter is removed.

PLAN

E

SECTION E - E

Exploded views- Special features

An assembly can be exploded orthographically or pictorially. Exploded views are important when describing how a product is put together. It can suggest the order in which components are to be assembled.
A worked example is shown on page 22 and an A3 worksheet is available online.

Positioning

The components should be shown exploded along an axis and, preferably, with clear space between components.

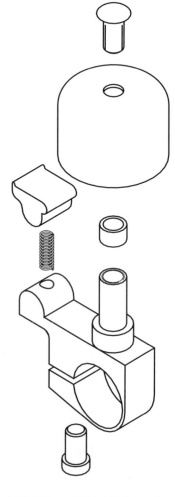

ORTHOGRAPHIC EXPLODED VIEW

PICTORIAL EXPLODED VIEW

Features of a revolved section

The handle bar is hollow and one way of showing this is by revolving a cross-section within the handle bar. A revolved section saves space on the drawing.

Features of a removed section

Another way to show a cross-section is by adding a cutting plane and sliding the sectional view away from the handlebar.

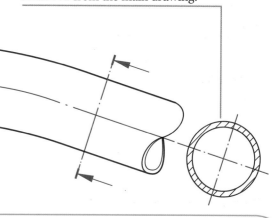

Revolved section

No cutting plane is used. A centre line is added and the section is rotated (revolved) around the axis. It shows a cross-section at this point in the component. It also saves space and helps declutter the drawing.

Removed section

A removed section performs the same task as the revolved section but this time a cutting plane is added and the section is **revolved** and then **removed** from the main drawing.

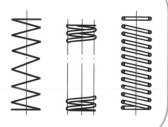
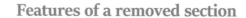

Standard Components

Nuts, bolts and screws and other fixings are used in most products.

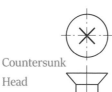

Hexagon Head Screw

Cylinder Head Screw

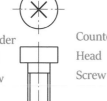

Countersunk Head Screw

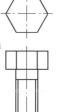

Countersunk Wood Screw

Hexagonal Nut

Springs

Springs are common standard components used in products.

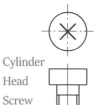

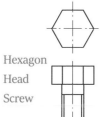

ASSEMBLIES, SECTIONS AND EXPLODED VIEWS - WORKED EXAMPLES AND EXAM PREP

Pictorial assemblies and component drawings of a bell for a bicycle are shown on this page and the next. You task is to draw, to a scale of 2:1, a sectional elevation 'A-A' of the assembled bicycle bell. The worked example, three pages over, will take you through the process but before you start you should read through the advice below and study the next two pages.

Before you begin it is important to have a method. Following these key points will enable you to draw or interpret any sectioned assembly.

1. Study the detail drawings carefully. This includes exploded or pictorial assembly views. These views give the best information about how an assembly should be put together.

2. Look for dimensioning clues about how components fit together.
    If there is a Ø6mm hole in a component, work out what fits inside the hole?
    Look for a Ø6mm screw, bolt, axle or spindle to fit inside it.

3. Start by drawing the main component first, then add a second component and a third etc. It's like assembling plastic building bricks one at a time.

4. Assemble the entire view before you section it.

5. Check each feature that the cutting plane slices through.

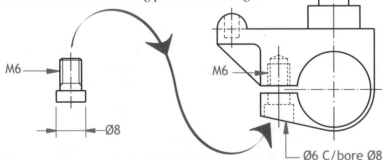

M6

Ø8

M6

Ø6 C/bore Ø8

The hole in the bottom of the handle bar clamp has three important pieces of information; the diameter is 6mm, the internal thread is M6 and the size of the counter bore is Ø8

The only screw thread that matches all three conditions is the clamping screw with an M6 thread and a Ø8 head. It is logical that these two components assemble together. The exploded view confirms this.

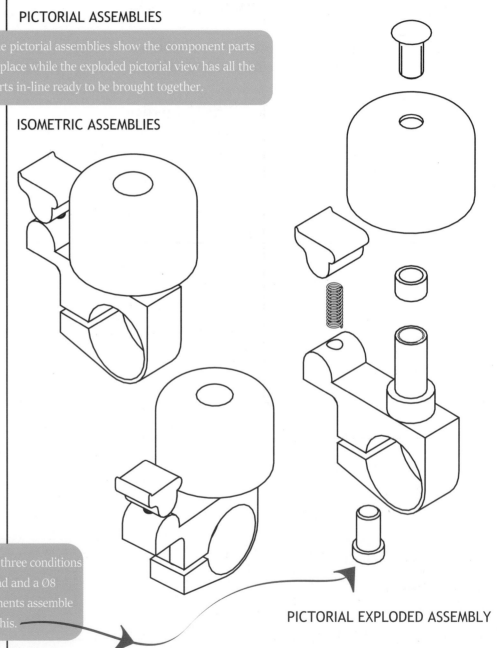

PICTORIAL ASSEMBLIES

The pictorial assemblies show the component parts in place while the exploded pictorial view has all the parts in-line ready to be brought together.

ISOMETRIC ASSEMBLIES

PICTORIAL EXPLODED ASSEMBLY

BICYCLE BELL - COMPONENT DRAWINGS

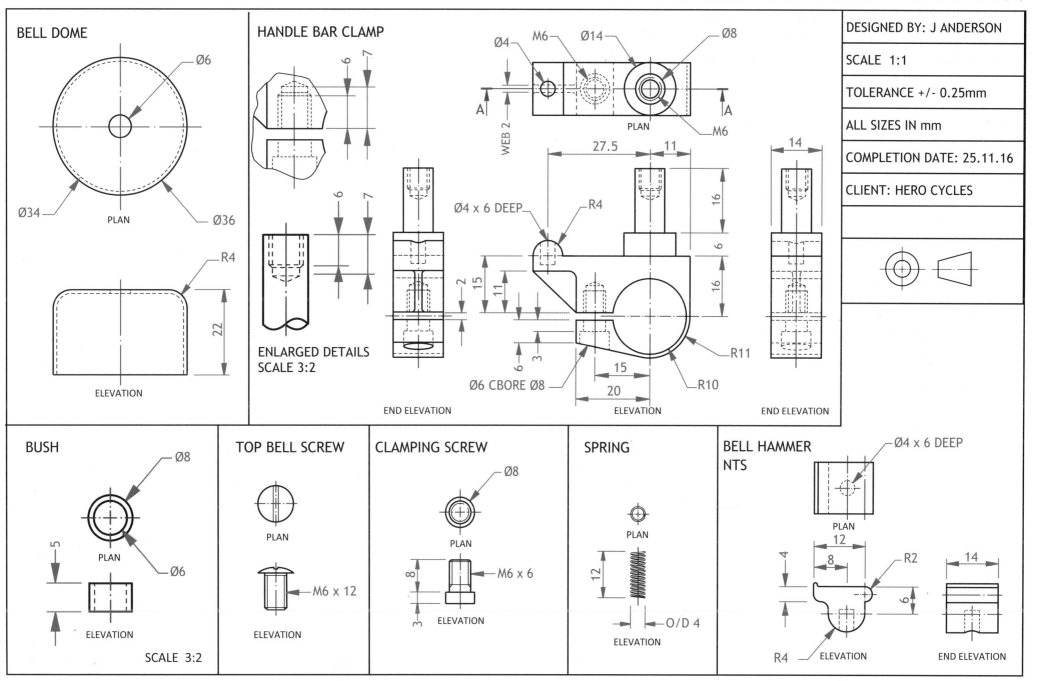

BELL DOME

Ø6
Ø34
Ø36
PLAN
R4
22
ELEVATION

HANDLE BAR CLAMP

6 7
6 7
ENLARGED DETAILS
SCALE 3:2

Ø4 M6 Ø14 Ø8
WEB 2
A A
PLAN
M6

27.5 11
16
6
16
14

Ø4 x 6 DEEP R4
15
11
2
6 3
Ø6 CBORE Ø8
15
20
R11
R10

END ELEVATION ELEVATION END ELEVATION

| DESIGNED BY: J ANDERSON |
| SCALE 1:1 |
| TOLERANCE +/- 0.25mm |
| ALL SIZES IN mm |
| COMPLETION DATE: 25.11.16 |
| CLIENT: HERO CYCLES |

BUSH

Ø8
5
PLAN
Ø6
ELEVATION
SCALE 3:2

TOP BELL SCREW

PLAN
M6 x 12
ELEVATION

CLAMPING SCREW

Ø8
PLAN
8
M6 x 6
3
ELEVATION

SPRING

PLAN
12
O/D 4
ELEVATION

BELL HAMMER NTS

Ø4 x 6 DEEP
PLAN
12
4 8 R2
6
14
R4 ELEVATION END ELEVATION

ASSEMBLIES - USING OUR WORKED EXAMPLES

You can learn how assemblies are built by using CAD software or by drawing them on paper with drawing instruments. The commonest method is to use both approaches. This section provides worked examples of each type of drawing. A3 worksheets are available to support and speed up your drawing. The worksheets are also differentiated to give students the choice of either creating a drawing from scratch or tackling it using a partially completed worksheet. Some worksheets only require that cross-hatching and cutting planes are added, thus saving time while still providing ideal exam revision.

There are two main methods of drawing the sectional elevation A-A, the **construction method** and the **projection method.**

Construction method

The construction method involves building the view up from dimensions and features.

In this method you build the drawing from scratch using a grid. Sizes are taken from the component drawings and a grid is drawn and then the features and details are added.

Advantages of the construction method

It can be easier to tackle when the assembly is small or complex.

It is essential when you are drawing the assembly to a scale. In this case the scale is 2:1, twice actual size. However, on our worksheet we have provided the given views at twice actual size.

Either method can be used.

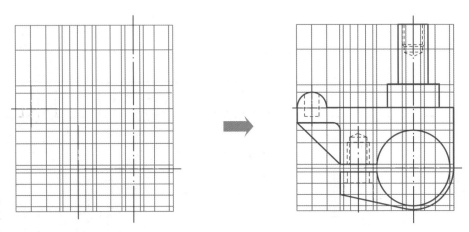

The construction method

In this method centre lines are positioned first and the grid is put together around them using sizes from the component drawings. Each component is built up in this way using a grid construction.

Projection method

This method enables you to project the section A-A from two other views. To use this method you can download the A3 worksheet from our website.

Advantages of projection

All the sizes you need are already in place on the other two views.

Your task is to identify each component on the given views and project them onto the sectional elevation. It can be quick and accurate but in some cases the detail is very small and it can be difficult to separate each component part in the given views. The handle bar clamp has been projected downward from the plan and across from the end elevation. Features are then picked out from the grid and drawn in before the next component is projected etc.

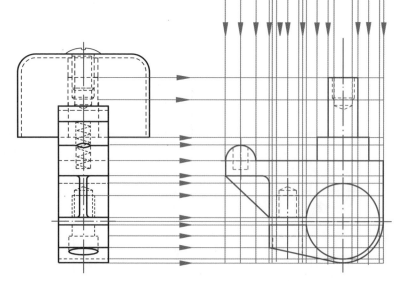

The projection method

The worked example on the next page uses the projection method and you can follow this example as a guide whichever method you choose when you complete the drawing.

EXAM PREP - SECTIONED ASSY

Draw, to a scale of 2:1, a sectional elevation A-A of the assembled bicycle bell.

SECTIONAL VIEW - WORKED EXAMPLE

Worksheet alert

You can download the worksheets online to support you with this task - see inside back cover for more information and website details.

1. Project the edges

- Project the handlebar clamp downwards from the plan and across from the end elevation
- Draw centre lines in first; this will enable you to work from the centre lines to build up the crate

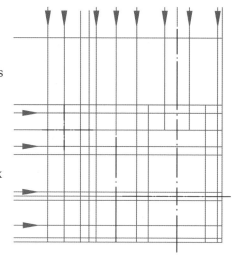

2. Draw the main component

- Set out features carefully; check the dimensioned component drawings
- Draw the screw threads in the holes
- Keep lines light at this stage

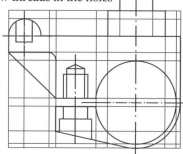

3. Assemble the second component

- Draw the bush in position. Add other components.
- Draw the spring and clamping screw in position
- Neither the screw or the spring will be sectioned

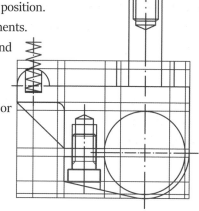

4. Draw the bell dome, hammer and top screw

- If you are using a worksheet the hammer is given

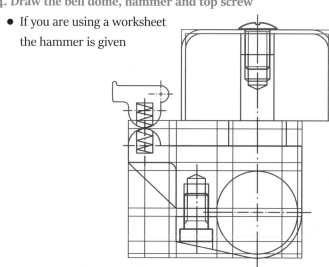

5. Firm-in the drawing.

- Take care to work out which parts are cut and which are not

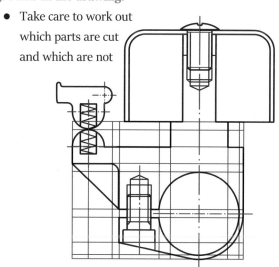

6. Cross-hatch the cut surfaces at 45°

- Change the direction of hatching on adjacent parts
- Do not show hidden detail
- Do not cross-hatch the web
- Note that the spring, bell post, clamping screw and top screw have not been cross hatched

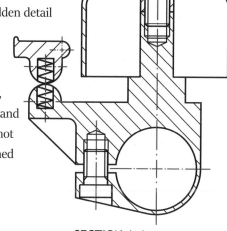

SECTION A-A

HIGHER GRAPHIC COMMUNICATION

EXPLODED VIEW - WORKED EXAMPLE

EXAM PREP - EXPLODED ASSY

Draw, to a scale of 2:1, an orthographic exploded view of the bell.

Worksheet alert

You can download the worksheets online to support you with this task - see inside back cover for more information and website details.

Exploded views - Special features

Assemblies can be exploded as a pictorial view or an orthographic view. The worked example below shows how to complete an orthographic exploded view of the bell assembly.

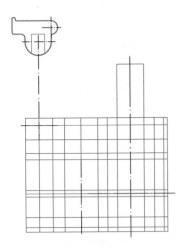

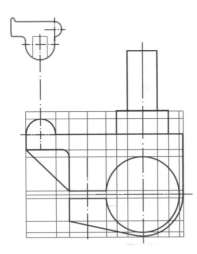

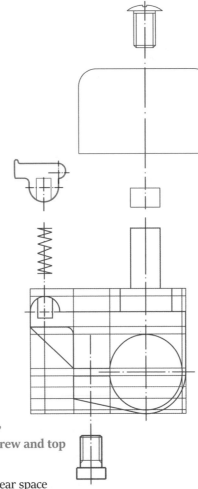

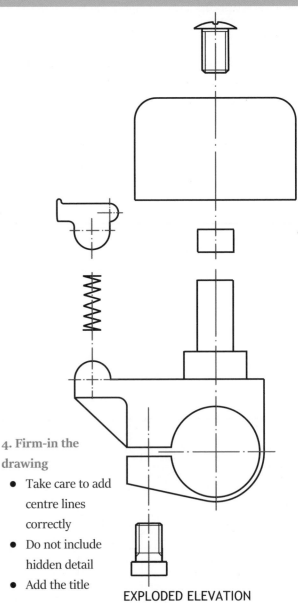

1. Construct the main component

- Draw centre lines in first; this will enable you to work from the centre lines to build up the construction of the grid
- The centre lines also provide the axis for exploding the components
- Remember you are working to a 2:1 scale

2. Draw the main component

- Keep lines light at this stage
- Take measurements from the centre lines
- There is no need to show hidden detail

3. Draw the spring, bell dome, bush, clamping screw and top screw

- Leave clear space between the components and the main part
- Extend centre lines to position the part
- Measure from centre lines to achieve accurate positioning

4. Firm-in the drawing

- Take care to add centre lines correctly
- Do not include hidden detail
- Add the title

EXPLODED ELEVATION

EXAM PREP - HALF SECTION

Draw the half-section, E-E, of the assembled bicycle bell to a scale 2:1.

Half-section - Special features

A half-section is used when there is a need to show both the inside and the outside of an assembly or component. This type of section normally removes one quarter of the assembly or part but it is called a half-section because the sectional view shows half the external and half the internal view. It requires a stepped cutting plane.

1. Project from the end elevation and plan views

- Project all the features from where the cutting plane slices through the assembly
- Remember you are working to a 2:1 scale

Worksheet alert

You can download the worksheets online to support you with this task - see inside back cover for more information and website details.

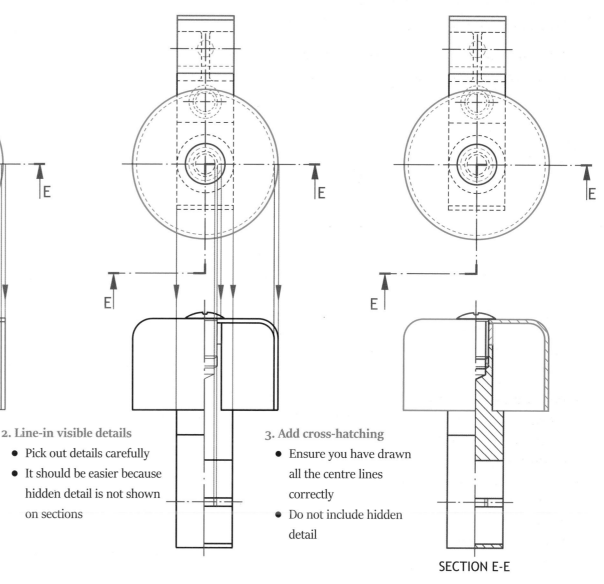

2. Line-in visible details

- Pick out details carefully
- It should be easier because hidden detail is not shown on sections

3. Add cross-hatching

- Ensure you have drawn all the centre lines correctly
- Do not include hidden detail

SECTION E-E

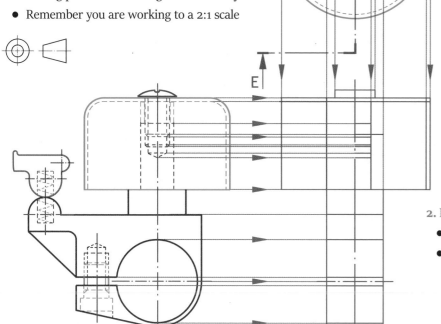

HIGHER GRAPHIC COMMUNICATION

EXAM PREP - STANDARDS AND CONVENTIONS

EXAM PREP - ASSEMBLIES

The internal screw thread for the clamping screw is deep enough so that the clamping screw doesn't reach the top of it.

Q1. Explain why the internal screw thread is deeper than the clamping screw can reach.

EXAM PREP

The handle bar clamp (the main part) and the hammer have been designed to allow the bell hammer to ring the bell easily and consistently.

Q4. Describe three features of these parts (shown on the elevation below) that make this possible.

The elevation below is missing the cutting plane C-C.

Q5. Add the cutting plane to the elevation taking care to ensure you apply the correct drawing standards and conventions.

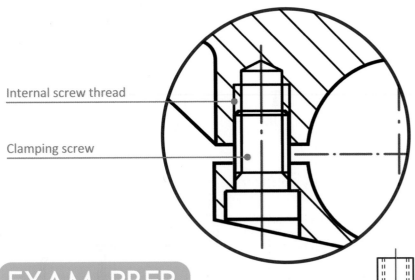

Internal screw thread

Clamping screw

EXAM PREP

The handle bar clamp includes a feature called a counter-bore.

Q2. Explain two functions of this counter-bore.

The clamp contains a 2mm gap.

Q3. Give two reasons for the inclusion of the gap.

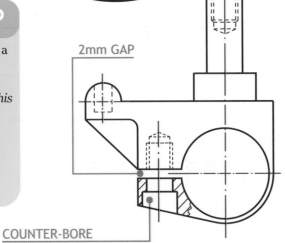

2mm GAP

COUNTER-BORE

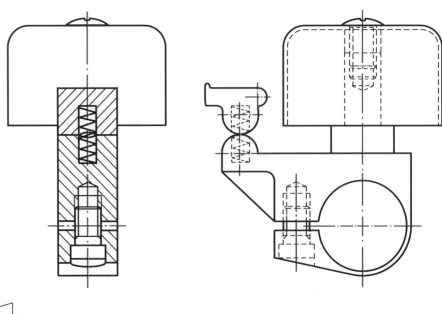

SECTION C-C

ELEVATION

Worksheet alert

You can download the worksheets online to support you with this task - see inside back cover for more information and website details.

EXAM PREP - SECTIONS

The drawings here are missing the cutting planes X-X and Y-Y.

Q1. Add both cutting planes to the drawings. The cutting planes should be added to different views. Take care to ensure you apply the correct drawing standards and conventions.

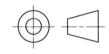

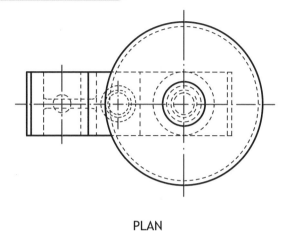

PLAN

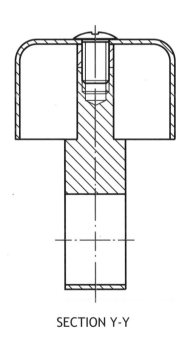

SECTION Y-Y

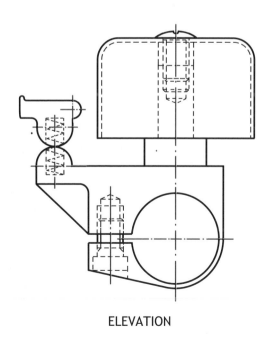

ELEVATION

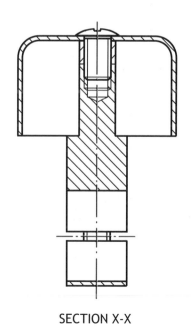

SECTION X-X

HIGHER GRAPHIC COMMUNICATION

MANUFACTURING TOLERANCES

When most products are manufactured, the component parts are made separately before being assembled into a product. If a component part is not made to the correct size it will not fit with other parts in the assembly.

A manufacturing tolerance added to the dimensions sets the limits of permissible manufacturing error in sizes that will still allow components to be assembled. Tolerancing dimensions is the way designers and architects ensure that components can fit together during assembly.

Example

An assembly requires that a support post is inserted into a boss and fixed with a screw. The nominal size of the hole in the boss and the insert on the post are the same; Ø6.

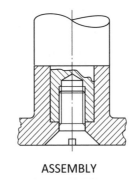

Support post

Post insert fits snuggly inside the boss.

A boss is a raised feature, usually cylindrical, that increases the thickness of material for screw fixings etc.

The fixing screw fixes the support post through the boss.

Boss and support post assembly

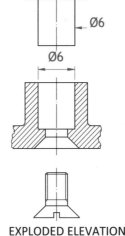

Ø6

Ø6

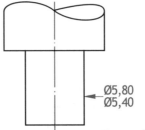

ASSEMBLY   EXPLODED ELEVATION

Why are tolerances required in this assembly?

- If both the hole and the post insert are exactly the same size, the insert will not fit inside the hole. This is called interference.

- It is not possible to mass produce components to exactly the correct size; some margin for manufacturing error is required.

- The hole and the post insert need to be dimensioned so that they can always assemble easily.

The process of putting limits on dimensions so that they ensure assembly is called dimensional tolerancing.

The drawings below show three different ways to tolerance the diameters. Note that the larger size is placed on top and the decimal point is always a comma. The manufacturer now knows that the parts must be kept within the limits shown in the tolerances.

Specific limits of size

This method specifies the limits of size directly. The upper limit is placed on top.

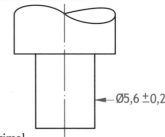

Ø5,80
Ø5,40

Ø6,40
Ø6,00

Symmetrical tolerance

This method shows the tolerance split evenly to either side of the nominal dimension.

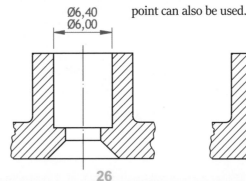

Ø5,6 ±0,2

Remember, a decimal point can also be used.

Ø6,2±0,2

Asymmetric tolerance

This method shows the tolerance split unevenly either side of the nominal size.

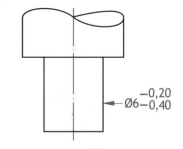

−0,20
Ø6−0,40

+0,4
Ø6 −0,0

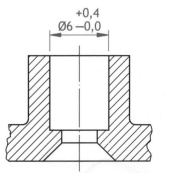

TOLERANCING DIMENSIONS - FUNCTIONAL AND NON-FUNCTIONAL DIMENSIONS

There are three reasons for applying manufacturing tolerances:

1. To ensure that parts can **assemble** correctly.

2. To give manufacturers leeway during production; it is impossible to **mass produce** components to **exactly** the correct size. The more precise the measurements the more expensive the components are to make.

3. To enable **interchangeability** of parts, for instance when one part wears out and needs replaced the new part should fit without modification.

Functional & non-functional dimensions

All dimensions are subject to tolerances. Tolerances are described as either **Functional** or **Non-functional.**

Functional tolerances are applied to dimensions that directly affect the function of the product e.g. dimensions that enable a product to assemble or enable moving parts to work. Functional tolerances are noted beside the dimensions on the drawings.

Non-functional tolerances are applied to all other dimensions that are not critical to the functioning of a product. Non-functional tolerances are normally found in the title block.

You will add both functional and non-functional tolerances to drawings in your coursework and you may be asked questions about tolerances on dimensions in your exam.

EXAM PREP

A metal bracket is designed to fix a mud guard to the frame of a bicycle. The bracket slides into a slot between two runners before being fixed to the mud guard with a screw.

Study the assembly drawings below and the component drawings on the next page and answer the questions on the worksheet that you can download from our website.

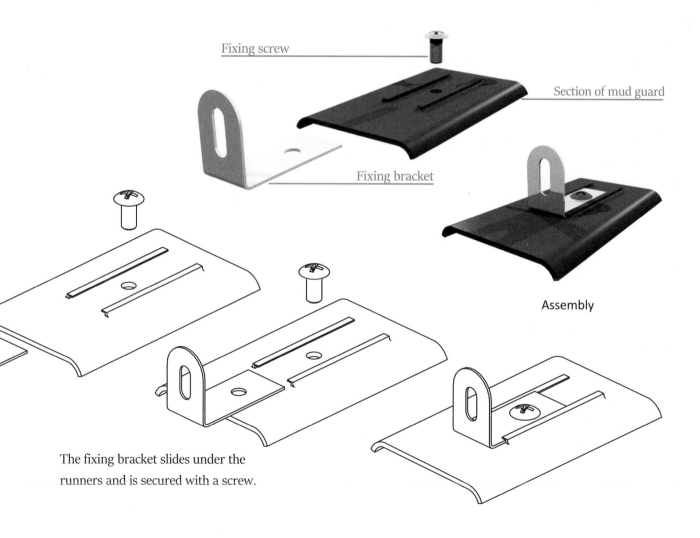

Fixing screw

Section of mud guard

Fixing bracket

Assembly

The fixing bracket slides under the runners and is secured with a screw.

EXAM PREP - TOLERANCING

Component drawings

The two components shown have been dimensioned. But before tolerances can be applied the engineer needs to identify and distinguish **functional** and **non-functional** dimensions.

Functional dimensions

The breadth of the bracket (20mm) is a functional dimension because it must fit between the two runners on the mudguard. If the breadth is too big it will fall off and if the space between the runners is too small it will not fit. A dimensional tolerance has been applied to both dimensions.

Non-functional dimensions

A non-functional dimension such as the overall length of the bracket is not a critical, or functional dimension. If it is a little bigger or smaller the product will still assemble. Non-functional dimensions are also limited by the tolerance shown in the title block; in this case +/- 0.5mm.

EXAM PREP

Q1. Identify two other functional dimensions and apply a suitable tolerance to each dimension.

Q2. Identify where parallel dimensioning has been used and explain why this method is used.

Q3. Identify one non-functional dimension and explain why it is non-functional.

Worksheet alert

You can download the worksheets online to support you with this task - see inside back cover for more information and website details.

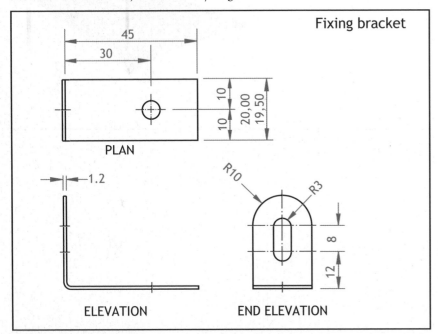

Fixing bracket

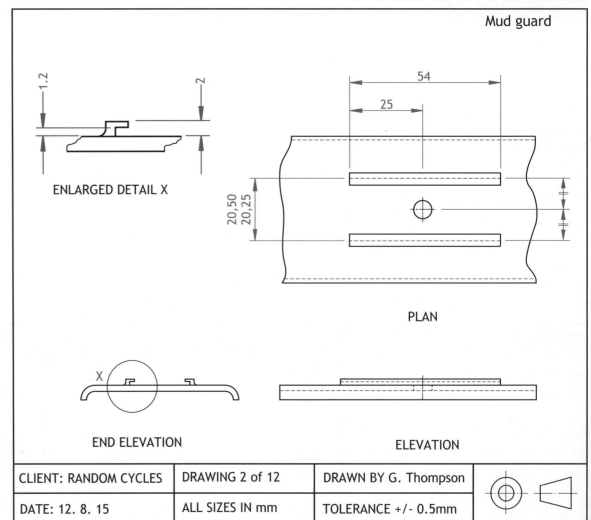

Mud guard

CLIENT: RANDOM CYCLES	DRAWING 2 of 12	DRAWN BY G. Thompson
DATE: 12. 8. 15	ALL SIZES IN mm	TOLERANCE +/- 0.5mm

THE ARC THE LINE AND THE TANGENT

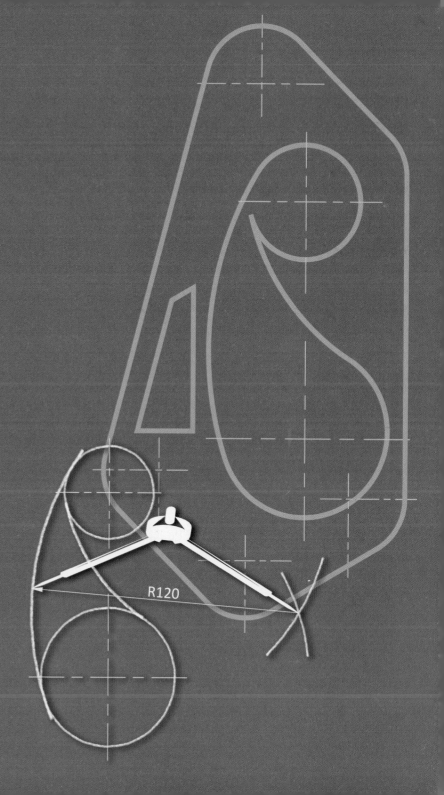

Tangency is the process of drawing circles and arcs that blend into other arcs or blend into straight lines.

The problem solving challenge is to locate the centre of an arc in order to draw the arc in the correct position so that a smooth tangent is achieved.

Tangency skills are still very relevant in engineering and product design. Tangency drawings can be done using CAD or on a drawing board with drawing instruments.

The worked examples here are set out for the drawing board but can equally be done using 2D or 3D CAD software.

R120

TANGENCY - SKILLS

Tangency between arcs and straight lines

There are two techniques that you need to learn;

1. Drawing a tangent between a straight line and an arc

2. Drawing a tangent between two arcs or an arc and a circle.

Remember, your challenge is to find the centre point of each arc.

This worked example will show you how to use both techniques.

Worked example

A stylised door number plate, number 16, is to be drawn to a scale of 1:1. The drawing will be tackled in two stages: drawing the back-plate and drawing the numbers.

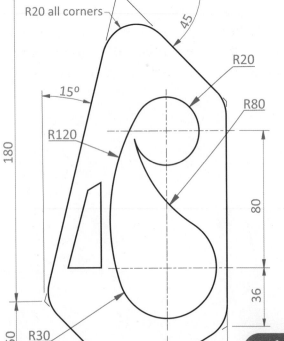

1. Draw the shape in straight lines. Use two set squares together to draw the 15° edge. The starting position is given below.

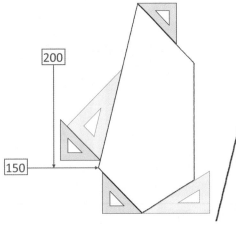

2. To find the centre of the top corner arc: set the compass to the arc radius (R20) and scribe an arc anywhere along each edge.

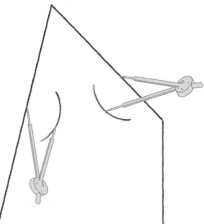

3. Draw lines parallel with the edges that skim the crown of the arcs. The centre of the arc is located where the lines cross.

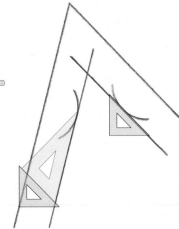

4. The centre is identified where the two straight lines cross. Draw the arc (R20).

5. The other corner arcs are completed using exactly the same method.

6. Firm in the outline and add centre lines. The wall plate is now ready to have the number 16 inserted.

> **Worksheet alert**
>
> You can download a worksheet online to support you with this task - see inside back cover for more information and website details.

TANGENCY BETWEEN ARCS

Tangency where two arcs merge is tackled differently. The challenge is to locate the centres of each connecting arc. To do this you will either add or subtract the radii.

This worked example is the number '6' on the number plate; sizes are on the previous page. It can be drawn on the drawing board or using CAD software.

You can be asked questions about tangency in the course exam.

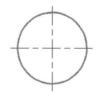
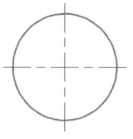
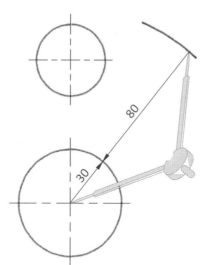
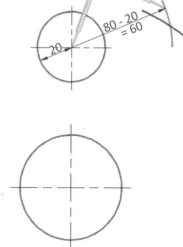
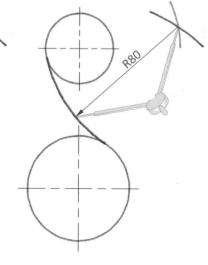

1. Position the circles accurately inside the outline. Draw the centre lines and circles.

2. Add the radius of the lower circle and the R80 arc: 30 + 80 = 110. Set the compass to R110 and scribe an arc.

3. Subtract the radius of the top circle from the radius of the connecting arc : 80 - 20 = 60. Set compass and scribe an arc to locate the centre where the arcs cross.

4. Set compass to R80 and draw the connecting arc. It should make a tangent with both of the circles.

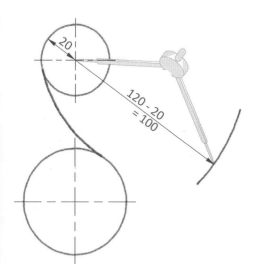
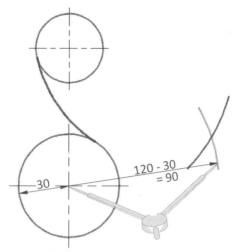
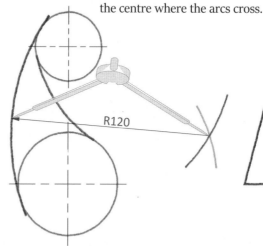
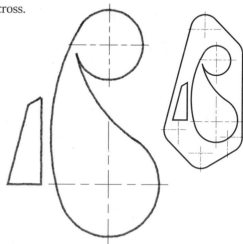

5. Subtract the radius of top circle from the radius of the connecting arc: 120 - 20 = 100. Set compass and scribe an arc.

6. Subtract the radius of the lower circle from the radius of the connecting arc: 120 - 30 = 90. Set the compass and scribe an arc. Crossing arcs locate the centre.

7. Set compass to R120 and draw the connecting arc between the two circles.

8. Firm in the outline and add the number 1. Estimate sizes for the number 1.

A GUIDE TO INTERSECTIONS & GEOMETRY

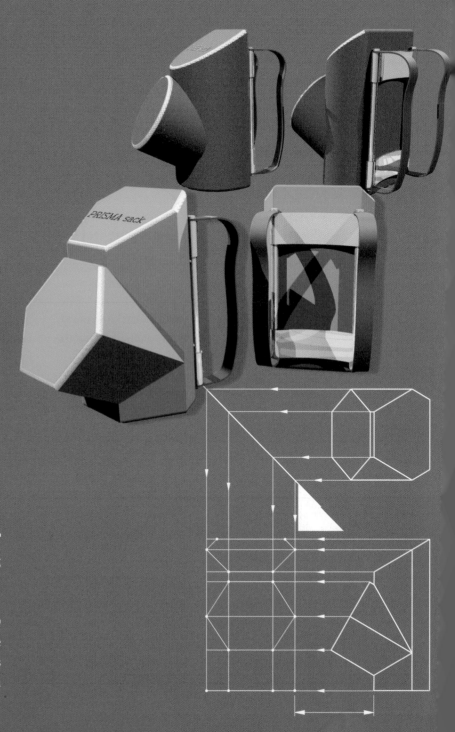

The manufactured world is built from geometric forms. Cuboids, cylinders, prisms, pyramids, cones and spheres feature heavily in our built environment and they certainly appear in installations and products that we make use of every day.

Many of these geometric products start life as flat sheets of paper, card, metals, plastics or fabrics and are made into 3D geometric forms before being joined to other geometric forms.

You need to understand the process of drawing 3D geometric forms as flat shapes (surface developments) and joining 3D geometric forms together (intersections). This chapter will take you through each process.

INTERSECTION OF GEOMETRIC SOLIDS

GEOMETRIC SOLIDS

Geometric forms (solids) are used widely in industries such as, engineering, construction, furniture manufacture, packaging and retail. The design of air conditioning and heating ducts, attic windows and roofs, upholstery, food packaging, clothing and fashion accessories all rely on intersection and surface development techniques.

In this topic you will learn how to construct intersecting geometric forms including cylinders and prisms and how to project useful 2D drawings including the true shapes of sloping surfaces and surface developments. These drawings are required whenever a product is made from flat sheet material.

Materials like steel, aluminium, cardboard, plastics, fabrics and plywood all have manufacturing properties that enable industries to create 3D products from flat 2D sheets.

DRAWING INTERSECTIONS
IMPORTANT TIPS

1. Treat the intersecting solids as a **main pipe** and a **branch pipe**.

2. The **main pipe** normally passes through the joint and out the other side.

3. The **branch pipe** normally (but not always) stops at the joint, though it can pass through.

4. To plot the line of intersection **divide up the branch pipe only**.

5. The **main pipe** has either a bigger diameter than the branch pipe or is the same size.

6. The **branch pipe** has a smaller diameter or is the same diameter as the main pipe.

In order to join both pipes together, the branch pipe requires to have one end shaped to fit the main pipe. The main pipe requires to have a hole cut to fit the branch pipe. This allows the pipes to fit together neatly so that the joint can be sealed and joined securely.

It is also true for materials such as fabrics or cardboard. The two intersecting solids must be shaped at the joint to form the line of intersection.

In this topic one of your challenges is to plot the line of intersection between intersecting solids.

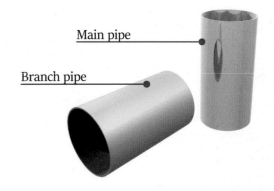

Main pipe

Branch pipe

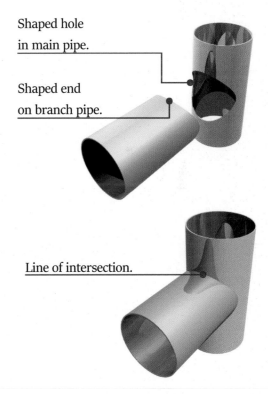

Shaped hole in main pipe.

Shaped end on branch pipe.

Line of intersection.

INTERSECTING CYLINDERS

BRIEF

Two designs for new lightweight rucksacks are at the preliminary design stage.

The clothing and accessories company **'Rags and Bags'** wants to offer two rucksack models.

The Tube Sack - made from intersecting cylinders

Target market: 8 - 12 years

Gender: Male & Female with different colour scheme and graphics for each.

Uses: School sack or casual use or sports wear.
And
The Prisma Sack - made from intersecting hexagonal prisms.

Target market: 12 - 18years

Gender: Male & Female with different colour scheme and graphics for each.

Uses: High School sack or casual use or sports wear.

'Rags and Bags' require the designer to complete production drawings for both rucksacks.

Worksheet alert

You can download a worksheet online to support you with this task - see inside back cover for more information and website details.

EXAM PREP

Draw to a **1:5 scale**:

The Plan

The complete Elevation showing the line of intersection.

The left end Elevation.

The true shape of the sloping surface on the main cylinder.

A symmetrical half of the Surface Development of each cylinder.

The TUBE sack

Note: The dimensions in red are layout sizes and should be measured from the edge of your drawing sheet. They help ensure your drawings fit on the sheet if you are not using a worksheet. Do not scale the sizes in red.

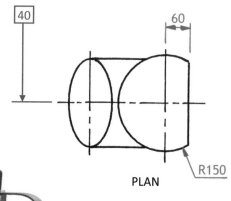

40

60

R150

PLAN

30°

Ø250

30°

500

265

120

70

200

ELEVATION

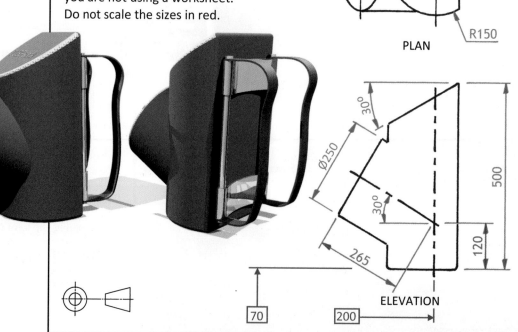

PROJECTING THE LINE OF INTERSECTION

1. Draw the plan and project the elevation.

Add a semi-circle to the branch cylinder.

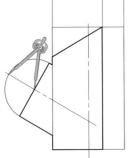

2. Divide up the semi-circle and project the end of the branch cylinder up to the plan.

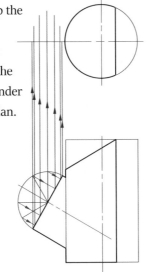

3. Transfer breadths from the semi-circle onto the plan and construct the ellipse.

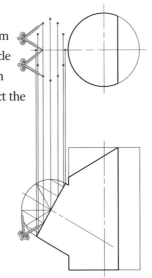

4. Project all 12 points from the ellipse back to the main cylinder and down to the elevation to construct the line of intersection where the generators meet.

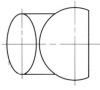

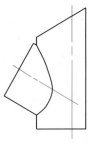

5. Firm in the drawing.

DRAWING THE TRUE SHAPE OF THE TUBESACK LID

1. Divide the plan and project surface generators down to the sloping lid.

2. Project generators at 90° to the sloping surface.

Datum Line

Add a datum line at 90° to the generators.

Identify the datum line on the plan. You now have two views of the same datum line.

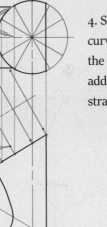

3. Step breadths from the plan onto the true shape.

Take your breadths from the datum line on the plan and step off from the datum on the true shape.

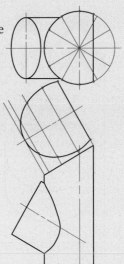

4. Sketch in the curve through the points and add the straight line.

5. Firm in the drawing.

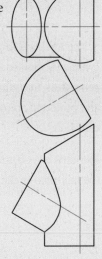

PROJECTING THE END ELEVATION

1. Draw the main cylinder of the end elevation using the half-plan (semi-circle) method.

Divide the top face of the branch cylinder as shown and projected to the end elevation.

Transfer breadths from the elevation to the end elevation. Sketch the ellipse.

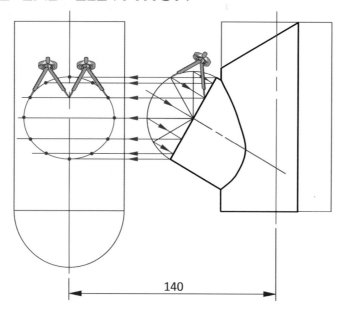

140

2. On the elevation, project generators down to the join line and then across to the end elevation.

On the end elevation, project each of the 12 points on the ellipse downward to meet the lines from the elevation.

Mark the points where the projection lines meet and sketch a smooth curve.

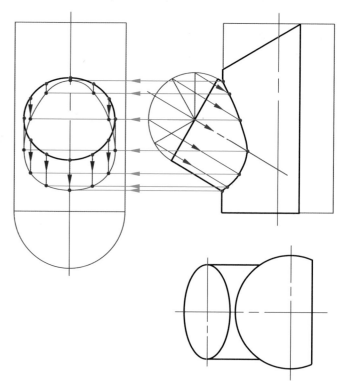

PLAN

3. The top surface of the main cylinder is divided using generators from the half-plan and projected across to the end elevation.

Breadths are transferred from the half-plan to the end elevation.

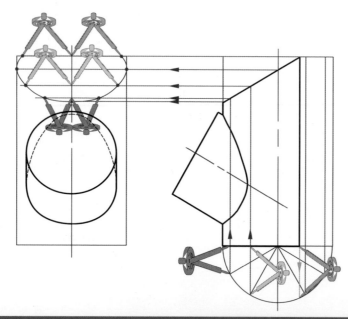

4. Firm in the outlines and hidden detail and add titles.

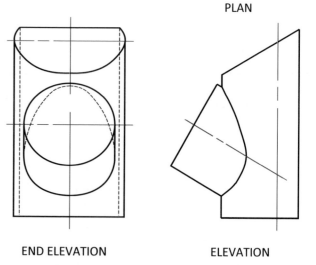

END ELEVATION

ELEVATION

SURFACE DEVELOPMENTS

Surface developments are required when a product is made from a flat sheet.

Follow the step-by-step guide and complete the developments of both cylinders.

Step 1

Project the cylinders and step-off the circumference of half a cylinder (6 segments). Add surface generators and numbers.

Numbers added to adjacent views can help you follow projection lines accurately.

Step 2

Add the extra surface generators, X, Y & Z to the main cylinder and the surface development.

Generators x, y & z are required because the features they highlight lie between the other generators.

Step 3

Project features from the elevation to both surface developments using your numbering as a guide.

Plot the curves and sketch them in freehand.

Step 4

Firm in the drawings taking care to remember centre lines and the fold line.

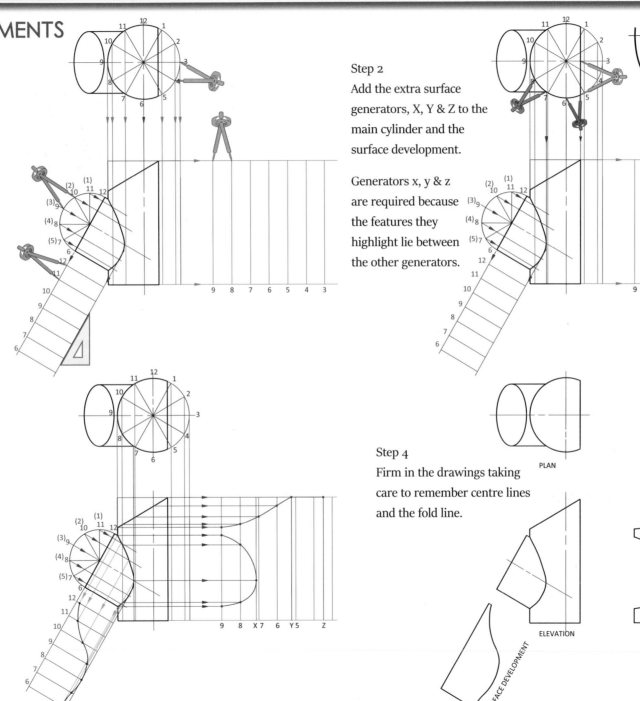

DRAWING INTERSECTING PRISMS

INTERSECTIONS WITH CAD

EXAM PREP

Draw to a 1:5 scale:

The plan, the complete elevation showing the line of intersection and the left end elevation

The true shape of the sloping surface of the main prism

A symmetrical half of the Surface Development of each prism

The PRISMA sack

Note: The dimensions in red are layout sizes and should be measured from the edge of your drawing sheet. They help ensure your drawings fit on the sheet if you are not using the worksheet. Do not scale the sizes in red.

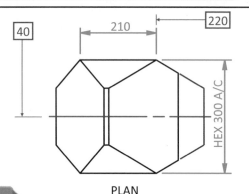

40 | 210 | 220

HEX 300 A/C

PLAN

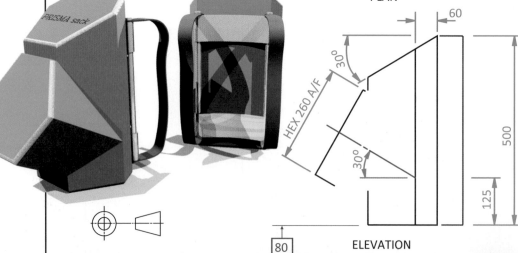

PRISMA sack

60

30°

HEX 260 A/F

30°

500

125

80

ELEVATION

Worksheet alert

You can download a worksheet online to support you with this task - see inside back cover for more information and website details.

60°

Create the 3D primitive that will be intersected.

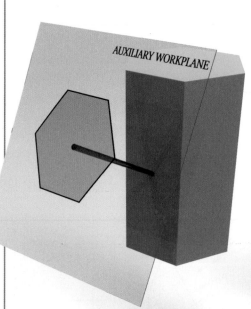

AUXILIARY WORKPLANE

Create a workplane perpendicular to the line you have drawn. This should create an auxiliary workplane at the angle you set the line. Draw the profile of your intersecting shape.

Select a vertical workplane that allows you to draw a line at the angle you want the intersecting prism to be at.

In this example, a line at 60° has been made.

The length of the line will determine how long the intersecting prism will be.

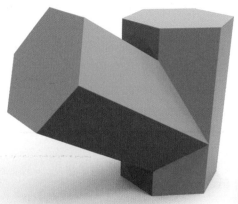

Extrude the profile on your auxiliary workplane until it intersects your first prism. Depending on your software, you will be able to generate the surface development of both prisms.

PLOTTING THE LINE OF INTERSECTION

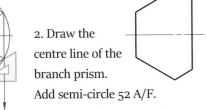

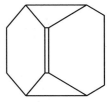

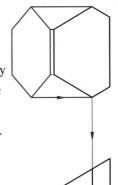

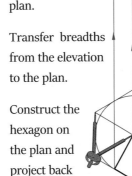

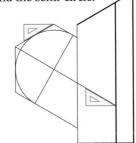

1. Draw the plan hexagon 60 A/C.

Project the elevation.

Add the sloping cut and the vertical cut.

2. Draw the centre line of the branch prism.
Add semi-circle 52 A/F.

Construct the hexagon around the semi-circle.

3. Project the hexagon up to the plan.

Transfer breadths from the elevation to the plan.

Construct the hexagon on the plan and project back to the main prism.

4. Plot the intersection by projecting the edges of the branch prism.

5. Firm in outlines.

PROJECTING THE TRUE SHAPE OF THE SLOPING FACE

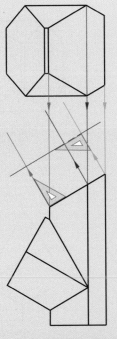

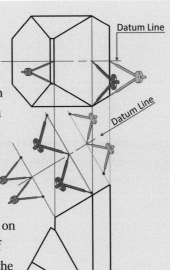

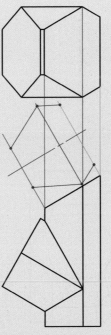

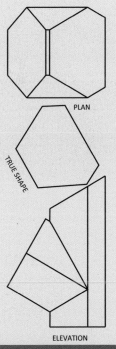

1. Project from the sloping surface at 90°.

Add a datum line at 90° to the generators.

2. Identify the datum line on the plan. You now have two views of the same datum line.

Take your breadths from the datum line on the plan and step off from the datum on the true shape.

Datum Line

Datum Line

3. Draw in the true shape of the sloping face (the lid of the PRISMA sack).

4. Firm in the outline and add titles.

PLAN

TRUE SHAPE

ELEVATION

PROJECTING THE END ELEVATION

1. Draw a 45° bounce line and project breadths from the plan and heights from the elevation.

Project both hexagons on the end elevation.

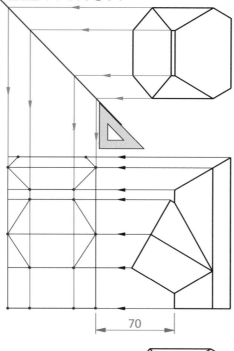

70

2. Project the additional corners to plot the lines of intersection on the end elevation.

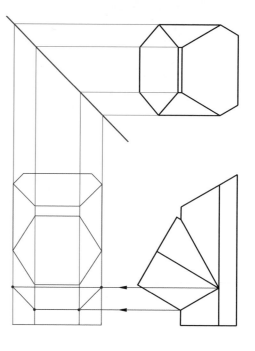

3. Firm in the outlines.

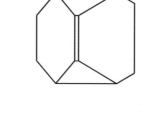

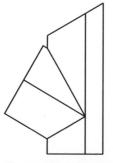
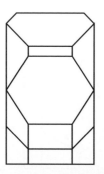

4. Add hidden detail and titles.

Remember the pocket is a separate compartment from the main bag.

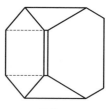

PLAN

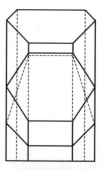
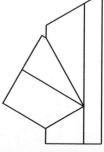

END ELEVATION

ELEVATION

SURFACE DEVELOPMENTS

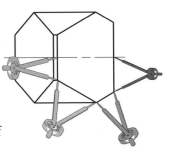

1. Project the ½ size surface development of the main prism.

Transfer the true length of each face from the plan to the surface development.

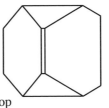

2. Project the height of each corner including the top face and the intersection.

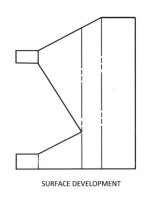

3. Firm in the outlines. Add fold lines and titles.

PLAN

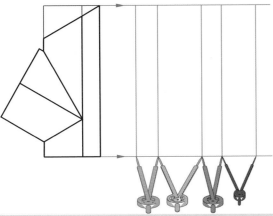

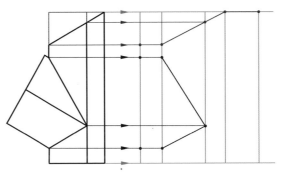

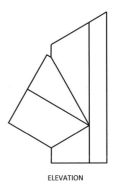

ELEVATION

SURFACE DEVELOPMENT

SURFACE DEVELOPMENT BRANCH PRISM

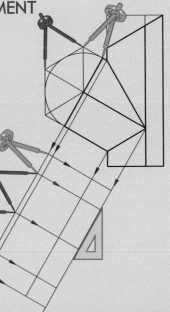

1. Project the ½ surface development of the branch prism (the pocket).

Transfer the true length of each face from the plan.

2. Mark each turning point (corner) and draw in the development.

3. Firm in the outlines. Remember to add fold lines.

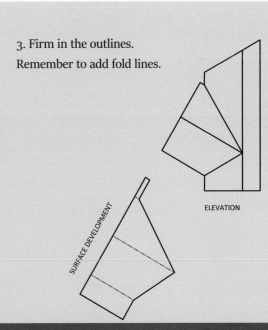

SURFACE DEVELOPMENT

ELEVATION

ISOMETRIC DRAWING LIFE IN 3D

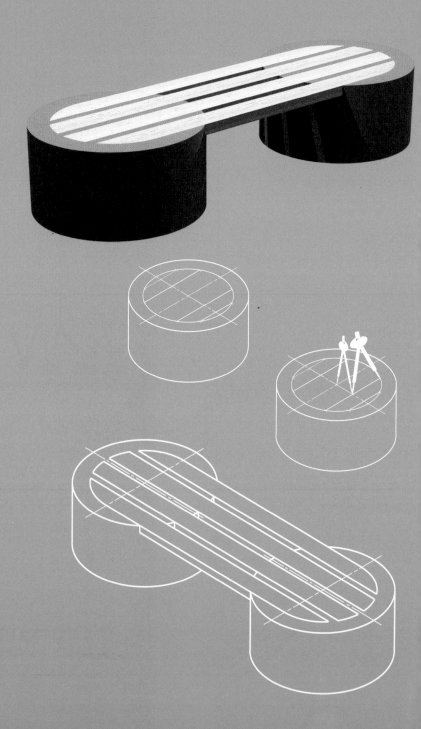

Isometric drawings are used in design, engineering and construction to show a 3D view of a component, product or building. These isometric drawings often appear less technical than orthographic drawings and can be easier to understand.

Isometric drawings are most often used in conjunction with orthographic views. Orthographic views show the technical detail while the isometric drawings help clarify the form of a product.

Isometric exploded views are often used to explain assembly details. Isometric drawings are classified as pictorial views.

The pictorial styles commonly used in engineering are isometric and oblique. Other pictorial styles, perspective and planometric drawings, are used in architecture. This book covers the two most common pictorial styles; isometric and planometric drawing.

PRINCIPLES OF ISOMETRIC DRAWING

There are two important features of isometric drawing:

1. Isometric drawing uses true dimensions on heights, lengths and breadths; isometric is Greek for 'equal measure'.

2. The the isometric drawing angle of all horizontal edges (lengths and breadths) is 30°. The angle of vertical edges remains vertical.

ORTHOGRAPHIC VIEWS

ISOMETRIC VIEW

OCULAR bench

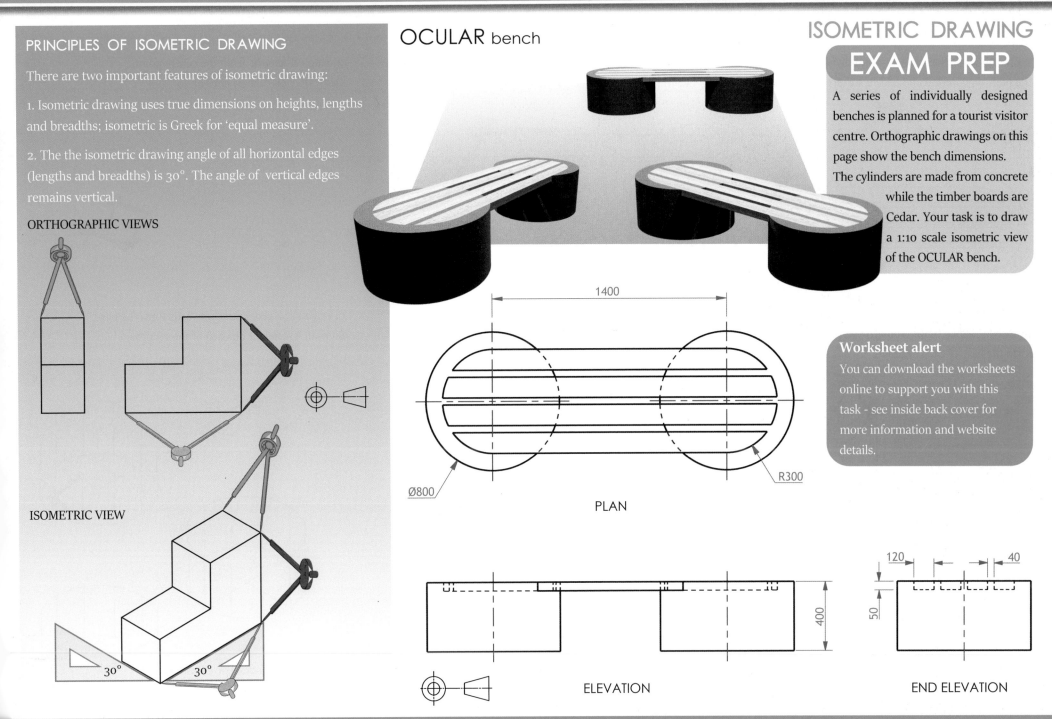

ISOMETRIC DRAWING

EXAM PREP

A series of individually designed benches is planned for a tourist visitor centre. Orthographic drawings on this page show the bench dimensions. The cylinders are made from concrete while the timber boards are Cedar. Your task is to draw a 1:10 scale isometric view of the OCULAR bench.

Worksheet alert

You can download the worksheets online to support you with this task - see inside back cover for more information and website details.

1400

Ø800

R300

PLAN

ELEVATION

END ELEVATION

120   40

50

400

ISOMETRIC DRAWING

1. Use the worksheet provided and divide a circle on the plan view into 12 and add 12 surface generators.

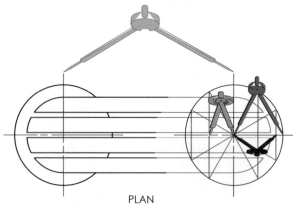

PLAN

2. Draw the centres of each circle spaced correctly. Use the isometric angle, 30° to construct the centre lines.

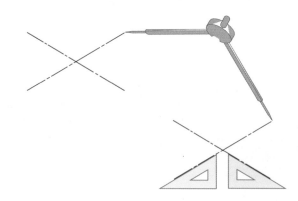

3. Step-off lengths from the centre points. Draw in construction lines at 30°.

4. Transfer breadths from the plan view on to the isometric. Sketch in the isometric ellipse. This will form the base of each cylinder.

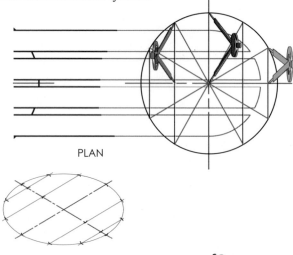

PLAN

5. Project the generators down from plan to elevation and measure the height.

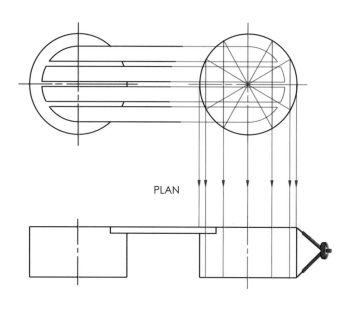

PLAN

ELEVATION

6. Project the generators upwards from the base. Step-off the height on each of the verticals.

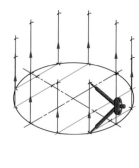
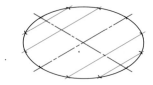

7. Sketch in the isometric ellipses.

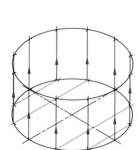

DRAWING THE SPARS

8. Add the tangent lines up the outsides of the cylinders.

9. To draw the small circle at the end of the wooden spars. Divide the circle into 12 the same as before.

10. Transfer the divided circle onto the isometric view the same way as before. Sketch the circle through the 12 points.

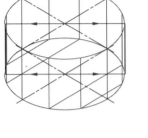
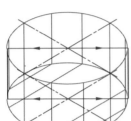
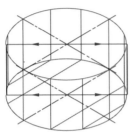

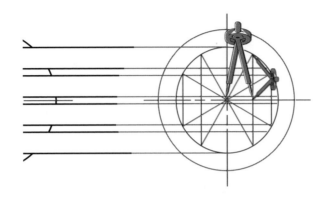
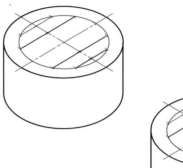

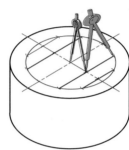

11. Measure the positions of the spars. Draw the spars on the top surface.

12. Add a thickness to the spars.

13. Line in the drawing and add a title.

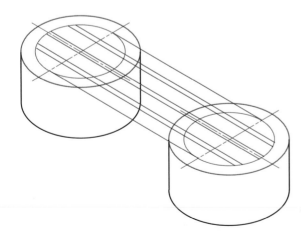

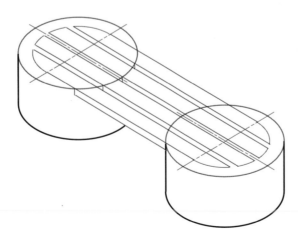

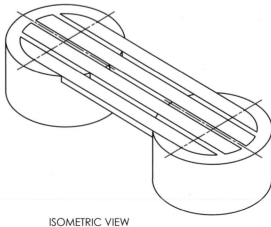

ISOMETRIC VIEW

PLANOMETRIC

DRAWING FROM THE BOTTOM UP

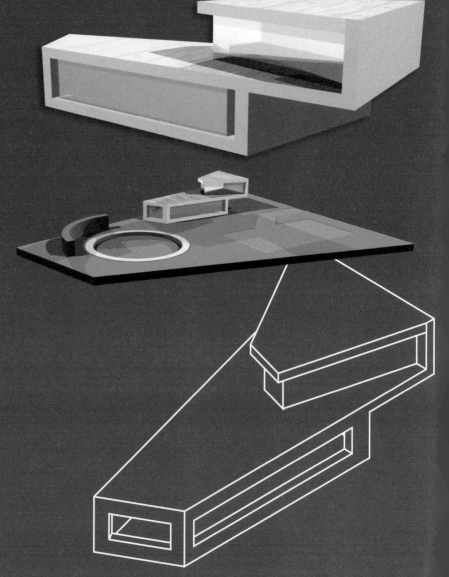

Planometric drawings are not intended to be realistic but to give a clear view of a 3D environmental space. They assume the viewer to be hovering above the space and are often used to depict interior as well as outdoor spaces.

Planometric drawings use true sizes along both horizontal axis' and vertical heights. Hidden detail should not be shown on planometric views.

The drawings here are planned for a drawing board but they can also be completed using CAD.

Completing these drawings will develop your visualisation skills and improve your understanding of planometric drawing. At the very least you should consider working through the drawing in this book. It will give you an understanding of the process and style of drawing.

PLANOMETRIC DRAWING

PRINCIPLES OF PLANOMETRIC DRAWING

Planometric drawing uses the plan view as a starting point.

The plan is rotated to either 30° by 60° or 45° by 45°.

The planometric view is then projected upwards from the rotated plan.

ORTHOGRAPHIC VIEWS

1. Plan is drawn in a rotated position.

2. Heights are projected upwards.

3. Breadths complete the view.

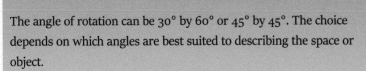

45°   45°   60°   30°

The angle of rotation can be 30° by 60° or 45° by 45°. The choice depends on which angles are best suited to describing the space or object.

EXAM PREP

A tourist visitor centre with an upstairs cafe is being planned. The architect needs a view that shows the visitor centre on the site with the sunken patio, curved wall and car park in place. He has requested a planometric view of the entire site.

It is your task to draw a planometric view with the building in position on the site.

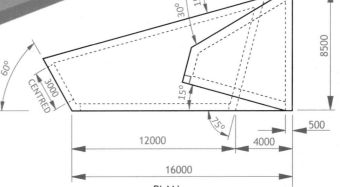

NEW VISITOR CENTRE ON PROPOSED SITE

DETAILS OF THE VISITOR CENTRE

See details and dimensions of the site plan on the next page.

15°
30°
15°
60°
75°
3000 CENTRED
8500
12000
4000
500
16000

PLAN

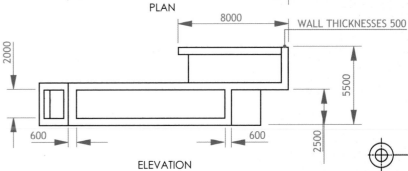

8000
WALL THICKNESSES 500
2000
5500
600
600
2500

END ELEVATION

ELEVATION

COMBINING SET SQUARES

There is a worksheet available from our website that will speed you through this drawing. But should you wish to draw the planometric from scratch, the task is made easier by combining set squares to achieve a 15° angle.

The graphic shows the standard 30°, 60° and 45° angles using set squares and 'T' square.

It also shows how to combine the set squares to achieve 15°, 75° and 105° angles. You will use these techniques when you complete this drawing.

Worksheet alert

You can download the worksheets online to support you with this task - see inside back cover for more information and website details.

You can complete the task from scratch but you will need to draw the plan and elevation first to a scale of **1:200** and step-off sizes onto the planometric view. Be smart, download the workheet!

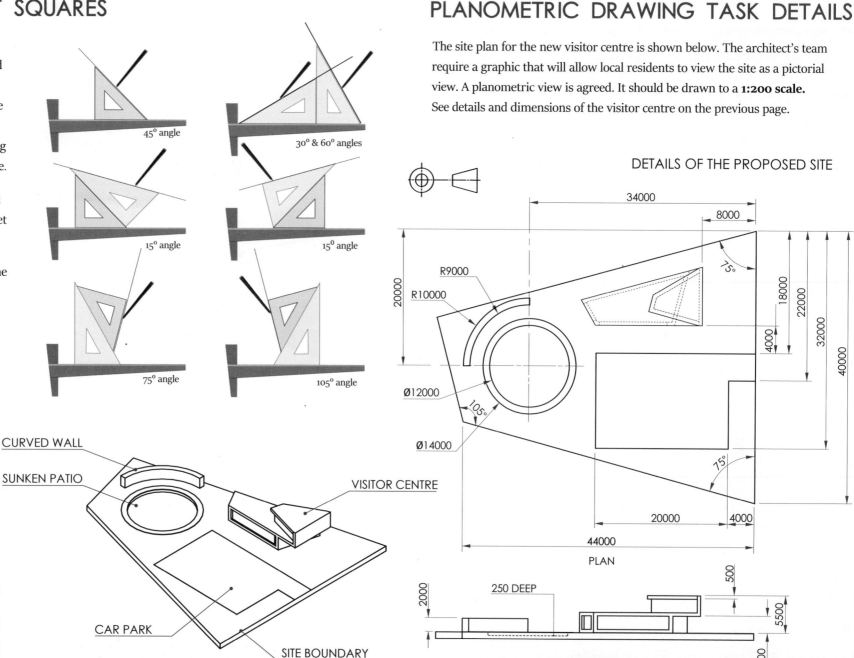

45° angle

30° & 60° angles

15° angle

15° angle

75° angle

105° angle

CURVED WALL

SUNKEN PATIO

VISITOR CENTRE

CAR PARK

SITE BOUNDARY

PLANOMETRIC DRAWING TASK DETAILS

The site plan for the new visitor centre is shown below. The architect's team require a graphic that will allow local residents to view the site as a pictorial view. A planometric view is agreed. It should be drawn to a **1:200 scale.** See details and dimensions of the visitor centre on the previous page.

DETAILS OF THE PROPOSED SITE

34000

8000

75°

R9000

R10000

20000

18000

22000

32000

40000

4000

Ø12000

105°

Ø14000

75°

20000

4000

44000

PLAN

500

2000

250 DEEP

5500

2500

ELEVATION

PLANOMETRIC DRAWING

DRAWING THE SITE

1. Work to a scale of 1:200 from the site plan and draw a rectangle (240 x 200) to enclose the site boundary rotated to 30° by 60°.

Or, step-off sizes from the worksheet available on our website.

It is important, when you are drawing irregular or angled shapes to work with a simple rectangle first.

DRAWING THE BUILDING

3. Project the outline of the visitor centre upwards to the height of the first floor.

Use your compass again to step off heights from the elevation.

Line in the first floor roof lightly.

2. Draw the plan view of the site inside the rectangle. Position each of the features.

Step-off sizes from the worksheet using a compass. Work from the rectangle to locate each corner and transfer each size to the planometric view (construction shown here in blue).

Notice that the circles and arcs are drawn using a compass.

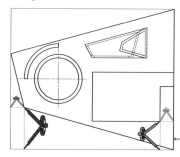

WORKSHEET

4. Project the upper roof. Take the height from the ground line.

Draw in the outline of the roof lightly.

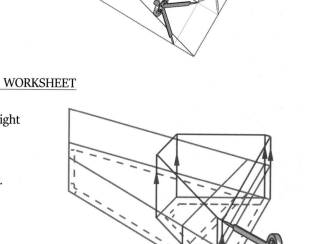

PLANOMETRIC DRAWING

5. Draw the thickness of the walls.

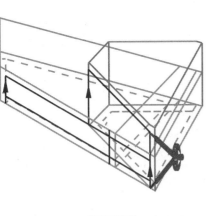

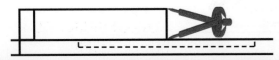

6. Draw the window glass by projecting the hidden lines on the rotated plan and stepping sizes from the elevation.

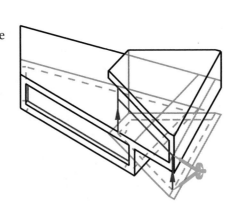

7. Line in the planometric view. Do not show hidden detail.

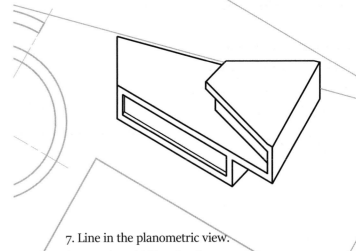

DRAWING THE CURVED WALL

8. Project the centre point upwards to match the height of the wall.

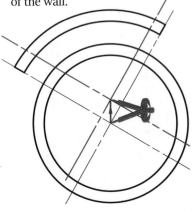

9. Draw both arcs with your compass.

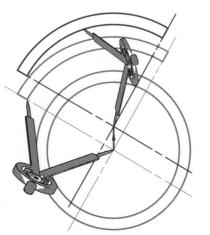

10. Project the vertical edges.

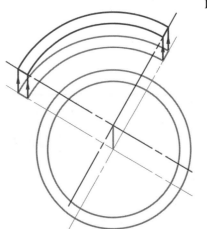

11. Firm-in the outline. Do not show hidden detail.

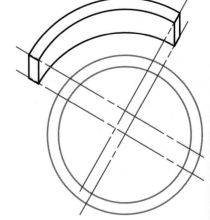

PLANOMETRIC DRAWING

DRAWING THE SUNKEN PATIO

12. Project the centre point downwards to match the depth of the patio.

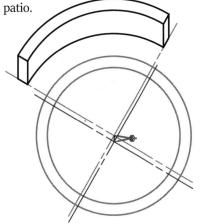

15. Firm-in the entire site layout. Add the scale.

13. Draw the arc from the new centre using the radius of the inner circle.

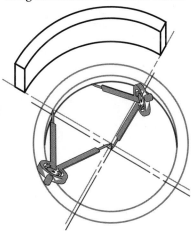

14. Firm in the sunken patio. Do not show hidden detail.

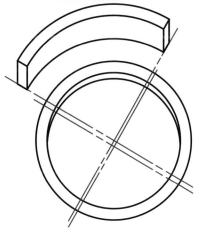

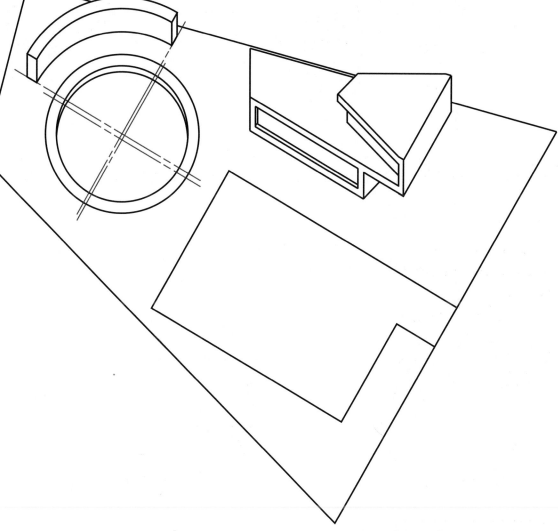

PLANOMETRIC VIEW
SCALE 1:200

AUXILIARY VIEWS

ALL ANGLES COVERED

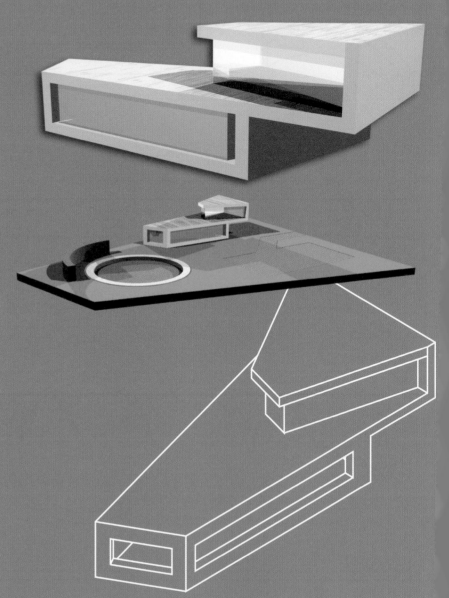

Auxiliary views are simply additional or extra orthographic views. They help to provide information that can't be seen in the normal orthographic views; Elevation, Plan and End Elevations.

Auxiliaries are commonly used by architects in construction drawings but they are also useful in engineering when the true shape of a surface or a special feature needs to be shown.

Auxiliary views are projected just like other orthographic views but they are not projected vertically or horizontally. They are projected at an angle to provide a different view point.

The drawings here are planned for a drawing board but they can also be completed on 3D CAD. Completing these drawings will develop your visualisation skills and improve your understanding of orthographic projection.

AUXILIARY PROJECTION

EXAM PREP

A tourist visitor centre with an upstairs cafe is being planned. The architect wants to view his design from several vantage points. An auxiliary elevation and an auxiliary plan are required so that the design can be evaluated from different view points. Draw an auxiliary elevation and an auxiliary plan to 1:100 scale.

NEW VISITOR CENTRE ON THE PROPOSED SITE

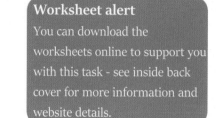

Worksheet alert

You can download the worksheets online to support you with this task - see inside back cover for more information and website details.

ORTHOGRAPHIC DETAIL DRAWINGS

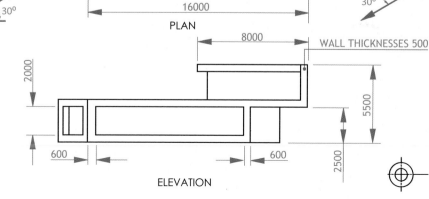

POSITION OF AUXILIARY ELEVATION

30°

POSITION OF AUXILIARY PLAN

30°

PLAN

30° 15°
8500
60°
3000 CENTRED
15°
75°
500
12000
4000
16000

WALL THICKNESSES 500

8000
2000
5500
2500

END ELEVATION

600

ELEVATION

600

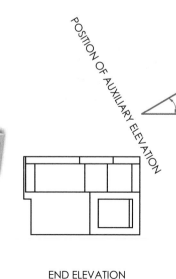

AUXILIARY ELEVATION

COMBINING SET SQUARES

There are worksheets available from our website that will speed up this drawing task. But should you wish to draw the elevation and plan from scratch, the task is made easier by combining set squares to achieve a 15° angle.

The graphic shows the standard 30°, 60° and 45° angles using set squares and 'T' square.

It also shows how to combine the set squares to achieve 15°, 75° and 105° angles. You will need these techniques to complete the elevation and plan.

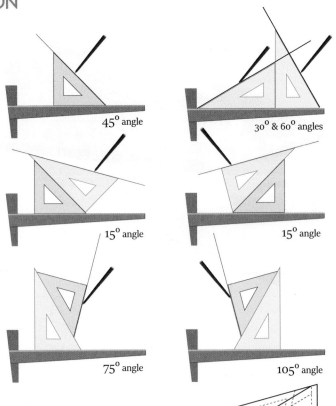

45° angle

30° & 60° angles

15° angle

15° angle

75° angle

105° angle

PROJECTING ONE SURFACE AT A TIME

1. Auxiliary elevations are always projected from the plan.

Project a single flat surface, it makes the drawing process simpler.

Project the surface facing the direction of viewing, in this case 30° down to the left.

Draw in a datum line at 90° to the projection lines.

Establish the datum line on the elevation (normally the ground line).

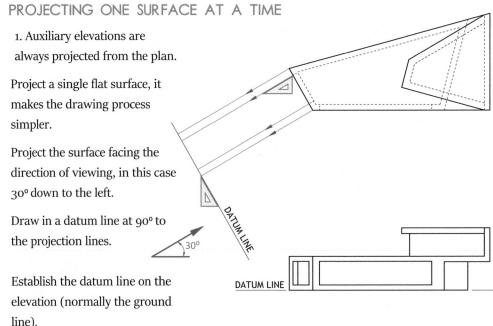

DATUM LINE

30°

DATUM LINE

2. Step-off heights that apply to the surface you have projected.

The heights come from the elevation and can be transferred using a compass. Work from the datum lines to lift and place heights from the elevation onto the auxiliary view.

Line in the surface.

Note: at this stage the technique is the same as drawing a true shape. In fact a true shape is an auxiliary view that shows only one surface.

3. Project the second surface in the same way as before.

Transfer heights that apply to the second surface, from the elevation.

Line in the second surface.

Do the same with the upper floor cafe roof.

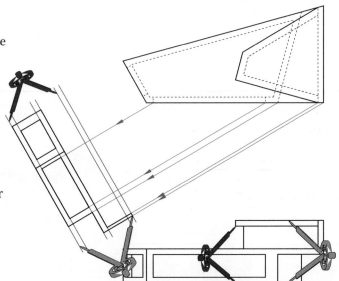

AUXILIARY ELEVATION

4. Project all remaining surfaces, in this case the roof.

Project the depth of the window through the wall.

Firm in the edges.

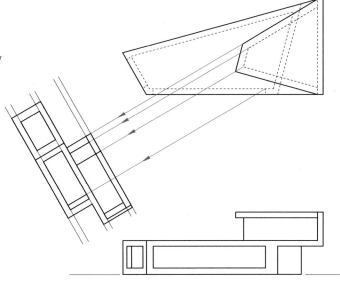

5. Firm in the outlines and label the views.

Do not show hidden detail on the auxiliary elevation.

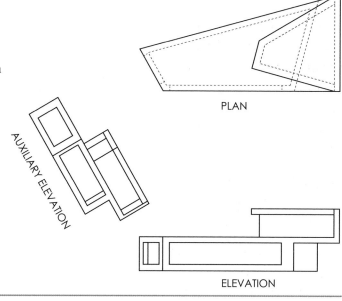

PLAN

AUXILIARY ELEVATION

ELEVATION

AUXILIARY PLAN

1. Auxiliary plans are projected from the elevation.

Project a surface facing in the direction of viewing, in this case the end wall, at 30° up and to the right.

Draw in a datum line at 90° to the projection lines.

Add a datum line to the plan view.

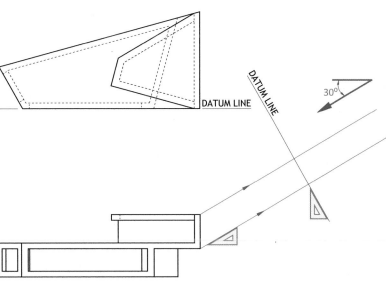

DATUM LINE

DATUM LINE

30°

2. Transfer the breadth of the end wall from the plan onto the auxiliary view.

Work from the datum lines to lift and place breadths from the plan onto the auxiliary view.

Firm in the surface.

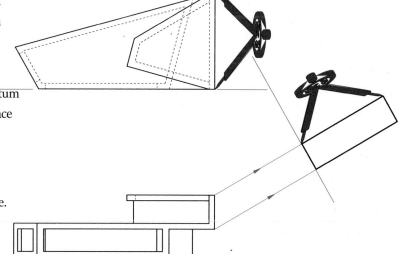

AUXILIARY PLAN

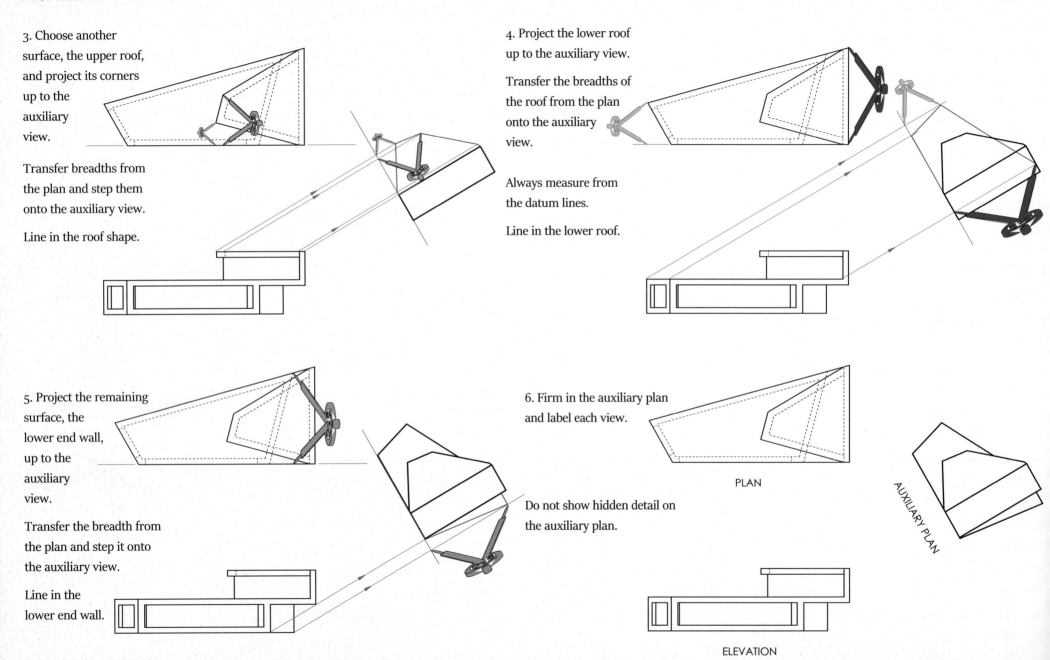

3. Choose another surface, the upper roof, and project its corners up to the auxiliary view.

Transfer breadths from the plan and step them onto the auxiliary view.

Line in the roof shape.

4. Project the lower roof up to the auxiliary view.

Transfer the breadths of the roof from the plan onto the auxiliary view.

Always measure from the datum lines.

Line in the lower roof.

5. Project the remaining surface, the lower end wall, up to the auxiliary view.

Transfer the breadth from the plan and step it onto the auxiliary view.

Line in the lower end wall.

6. Firm in the auxiliary plan and label each view.

Do not show hidden detail on the auxiliary plan.

PLAN

AUXILIARY PLAN

ELEVATION

CONSTRUCTION DRAWING

BUILDING THE FUTURE

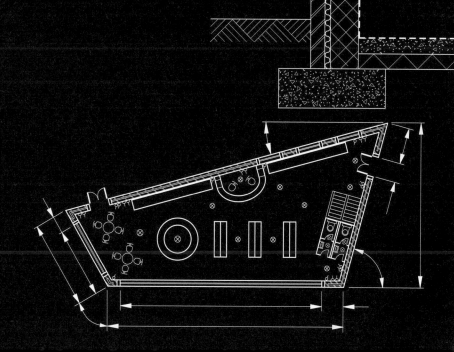

Like every other man-made product, buildings require a set of drawings to guide the builder and other trades people through the construction process. These drawings have differences to say, production drawings for a chair or a bicycle.

The size of a building means it will need to be drawn to a different scale, in reality, several different scales, and there is more emphasis on plan views. Additionally, there is not the same requirement for hidden detail or exploded views in construction drawings. Otherwise the drawings are pretty similar; some will have dimensions attached and there is a similar reliance on technical detail such as sectional views.

THE PROJECT SET OF CONSTRUCTION DRAWINGS

The project set of drawings required before building work can begin include:

Location plan (Block Plan) - Scale 1:1250 or 1:2500

Site Plan - Scale 1:200 or 1:500

Floor Plans - Scale 1:50

Elevations - Scale 1:100 or 1:50

Sections - Scale 1:20

The drawings will be produced by an architectural team that includes building technicians led by an architect.

The drawings are required for a number of reasons:

Drawings guide trades-people including builders, plumbers, joiners and electricians. Drawings are also required by the local building standards department who check that the construction is sound, safe and energy efficient. And by the planning department who check that the appearance of the proposed building does not conflict with its surroundings.

The building standards and planning departments have the final say in whether the building project can go ahead. The owners of buildings on neighbouring plots are also entitled to view the drawings and give their approval or objections to the plans.

Location Plan (Block Plan)

The location plan is the first drawing in the project set and the drawing that has the biggest scale. Ordinance survey (OS) maps are available at 1:1250 scale and these are often used as the basis for the location plan. The site with the proposed development is highlighted by colouring it or adding a thick outline.

The location plan normally includes:

- The building plot with neighbouring plots shown and identified
- Pavements, roads, footpaths, parks and fields
- Street names and plot (house) numbers
- A north direction arrow and drawing scale.

LOCATION PLAN

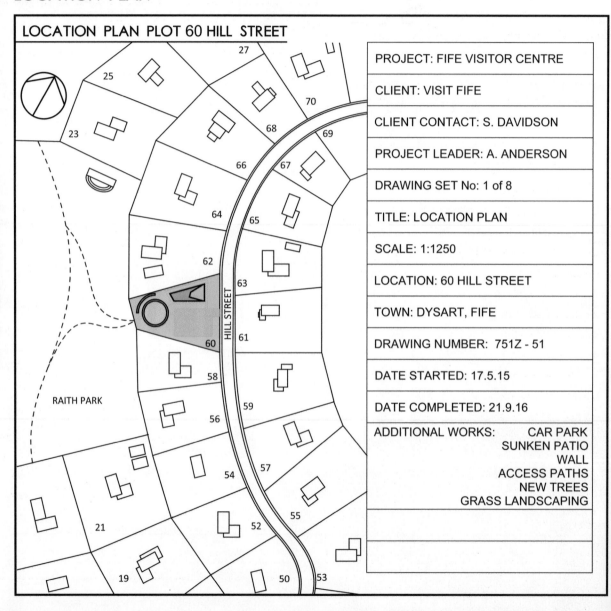

LOCATION PLAN PLOT 60 HILL STREET

| PROJECT: FIFE VISITOR CENTRE |
| CLIENT: VISIT FIFE |
| CLIENT CONTACT: S. DAVIDSON |
| PROJECT LEADER: A. ANDERSON |
| DRAWING SET No: 1 of 8 |
| TITLE: LOCATION PLAN |
| SCALE: 1:1250 |
| LOCATION: 60 HILL STREET |
| TOWN: DYSART, FIFE |
| DRAWING NUMBER: 751Z - 51 |
| DATE STARTED: 17.5.15 |
| DATE COMPLETED: 21.9.16 |
| ADDITIONAL WORKS: CAR PARK SUNKEN PATIO WALL ACCESS PATHS NEW TREES GRASS LANDSCAPING |

SITE PLAN FEATURES

The site plan is the second drawing in the project set. The scale used for a site plan is normally 1:200 for domestic buildings. Larger public and commercial buildings may be drawn to a larger scale; perhaps 1:500.

The site plan focuses on the building site and shows the exact position of the building on the site. It also shows details of other building features such as access paths, walls, trees, land contours and any landscaping to be completed.

A site plan includes:

- The building plot boundary with neighbouring plots identified.
- The plan view of the building in situation.
- Dimensions to position the building on the site.
- Contour lines to show the slope of the ground.
- Street names and plot (house) numbers.
- A north direction arrow.
- The drawing scale.
- Drainage runs (pipes) and manholes.
- Existing and new trees & trees to be removed.

EXAM PREP

The waste pipe run is shown on the site plan.

Q1. Explain why it is located in this position.

The waste pipes change direction between the building and the main sewer pipe.

Q2. Explain why this was done.

Q3. Of the trees shown, how many are new trees and how many require removing.

TIP Look at the drawings on pages 58 to 63 before you answer the exam prep questions in this chapter.

SITE PLAN

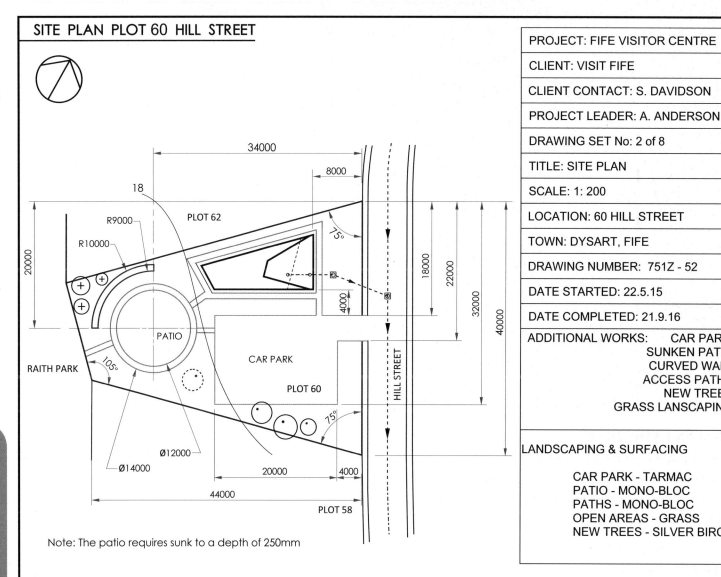

SITE PLAN PLOT 60 HILL STREET

PLOT 62

R9000

R10000

PLOT 60

CAR PARK

PATIO

RAITH PARK

HILL STREET

PLOT 58

Ø12000

Ø14000

34000
8000
18
20000
18000
22000
32000
40000
4000
20000
4000
44000
75°
105°
75°

Note: The patio requires sunk to a depth of 250mm

| PROJECT: FIFE VISITOR CENTRE |
| CLIENT: VISIT FIFE |
| CLIENT CONTACT: S. DAVIDSON |
| PROJECT LEADER: A. ANDERSON |
| DRAWING SET No: 2 of 8 |
| TITLE: SITE PLAN |
| SCALE: 1: 200 |
| LOCATION: 60 HILL STREET |
| TOWN: DYSART, FIFE |
| DRAWING NUMBER: 751Z - 52 |
| DATE STARTED: 22.5.15 |
| DATE COMPLETED: 21.9.16 |

ADDITIONAL WORKS: CAR PARK
SUNKEN PATIO
CURVED WALL
ACCESS PATHS
NEW TREES
GRASS LANSCAPING

LANDSCAPING & SURFACING

CAR PARK - TARMAC
PATIO - MONO-BLOC
PATHS - MONO-BLOC
OPEN AREAS - GRASS
NEW TREES - SILVER BIRCH

FLOOR PLAN

Floor plans come in a number of forms. They are often fully dimensioned to give the builder accurate information about the size of rooms and positions of features such as doors and windows. They may include fixtures and fittings such as shelving and display cases or tables and chairs. They can also come without dimensions and are intended to be shown to a client. Floor plans are often used in promotional materials to help sell a property or to promote a public building to the community.

A floor plan includes:

- Arrangement of rooms.
- Positions of doors and windows.
- Positions of light fittings, electrical sockets and switches.
- Kitchen and bathroom fixtures and fittings.
- Plumbing and drainage runs.
- Dimensions and notes.

EXAM PREP

It was a challenge for the architect to find a discrete position for the toilets in the open-plan space.

Q1. Explain how he resolved this problem.

When an interior space is designed it is important that the building and its contents are drawn to the same scale.

Q2. Explain why this is important.

FLOOR PLAN

FLOOR PLANS PLOT 60 HILL STREET

NOTE:

THE RH VERTICAL WALL ON THE UPPER FLOOR IS STEEL REINFORCED CONCRETE.

ALL INTERIOR FURNITURE TO BE IN LIGHT OAK WOOD AND FROM THE AKEA OAKLAND RANGE.

CAFE WORKTOPS TO BE MARBLE EFFECT WITH FULLY ROUNDED EDGES.

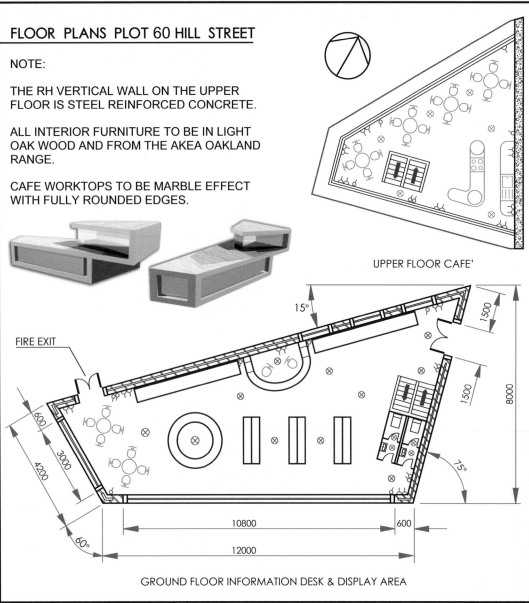

UPPER FLOOR CAFE'

FIRE EXIT

15°
1500
1500
8000
75°
600
4200
3000
60°
10800
600
12000

GROUND FLOOR INFORMATION DESK & DISPLAY AREA

PROJECT: FIFE VISITOR CENTRE	
CLIENT: VISIT FIFE	
CLIENT CONTACT: S. DAVIDSON	
PROJECT LEADER: A. ANDERSON	
DRAWING SET No: 3 of 8	
TITLE: FLOOR PLANS	
SCALE: 1: 50	
LOCATION: 60 HILL STREET	
TOWN: DYSART, FIFE	
DRAWING NUMBER: 751Z - 53	
DATE STARTED: 22.5.15	
DATE COMPLETED: 21.9.16	

FLOOR COVERINGS and DECOR:

    FLOOR - LAMINATED OAK FLOOR THROUGHOUT
    WALLS - SATIN EMULSION

FIXTURES and FITTING

GROUND FLOOR:
    RECEPTION DESK CURVED TYPE 2
    2 DISPLAY CABINETS TYPE 6
    3 DISPLAY CABINETS TYPE 4
    1 CIRCULAR DISPLAY TYPE 12

CAFE
    ISLAND COOKING UNIT TYPE 7
    WALL BASED SINK UNIT & WORK SURFACE TYPE 9

SECTIONAL VIEW FEATURES

Sectional views show a slice through a part of the building, normally to a scale of 1:20. This example shows a section through the eaves, a window and the foundations of the building.

The project set of drawings will include several sectional views showing all the relevant materials and joining methods. Materials are shown either by annotation or by using a BS symbol to describe the material.

Sectional views are vital when describing how a building is to be constructed. The building standards department will check the sectional drawings to ensure the design is sound.

Sectional views include:
- Technical details of eaves and foundations.
- Technical details of doors and windows.
- Technical details of floors and ceilings.
- Dimensions.
- Details of the materials to be used throughout the build.
- Ground levels outside and underneath the building.

EXAM PREP

A new building has to be energy efficient and conform to government regulations on heat loss.

Q1. Explain how a new building design can be tested for energy efficiency prior to being built.

SECTIONS

SECTION THROUGH EAVES, WINDOW & FOUNDATIONS PLOT 60 HILL STREET

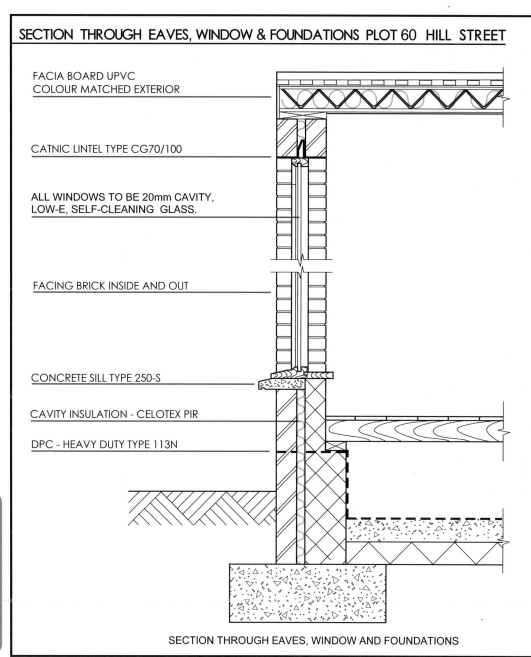

FACIA BOARD UPVC
COLOUR MATCHED EXTERIOR

CATNIC LINTEL TYPE CG70/100

ALL WINDOWS TO BE 20mm CAVITY,
LOW-E, SELF-CLEANING GLASS.

FACING BRICK INSIDE AND OUT

CONCRETE SILL TYPE 250-S

CAVITY INSULATION - CELOTEX PIR

DPC - HEAVY DUTY TYPE 113N

SECTION THROUGH EAVES, WINDOW AND FOUNDATIONS

PROJECT: FIFE VISITOR CENTRE	
CLIENT: VISIT FIFE	
CLIENT CONTACT: S. DAVIDSON	
PROJECT LEADER: A. ANDERSON	
DRAWING SET No: 4 of 8	
TITLE: SECTION THROUGH WINDOW	
SCALE: 1: 20	
LOCATION: 60 HILL STREET	
TOWN: DYSART, FIFE	
DRAWING NUMBER: 751Z - 54	
DATE STARTED: 22.5.15	
DATE COMPLETED: 21.9.16	

FRAMES AND SILLS:

ALL WINDOW FRAMES IN LIGHT OAK WITH CLEAR, BREATHABLE POLYURETHANE FINISH.

ROOF CONSTRUCTION:

THE FLAT ROOFS ARE TO BE BUILT USING OPEN WEB JOISTS - TYPE OW-77523A

ROOF CONSTRUCTION TO TAKE THE LOAD FROM A GREEN SEDUM ROOF, DEPTH 100mm

FLOOR CONSTRUCTION:

SUSPENDED TIMBER FLOOR JOISTS WITH 21mm T&G OAK FLOORING

ELEVATIONS

Elevation drawings are submitted to the planning department so that they can check that the building conforms to local planning standards. Occupiers on neighbouring plots will also be sent a copy and asked to ensure the design does not spoil their outlook. Elevations also give the builder the additional information needed to construct the building from the ground up.

Elevation drawings include:

- Orthographic views from each direction.
- The external features of the building.
- Main dimensions, especially heights.
- The style of roof; this one has a flat, green roof.
- The style and positions of doors and windows.
- The hinge position on windows.

ELEVATIONS PLOT 60 HILL STREET

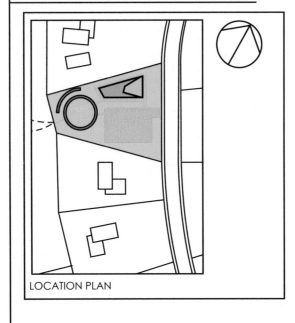

LOCATION PLAN

PROJECT: FIFE VISITOR CENTRE	
CLIENT: VISIT FIFE	
CLIENT CONTACT: S. DAVIDSON	
PROJECT LEADER: A. ANDERSON	
DRAWING SET No: 5 of 8	
TITLE: ELEVATIONS	
SCALE: 1:100	
UNITS: ALL SIZES IN mm	

LOCATION: 60 HILL STREET
TOWN: DYSART, FIFE
DRAWING NUMBER: 751Z - 55
DATE STARTED: 22.5.15
DATE COMPLETED: 21.9.16
WALLS:
BRICK - WATERSTRUCK 2601 DISTRESSED DRY WEIGHT - 3.2kg TYPE - BS EN 771-1

Note: ALL WINDOWS TO BE FIXED
EXCEPT THE THREE SMALL WINDOWS.

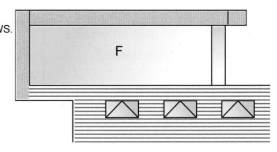

SMALL WINDOW DETAIL

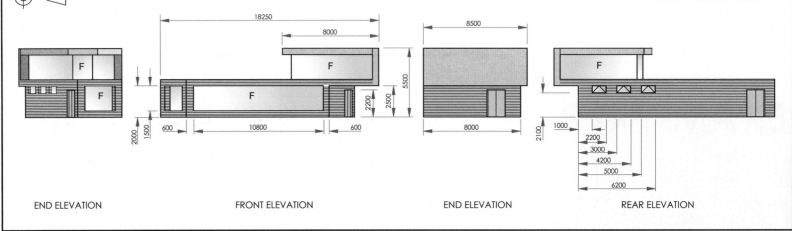

END ELEVATION   FRONT ELEVATION   END ELEVATION   REAR ELEVATION

CONSTRUCTION DRAWING SYMBOLS

WHY USE SYMBOLS?

The use of British Standard symbols in construction drawing is every bit as important as for engineering drawing. Symbols describe complex features using simple graphics and provide a common language that all users of the drawings can understand.

Standard symbols provide:

- Consistency of input.
- A common application that all users understand.
- Simplification of complex features leading to increased speed of drawing.
- Drawings that can cross language barriers; important in a growing international market.

The symbols shown here are a small selection of those used everyday in construction drawings. These are the ones you will need to understand and remember for your course exam.

ELECTRICAL

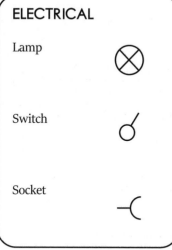

Lamp

Switch

Socket

LANDSCAPING

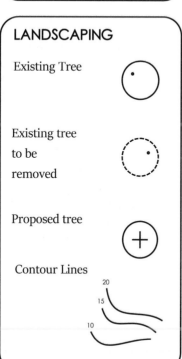

Existing Tree

Existing tree to be removed

Proposed tree

Contour Lines

INTERIOR FITTINGS

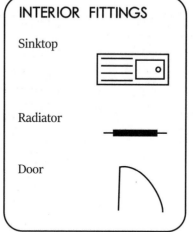

Sinktop

Radiator

Door

BATHROOM FITTINGS

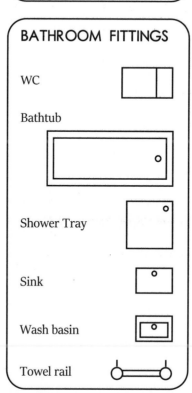

WC

Bathtub

Shower Tray

Sink

Wash basin

Towel rail

WINDOWS

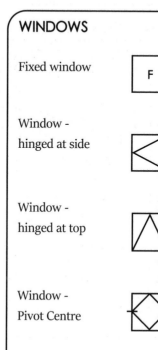

Fixed window

Window - hinged at side

Window - hinged at top

Window - Pivot Centre

Window - Sliding horizontally

Window - hinged at bottom

DIRECTION

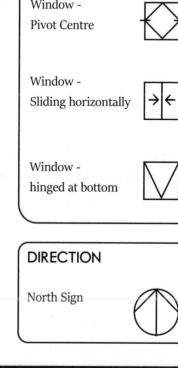

North Sign

STRUCTURAL

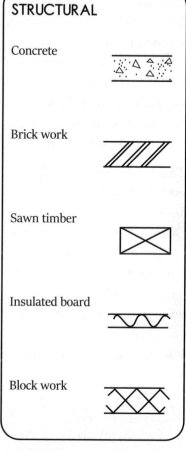

Concrete

Brick work

Sawn timber

Insulated board

Block work

DRAINS & WASTE PIPES

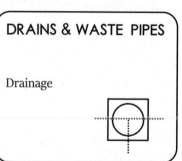

Drainage

DO
SOMETHING
USEFUL:
SKETCH!

Of all the skills you will develop in this course perhaps the most crucial is freehand sketching. It is a design skill from which all other skills spring. If you can master the means of communicating graphically with just a pencil and paper and develop an eye for proportion and perspective, then all the other course skills will follow.

Sketching is immediate, fluid and necessary when developing and recoding design ideas. Sketching is also a skill that, once the basics are mastered, is satisfying and rewarding. This section assumes that you have developed some sketching skills in your N5 course and that you are familiar with vanishing points and perspective techniques.

WHAT IS IT?

Of all the skills you will learn in this course freehand sketching is the most essential. It is the skill on which the other skills are built. It will develop your eye, train your hand, improve your creativity and satisfy your emotions when you master it.

Learning to sketch requires two things:

1. Effective demonstrations (your teacher should provide these).
2. Practice (only you can do this).

This section in the book cannot teach you how to sketch but can encourage you to think about technique and learn the process so that you can practice the skills.

HOW TO PRACTICE

You don't need special equipment to practice sketching. A3 paper, a 2B pencil and a flat surface to work on are all that are required.

Choose everyday items from your house, including furniture, and practice your freehand sketching technique by making three types of sketches:

- Orthographic sketches
- perspective sketches
- technical detail

BICYCLE HANDLEBAR TORCH

The torch shown here will allow us to demonstrate the process behind each method of sketching. You can work from these pages and sketch the torch but you should work from real items whenever you can. These skills are vital to your development as a graphics specialist; practice and master them.

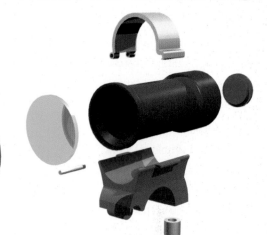

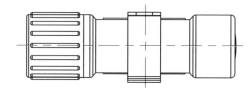

PLAN

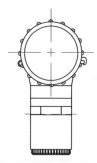

END ELEVATION

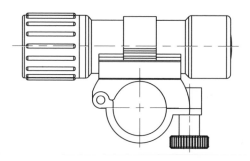
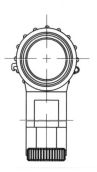

ELEVATION

END ELEVATION

Worksheet alert
You can download the worksheets online to support you with this task - see inside back cover for more information and website details.

ORTHOGRAPHIC SKETCHING

WHAT IS IT?

Sketching an item in 2D is a basic skill. Orthographic sketching, creating sketches of related views, is an important skill to master in this course.

A similar process to orthographic projection on a drawing board is used when sketching. Sizes are not important but establishing good proportion is.

1. STARTING A SKETCH

- Select a simple 2D view and construct the sketch.
- Ensure you sketch each feature in good proportion.

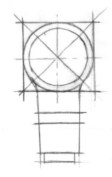

2. ADDING VIEWS

- Project the adjacent view taking care to keep freehand lines straight.
- Use simple box shapes to construct the main features.
- Project the plan view.

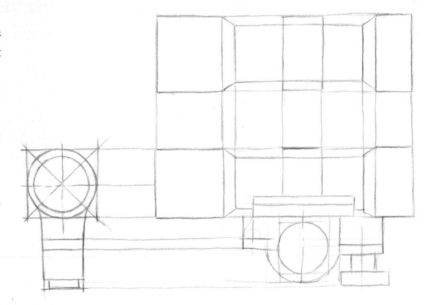

3. ADDING DETAIL

- Details can be picked out individually.
- Firm in the outlines.
- Add centre lines as required.
- Component views can be dimensioned. This assembly sketch should not be dimensioned.

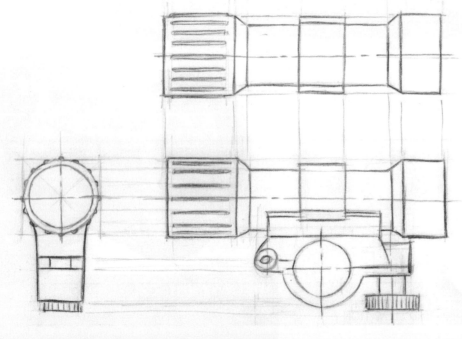

4. ENLARGED VIEW

- Orthographic enlarged views can be sketched to show smaller features in more detail.
- Annotations can be added to clarify features.
- Well chosen annotations can also pick up extra marks in an assessment.

16 x Ø2 Raised semi-circles on a 30 PCD

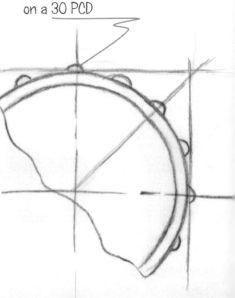

PERSPECTIVE SKETCHING

WHAT IS IT?

2-point perspective is the style of choice when you need a sketched graphic that looks realistic. We see things in perspective but it can be challenging to sketch in perspective.

Practice will train your eye to identify good perspective and train your hand to create it. Designers work in perspective because of its realism.

SKETCHING THE TORCH

1. SELECT A FACE

- Construct the perspective ellipse.
- Use construction lines to plan the size and angle it towards the vanishing point.

2. PROJECT THE LENGTH

- Project towards the second vanishing point
- Take care with this curve; it should be 'rounder' than the front curve.

3. ADD THE OTHER SECTIONS

- Project towards the vanishing point; ensure your proportions are accurate.

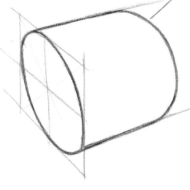

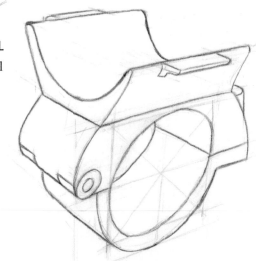

4. ADD DETAIL

- Make careful use of the VP.
- Ensure good proportions.
- Firm in the outline.

SKETCHING THE HANDLEBAR CLAMP

1. SKETCH THE FLAT FACE

- Construct the perspective ellipse.
- Use construction lines to plan the proportion and size.
- Be sure to aim towards the vanishing point.

2. PROJECT THE BREADTH

- Project towards the second vanishing point.
- Take care with proportions.

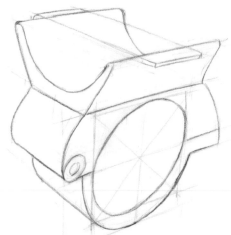

3. ADD DETAIL

- Make careful use of the VP.
- Firm the outline.

SKETCHING TECHNICAL DETAIL

WHAT IS IT?

You will become familiar with technical detail in other areas of the course and you need to be able to identify, understand and produce technical details in your assessments. This section covers; exploded views, sections, sub-assemblies, enlarged and partial views and details of moving parts. You should focus on these when you produce technical sketches in your project work.

TASK

Sketch four examples of technical detail using the cycle torch or another product. The construction work followed by the final sketches shown here will help guide you through the process.

WHY IS SKETCHING TECHNICAL DETAIL SO IMPORTANT?

Sketching is the designers most important skill. Technical detail are sketches a designer uses to explain how a product assembles and works.

Sketching technical detail will help you to analyse a product and ensure you can describe how products assemble in your assignment task and in the course exam.

You can practice these actual sketches by downloading our worksheets from the website. Or, practice by sketching other everyday items.

EXPLODED VIEW

1. CONSTRUCTION

- Try to sketch a view exploded in two planes.
- Use projection lines to position your exploded parts.

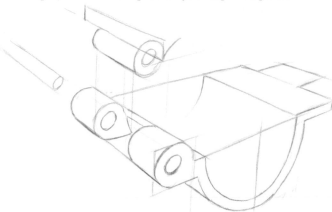

SECTIONAL VIEW

1. CONSTRUCTION

- Construct the part view using boxes.
- Ensure you establish good proportion.

2. ADD DETAIL

- Add the screw thread and check each part is correctly positioned.
- Cross-hatch and firm in outlines.

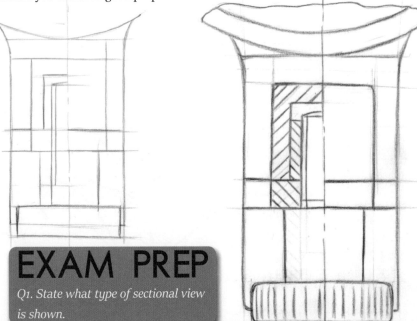

EXAM PREP

Q1. State what type of sectional view is shown.

The pin is brass to prevent wear

The top cover is held in position and the hinge pin is slid through

2. FIRM IN

- Check your lines of perspective and adjust as required.
- Firm in the outline and annotate...

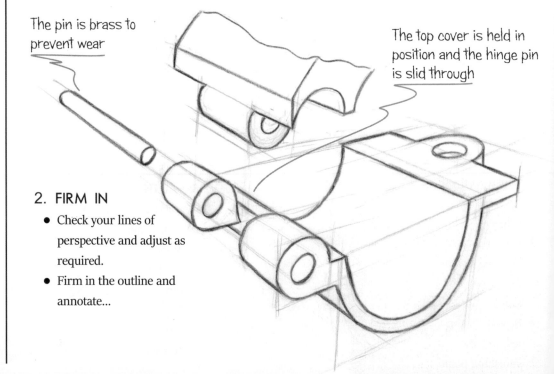

MOVING PARTS

1. CONSTRUCTION

- Study the movement and construct a sketch in the open position.

2. FIRM AND ANNOTATE

- Add arrows to indicate movement.
- Colour can help distinguish different parts.

Tips
- Sketch arrows to indicate movement.
- Annotations demonstrate your knowledge and help create a busy, detailed layout; annotations can be visual as well as informative.

EXPLODED PICTORIAL PART SECTION

1. CONSTRUCTION

If you feel confident try this sketch. Don't worry about the screw threads. Just try to get the proportions and alignments right.

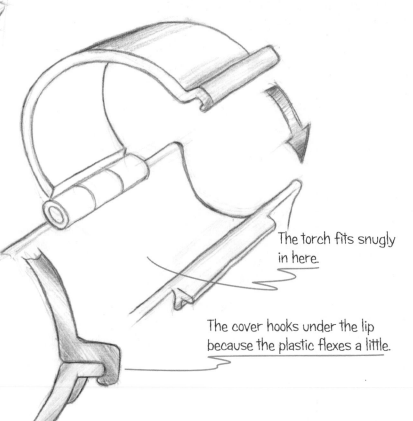

The torch fits snugly in here.

The cover hooks under the lip because the plastic flexes a little.

SKETCHING TECHNICAL DETAIL

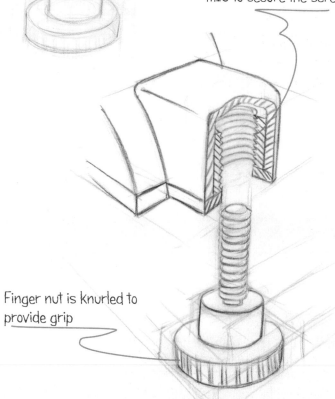

2. ADD DETAIL

- Add knurling details, cross-hatching and screw threads if you are confident.
- It's never going to be perfect but it's not intended to be.

The brass insert is threaded M10 to secure the screw.

Finger nut is knurled to provide grip

MANUAL ILLUSTRATION
RENDER
IT
COOL

SPIRIT MARKER

Manual illustration lies just behind sketching in the list of most important design skills. Illustration is an integral part of preliminary graphics. Being able to colour and render a sketch quickly will allow you to communicate an idea or evaluate a design more effectively.

Adding colour and tone can enhance the realism of a sketch and give it more impact in a page of design ideas. A well rendered image can sell an idea, convince a client and prove to you that your design has potential. Learn to illustrate and be able to communicate your ideas effectively.

MANUAL ILLUSTRATION

WHAT IS IT?

Manual illustration is applying colour, tone and surface texture to a line drawing or sketch. The common mediums used are: coloured pencil and spirit marker. What are the differences and what should you learn?

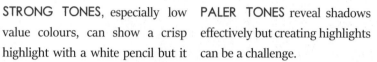

MARKER PENS

PROS...

Markers come in a vast range of PANTONE colours. Their tonal range and variety of tints and shades is massive. Designers like them because the application of colour is immediate, the quality is very good and because of the vast range of tones and colours.

...AND CONS

Good quality spirit markers are expensive. The range of colours and tones you will use in school will be limited by the cost. Some pens are refillable and some are designed to be recycled.
Re-fill inks are also expensive so take care of the pens and ensure the cap is secured before you put the pens away.

COLOURED PENCILS

Coloured pencils are cheap and come in a wide range of colours. They will likely be the medium of choice in most schools. The down-side is that they produce a grainy texture and it can be difficult to get a really dark tone without it becoming shiny. The best solution is to use marker pens and coloured pencils together.

WHAT COLOURS AND TONES SHOULD I USE?

The range of tones is large. In school you may only have strong, saturated colours. Paler (pastel) and mid-tones are available as well and these are often more useful when completing illustration work for this course. So, choose carefully.

STRONG TONES, especially low value colours, can show a crisp highlight with a white pencil but it can be difficult to get shadows (darker tones) to show up.

PALER TONES reveal shadows effectively but creating highlights can be a challenge.

STRONG TONE with both black and white rendering pencils added.

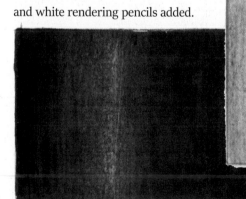

PALER TONES come into their own when reflective, textured or plastic surface finishes are required.

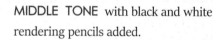

MIDDLE TONE with black and white rendering pencils added.

MARKER PEN TECHNIQUES

THREE COMMON ILLUSTRATION TECHNIQUES

1. Blocking in
2. Strike through
3. Striping

IMPORTANT TIP

The techniques shown on this and subsequent pages are not intended to represent presentation work. These examples cover techniques employed to emphasise or enhance design sketches. They reveal materials or suggest form. These are the techniques that will be useful to you when you are designing or exploring a product when you begin your assignment task.

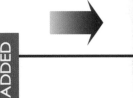

SPIRIT MARKER

BLOCKING IN

Use the pen in multiple directions to cover the area evenly. You may need to cover the area more than once. This creates an even base tone.

BLOCKING IN

STRIKE THROUGH

Start the strokes at the bottom right and pass fully over the shape, crossing the outline. Alter the angle of strokes as you move over the shape, this creates a textured look. Leaving small gaps can help achieve a reflective or shiny appearance.

STRIKE THROUGH

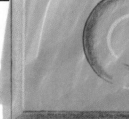

WITH COLOURED PENCIL TONAL SHADING ADDED

CYLINDRICAL STRIPING

Apply the strokes in one direction and leave gaps to suggest a cylindrical effect. Don't worry about errors; look at this example, it's not perfect. Read the tip at the top right.

STRIPING

STRIKE THROUGH

WHY USE IT? Strike through is suitable for 2D illustrations such as the elevation of the torch. Choose your colour and tone carefully when representing plastic products.

1. THE SKETCH OR DRAWING

The line sketch can be in pencil or, for best effect, in coloured pencil. This one is sketched freehand and was tidied up with a straight edge.

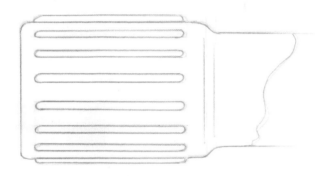

3. ADD SHADOWS WITH THE MARKER PEN

Apply darker tones with the marker using the bullet tip where necessary. Below the ribs and at the top and bottom of the curved surface are important areas to shade. This will create tonal contrast and suggest curving.

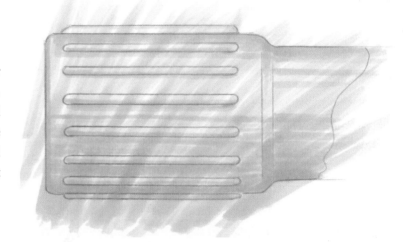

2. APPLY THE STRIKE THROUGH

Begin at the bottom right and apply strokes as you progress to the top left. Try to vary the angle and curving of the strokes to achieve a realistic effect.

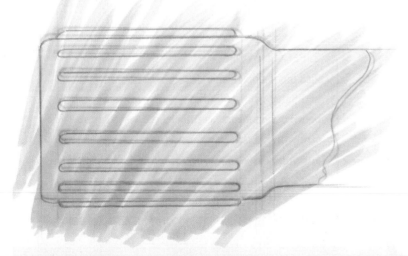

4. ENHANCE TONES WITH COLOURED PENCIL

Shadows are picked out and enhanced using coloured pencil. You can choose black or a colour to match the marker pen. This one uses a blue pencil to match the marker. The dark shadows create contrast with the crisp highlights. No white highlighter has been used. It does not show up well on the pale marker tone.

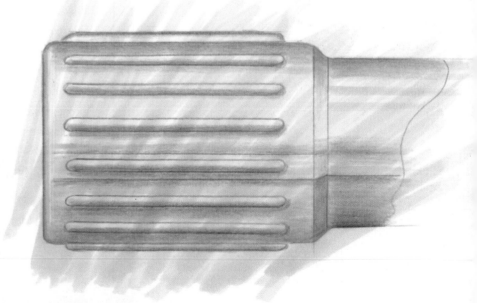

STRIPING

1. MARKER STROKES

Pen strokes are applied to the technical detail leaving gaps where the highlights should be. Work freehand and take care to follow the line of perspective.

Don't get hung up about the odd mistake. This one has several. Remember, it's a preliminary graphic not a piece of art

2. PENCIL WORK

Tone from a coloured pencil finishes the graphic. Add darker tones where the light disappears around the curved surfaces. Finish with a strong outline.

PARTIAL BLOCKING IN

1. PARTIAL BLOCKING IN

Select one or two surfaces on each component and block them in carefully.

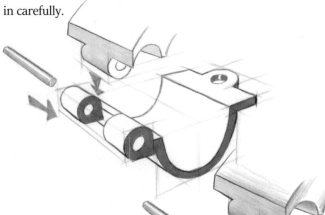

2. OPTIONAL FINISHING

Either apply tonal scale with coloured pencil.
Or
Add more marker pen to darken tones and create shadows.
Outline it with a fine line pen.
This illustration uses no coloured pencil at all.

BLOCKING IN

1. BLOCKING IN

Block in each part carefully. Using different colours helps distinguish separate components.

2. PENCIL WORK

Pick out shadows and highlights using coloured pencils. Detail such as the screw thread and knurling are emphasised in strong tones. A white pencil is used to create highlights on the darker areas.

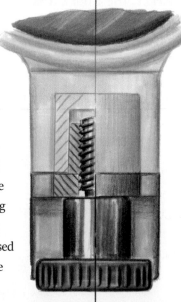

This shows what a preliminary graphics page may look like. Sketching and illustration are brought together either to support design work or to analyse an existing product by deconstructing it graphically.

Try overlapping one or two of your graphics to create a dynamic, 3D look.

Annotations are important, they demonstrate your knowledge and understanding of the product and how it assembles.

This work is mainly freehand; though you can use a straight edge and instruments if you wish.

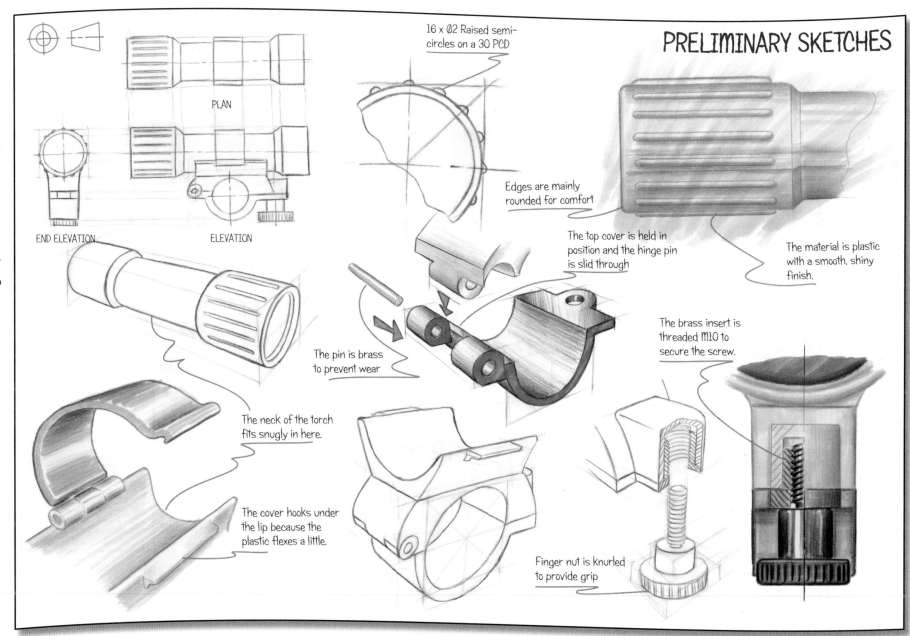

PRELIMINARY SKETCHES

PLAN

END ELEVATION

ELEVATION

16 x Ø2 Raised semi-circles on a 30 PCD

Edges are mainly rounded for comfort

The top cover is held in position and the hinge pin is slid through

The material is plastic with a smooth. shiny finish.

The pin is brass to prevent wear

The brass insert is threaded M10 to secure the screw.

The neck of the torch fits snugly in here.

The cover hooks under the lip because the plastic flexes a little.

Finger nut is knurled to provide grip

MANUAL ILLUSTRATION

PRELIMINARY GRAPHICS PAGE

PRELIMINARY SKETCHES

GRAPHICS IN SOCIETY

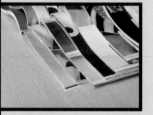

WHAT IS THE IMPACT? HOW ARE WE INFLUENCED?

Graphics, Sketches, Drawings, Logos, Videos, Slides, Illustrations, Art, Diagrams, Signs, Plans, Apps, Photographs, Movies, Magazines, Posters, Adverts, Flyers, Leaflets, Decals, Wraps, Images, Cartoons, Graffiti, Maps, Patterns, Decorations, Computer games, Dials, Detailing, Screens, Geometry, Stained Glass, Websites, Graphs, Banners, Wallpaper, Packaging, Flags and Tattoos.

They are all types of graphic or contain or display types of graphic. These graphics can be informative, educational, entertaining, beautiful, commercial or provoking. One thing is for certain; we are surrounded by graphics of every sort. It is important to understand these graphics and the impact that they are intended to have on us.

GRAPHIC IN SOCIETY

The importance of graphics to manufacturing industries is well covered elsewhere in this book. It is the use and influence of graphics in wider society that we are covering in this chapter.

Understanding how graphics are produced and applied using multi-media technologies will shed light on issues we should be aware of. These are technologies that deliver graphics to our homes, workplaces and our public spaces every day. Many of these technologies have become very familiar and indeed essential to us. Others are more subtle in their purpose and influence. It is not possible to cover every area of impact that graphics have on society but those covered here are some of the main areas of influence.

Graphics are designed to: Promote, Persuade, Present, Sell, Stimulate, Inform, Identify, Create, Contact, Communicate, Entertain, Locate, Direct, Simplify, Organise, Make, Build, Protect and Attract Attention. There are as many different forms and styles of graphic as there are means of delivering them. Your task is to be aware of and understand the impact of graphics on us all.

GRAPHICS AND COPYRIGHT

The copyright of an image, whether it is a photograph, drawing, illustration, logo, 3D model or promotional layout automatically belongs to its creator. The copyright may be sold to or licensed to another party. This means that the image cannot be used without permission from the copyright holder.

You should be aware of copyright because, when you use an image in your coursework it is, technically, an offence to copy the work, show the work in public or adapt the work without permission. However, under the 'Fair Dealing' rule, the use of images **for educational purposes** is normally permitted. The owner of the work also has the right to be identified as the author. So remember to acknowledge the owner of any images you use in your project work. All of the above applies to any photographs that you may take yourself and images that you create yourself; you have automatic copyright of them. An image or document may be registered and a copyright symbol can be applied to make it clear that the item is copyright protected.

MOBILE TECHNOLOGY

What is it?

Portable devices such as smart phones, laptops, tablets, pads, notebooks, GPS devices and digital cameras.

What types of graphics are used?

Digital photographs, 3D models, animations, 2D vectors, digital videos, bar codes and QR codes. The image types and sizes that are commonly used for mobile technologies are: JPEG, PNG and GIF. The image resolution of mobile devices determines image quality and is partly governed by the screen size, resolution (how many pixels the screen contains) and the pixel density PPI (how many pixels it can display along one inch). Smartphone screens vary in size between 4in and 5in (screens size is still stated in inches) and the resolution is around 1,920 x 1,080 pixels. The pixel densities vary between 468ppi and 326ppi.

Impact on society

Mobile technology is accessible anywhere there is a compatible signal. Available at any time of day, it can remotely connect and network with your home, office and the internet. Banking and other finance can be managed remotely. E-tickets make booking travel and events more convenient and GPS navigation aids travel. Networking and social media sites are available wherever there is a signal. The speed with which breaking news is spread across the internet through social media makes the smartphone an essential item for millions. Cloud computing means that mobile devices can support flexible working. QR codes (quick response codes) can be scanned by a smartphone to provide information about the product it is attached to, usually via a web-page.

Issues?

Devices require a signal and a charged battery or power source. Security of your personal information and data can be at risk from criminals when using wireless systems. Security has to be tight and this can be expensive to maintain. If your GPS device and your cell phone are both fitted with Satnav, then satellites can pinpoint your exact position at any given time. It raises concerns about your rights and your privacy.

PUBLIC INFORMATION SIGNS AND SYMBOLS

What is it?

The use of graphical and digital technologies to provide public information signs. Public signs can be made from metals, plastics, neon glass and digital electronic display systems.

Types of graphic used.

Public signs perform one or more of five functions:

Information: signs giving information about locations, services and facilities, such as maps, directories, timetables, departure and arrival displays and instructional signs.

Identification: Signs indicating services, shops and features such as building numbers and names, public toilet signs, or floor names and numbers.

Direction: Signs showing the locations of public spaces, services and facilities.

Safety: Warning or safety instructions, such as traffic, warning and exit signs.

Regulatory: Signs conveying rules and regulations (e.g. keep left).

Impact on society

Public signs help to make our lives safer, better organised and more convenient. Consistency and standardisation of signage across many areas helps ensure that signs are understood across cultures, languages and borders. Signs also can be efficient by providing information with little or no words.

Digital signs can be changed remotely without having to print a new sign. The message can be updated regularly. There is no paper waste. It can be dynamic and can command attention. Advertising and information can be rotated or 'rolled' to make best use of the space and time available and to catch the eye of the potential customer. Changes can be controlled remotely.

Issues

Advertising signs are controlled so that they meet criteria specified by the government. They must be safe, clean and tidy, permitted by the landowner and not obscure official road signs etc. Illuminated signs can cause stress to people living near-by.

MEDICINE & HEALTH

What is it?

The use of digital and graphical technologies in medicine and health care.

Types of graphic used:

- Scanning of the body, MRI , X-Ray, Ultrasound and 3D scanning.
- 3D CAD modelling and printing of prosthetic limbs and body parts.
- 3D CAD modelling and machining of dental implant crowns.
- Simulation of medical operations using an interactive 3D CAD simulation.

Impact on society

Laser scans of organic forms and the resulting 3D scan can be converted to an STL file so that prosthetic body parts can be designed and modelled around it. 3D Printing prosthetic limbs is a cheaper, faster and more accurate method of making artificial limbs. It tailors prosthetics to better suit the amputee, improving comfort and function. The prosthetics are durable and lightweight and are custom made for the user.

Dental crowns and implants are made to fit the recipients mouth accurately. 3D imaging scans the mouth and a 3D model of the mouth is taken. Teeth are modelled using 3D CAD and the model is emailed to the lab where it is milled (cut) from a solid block. It gives a more precise fit and saves time.

Training surgeons using simulated operations leads to safer operations performed by more experienced professionals. 3D simulations give surgeons experience without putting a patient at risk. Ultra-sound and MRI scans are now standard practice in the NHS and help provide accurate diagnosis and save lives.

Issues

Around 34 million people around the world have lost one or more limbs and it is clear that relatively few amputees will get the opportunity to have a prosthetic limb fitted. CAD designed and 3D printed prosthetics make the process much cheaper and, as the technology develops, it is hoped that many more people, including those in developing countries, will have this and other CAD enhanced treatment available to them.

TEXTILES AND FASHION

What is it?

The use of graphic designs on garments, textiles, fabrics and footwear.

Types of graphic used.

Knitted and woven textiles. Printed fabrics using screen printing. Graphic input into sports clothing and sports shoe design. Shop front and interior design.

Impact on society

Textile and fashion design are vital parts of the fashion and textile retail industries. Graphics in the textile industry has a significant impact on customer appeal and sales success.

The textile and fashion industry:

- Is responsible for clothing the entire population; we all need clothes.
- Employs workers on many levels; garment workers, pattern makers, textile designers, graphic designers, marketing teams, advertising agencies and packing companies — all employing a large workforce.
- Contributes billions to the national and global economies.
- Brings innovation and creativity to mainstream society.
- Gives consumers choice and opportunity to express themselves through what they wear.
- Helps fuel new technology by its demand for new materials and manufacturing methods.
- Provides fashion shop outlets which are often cleverly designed, hi-impact retail buildings, bringing skilled jobs to architects, joiners, electricians and shop-fitters.

Issues

The textile and fashion industry is governed by trends that are artificially created to drive sales. Fashion (and consumers) often value clever graphics and styles before function, comfort and quality.

OUTDOOR COMMERCIAL BRANDING

What is it?

Vehicle wraps and decals, shop front signage, billboards etc.

Types of graphic used:

- Vehicle wraps, vehicle decals and cut vinyl displays.
- Shop front branding, signs and displays.
- Printed and electronic advertising billboards

Impact on society

Outdoor advertising is the most visual promotional tool for connecting with a target market. Unlike radio or TV it cannot be turned off or switched over. Outdoor displays can benefit because of scale and location. All three forms of outdoor graphic display give a company's identity more 'visual impact' and help reinforce the 'brand identity'.

The average business vehicle is seen by up to 3000 people per day. The cost of the vehicle wrap per 100 sightings is 4p. A far more cost effective form of advertising than radio (£1.20/100 listeners) or direct mail at £1.90 per 100. Vehicle branding can last 5 years as opposed to short lived radio or magazine advertising.

A shop front advertising display can set the right tone whether it be cheap and cheerful or elegant and sophisticated. Both types of display may contain the company name, logo, tag-line or slogan, colour scheme, corporate image and typeface, contact details, web address and open and closed times.

Billboards have 24 hour exposure. Impact of scale and can generate strong product awareness.

Issues

All of the examples listed above are more effective when teamed with other types of advertising media. Outdoor advertising displays should not appear cluttered and must make the key information easy to locate and remember. The vast majority of viewers are on the move when viewing. Outdoor advertising can be intrusive and unwelcome.

PRINTED MEDIA

What is it?

Printed media: newspapers, magazines etc. Publications prepared using DTP.

Types of graphic used

Photographs, Illustrations, Vector images, Page layouts.

Impact on society

There are six different printed media formats that advertisers use: newspapers, magazines, direct mail, customer magazines, door drop leaflets and catalogues.

Marketers and advertisers know that newspapers and magazines are the easiest way to reach targeted customers. Glossy, monthly magazines are the most effective advertising medium when targeting a particular audience.

Local newspapers are still the best way to promote local news and events and advertise products to a local market. Companies that print newspapers and magazines have developed their own websites. These websites publish news stories as they occur, matching the radio and TV speed for reporting news. They follow this up with in-depth reporting in a paper based format. Many readers take online subscriptions to their magazines or newspapers and read online.

Paper based printed magazines and newspapers are convenient, well presented and do not require technology or a power source to access. Many paper publications have a large and very loyal readership.

Issues

Until every small town has fast broadband access, newspapers will continue to provide a valuable news service, especially local news. Advertising using promotional graphics is a major factor in the success of paper publications. Businesses know they can target groups of society by placing promotions in selected publications.

Paper based publications can be costly to produce. Production methods can damage the environment, though sustainable production using recycled paper and safer vegetable inks are with us already and these sustainable methods are rapidly expanding.

Distribution is costly, publications need to be physically transported to the end user; collected or delivered. Printed media is not the best way of targeting a global market.

In magazine publishing the turn around time from writing an article to printing and publishing the magazine can be between 4 and 6 weeks. In news terms this is not quick enough. Blogs and social media websites can publish news electronically within a few hours.

EXAM PREP

In the Print v Pixels debate there are arguments that favour newspapers and magazines while other arguments favour online reading through websites and blogs.

Q. *Discuss the pros and cons of both platforms, printed media and digital media, regarding the choice of media for accessing news and entertainment publications.*
Make three clear points in your answer.

PACKAGING AND RETAIL BRANDING

What is it?

The use of graphics in product and food packaging industries.

Types of graphic used.

Promotional artwork and design work on product packaging.

Impact on society

Retail packaging has been described as *'The last and best chance to make a sale'* - Marty Neumeier. Good packaging design can increase sales, secure greater customer loyalty, generate fewer complaints, open up new markets, attract new customers and improve the business' identity.

Product packaging has several functions including:

- Containing and protecting the product without harming the environment.
- Drawing attention to a specific product in a crowded retail space.
- Positioning a product amongst a certain category and value.
- Differentiating a product from its competitors.
- To be stack-able, rack-able and durable in storage, transport and display.
- Representing a brand identity.
- Representing the creativity and advanced qualities the product may have.
- Making a connection with its target market.
- Providing nutritional information and instructions for use.

Studies of shopping behaviour raised two interesting theories:

1. Consumers make about 70% of their buying decisions at the point of sale.
2. Consumers spend around 3 seconds looking at packaging.

Issues

Packaging needs to be either recyclable or compostable (rot in an environmentally friendly way). Packaging should be made, where possible, from recycled materials. Graphics need to be able to adhere to a variety of surfaces such as plastics, paper and cardboard. Printing technology allows printing on all of the common packaging materials.

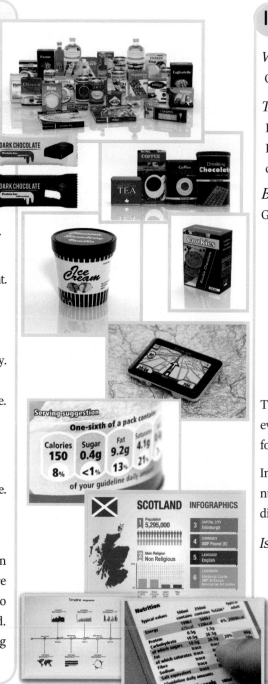

INFORMATION GRAPHICS

What is it?

Graphs and charts, tables, pictograms, diagrams and maps etc

Types of graphic used.

Bar Charts, Pie charts, Line Graphs, Tables, Timelines, Schematics, Maps, Planning Charts, and Pictograms. These are used to show and compare changes, to show and compare relationships and to bring facts to life.

Benefits to society

Graphs and charts benefit people by:

- Presenting information in a visual way that is less reliant on text or numbers.
- Making information more accessible and more likely to be read and understood.
- Emphasizing a main point.
- Engaging the audience.
- Giving raw data more visual impact.
- Allowing a quick way for the audience to visualize the data.

These graphics are among the most widely used in society and permeate every activity including; sport, banking, industry, building, health, labels, food and retail.

Information graphics provide real benefit to consumers by presenting nutritional information that can be used to help people achieve a healthier diet. Such information has to be simple, visual and easy to interpret.

Issues

- They can be technical in nature. Some members of the audience may still have difficulty interpreting or understand the information.
- Carefully prepared info graphics can lead to a product or service or data being made to look better than it is by simplifying the information, placing a skewed emphasis on the figures or adding carefully chosen graphics to convince the audience.

An extract from guidance given to food producing and packaging retailers by *The Department of Health* and the *Food Standards Agency*, is shown below. Four examples of draft designs for a nutrition label are shown, right.

'Guide to creating a front of pack (FoP) nutrition label for pre-packed products sold through retail outlets'

Colour
Only the lozenges (shapes) containing the information on fat, saturates, sugars and salt will be coloured. The colours used should be vibrant. The use of pastel colours should be avoided.

The colour management should deliver a good contrast between the traffic light colours, especially the amber and red.

The shade, tone and intensity of the traffic light colours that companies should aim to produce through their colour processes are:

Green: PANTONE® 375   or   C: 48% M: 0% Y: 94% K: 0%

Amber: PANTONE® 143   or   C: 0% M: 36% Y: 87% K: 0%

Red: PANTONE® RED 32   or   C: 0% M: 90% Y: 86% K: 0%

Contrast
There should be clear contrast between the background and the colour used for the font (numbers). Examples of good contrast are:
• white font on coloured background
• dark colour or black font on white background
• dark colour or black font on a coloured background

Terminology and order of nutrients
The name and order of the nutrients is set out in the EU FIC and will be presented on the front of pack as follows:

Energy / Fat / Saturates / Sugars / Salt
The Regulation does not allow any other nutrient in the repeat nutrition information on the front of food packaging.

Design a

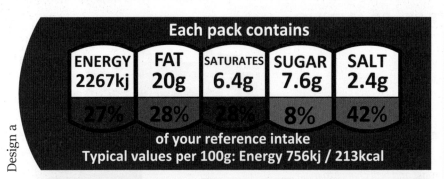

Design b

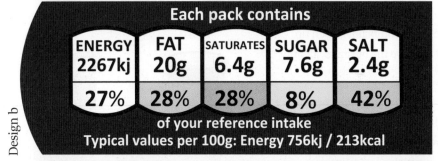

Design c

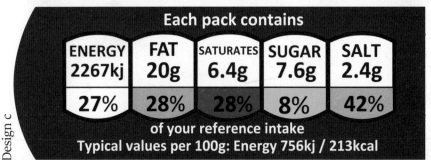

Design d

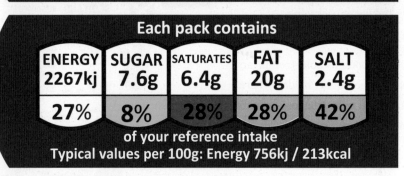

EXAM PREP

Pre-exam prep question task:
Using your DTP software, re-create the colours specified as CMYK in the guidance data.

Study the guide to nutritional information on the far left and the four draft nutritional labels left. Only one of the labels conforms to the guidance.

Q1. Identify the label that is designed correctly.

Q2. Explain the faults with the other three labels that cause lack of conformance with the guidance.

The specifications for use of colour, shade, tone and intensity refer to the terms 'Pantone®' and 'CMYK'.

Q3. Explain what is meant by these terms.

Q4. Explain why both 'Pantone®' and 'CMYK' are specified in the guidance.

The guidance refers to contrast several times.

Q5. Explain why contrast is so important in the design of these labels.

WHEN DESIGN GOES DIGITAL

Computers appear to be taking over everything! Not so long ago, designers and engineers laboriously created hand-drawings of incredible detail to ensure things could be built and manufactured.

This was all well and good, however hand drawings have lots of limitations and industry was quick to adopt the features that computers brought.

In this chapter you will discover how CAD changed the world of engineering and design...

THE IMPACT OF CAD

Almost every manufacturing and construction industry uses CAD files. In industry CAD files are created for two main purposes:

- Computer-aided design (CAD) files are used in the design of products and buildings.

- CAD files are used with computer numeric controlled (CNC) machinery to manufacture products, CADCAM (computer-aided design and manufacture).

CAD files can be created in-house or sub-contracted to a CAD technician or designer.

3D CAD was first invented in 1960s but in recent years it has developed rapidly and dominates design in engineering and architecture and, with the application of CADCAM and 3D printing, is increasingly used for manufacturing.

As new materials and printing technologies are created, more realistic prototypes will be printed directly from 3D CAD files. Printed buildings and cars have already been produced and full production is the next phase.

Precision engineering is the foundation of automotive and aeronautical manufacture and is increasingly used for creating personalised medical products, such as bone replacement. The demand for designers, architects, engineers and technicians who understand the process of CADCAM is more important than ever.

OPPORTUNITY

Opportunities for young designers, engineers, technicians and architects are many and varied and CAD skills are common to them all. You may well be at the start of a journey that leads you towards a career in which CAD skills are a significant part.

EMPLOYABILITY

3D CAD has become so important that it forms an industry in itself. Big manufacturing companies have their own CAD teams and there are many independent design studios that specialise in contract design work. From games developers to architects and engineers, CAD skills are in great demand and colleges and universities offer courses to support these industries.

Your experience of CAD began a year or two ago in Graphic Communication at National 5 level. Your CAD skills at Higher level will develop much further and much faster and it may be a route that you will continue towards a career. Even if it isn't, you will improve your problem-solving skills, your spatial awareness and graphical skills and your understanding of the manufactured world as you progress through your course.

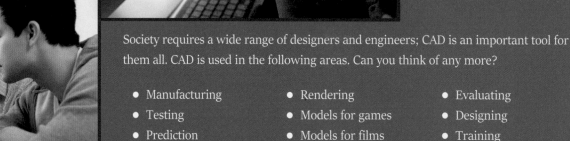

Society requires a wide range of designers and engineers; CAD is an important tool for them all. CAD is used in the following areas. Can you think of any more?

- Manufacturing
- Testing
- Prediction
- Animation
- Simulation

- Rendering
- Models for games
- Models for films
- Production drawings
- Prototyping

- Evaluating
- Designing
- Training
- Construction
- Communication

FILE MANAGEMENT

When you are doing any form of creative or design work using a computer you will inevitably generate lots of files - this book has required over 2000 separate files alone - and keeping track of your work is crucial.

In industry, you will be required to follow particular rules for opening and saving files. However, in school, college or university you will be left to manage your own projects. There are some simple rules to follow to manage your data.

Always use folders or 'directories' to organise your work. Make sure these have sensible names, calling something 'part1 thingy' is a sure-fire way of losing that critical file. Organise your files by separating them by type - whether DTP, CAD or Images - give each their own directory.

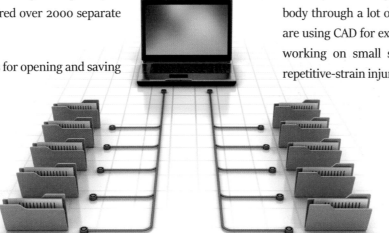

HEALTH+SAFETY

You may think using a computer is a fairly harmless activity, but you actually put your body through a lot of stress. Your eyes, back and arm muscles can be affected if you are using CAD for extended periods of time. Eye strain can occur, especially if you are working on small screens or in a dark environment. Your muscles can suffer repetitive-strain injury (RSI) if you are continually clicking a mouse - this can be painful and potentially life changing.

Take care of your body and take regular breaks - 15 minutes for every hour of use is a good guide. Do not work with screens that are too small or in an environment that is too dark. This is also true when playing computer games... You have been warned!

CAD LIBRARIES

CAD libraries are the backbone of professional 3D modelling. Most products that are commercially drawn using CAD will make use of 'Standard Components' - an item you may learn more about in Design and Manufacture - as these cut down on costs. CAD libraries are used by designers and engineers for a number of important reasons.

CAD libraries ward against technicians from repeatedly drawing the same item over and over. This is a huge waste of time and increases the likelihood that the technician will make an error.

Your CAD software may have a library pre-installed and you can find many free CAD libraries online.

IMPORT+EXPORT

Very few designers or engineers will use just one piece of software and when working in teams or between different companies, it is often necessary to share files. There are thousands of different file types used by a range of applications. Many of these can be 'imported' or 'exported' by software and allow people to share data.

There are some common files types that can help you. They can be broken into two categories - 2D files and 3D files. You will find these file types useful.

2D Files	3D Files
DXF	STEP
Drawing Exchange Format	Standard Exchange of Product model data
SVG	IGES
Scalar Vector Graphic	Initial Graphics Exchange Specification
	3DS
	3D Studio
	STL
	Standard Tessellation Language

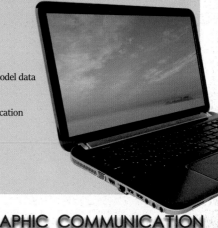

UNDERSTANDING 3D MODELS

Understanding how 3D models are created using a CAD package can help you overcome many problems - especially when using more than one software package to achieve your desired results.

All 3D modelling software relies on the mathematical relationships found in geometry. There are three important elements: **vertices**, **edges** and **faces**.

Vertices are the corners of edges and are perhaps the most important features as they control both edges and faces.

The position of a vertex will control the length of an edge and the shape of face. Three vertices will create three edges and one face (a triangle). This is called a polygon. In simple geometrically shaped, flat sided models, the number of polygons is not important.

However, when there are curves, the computer must generate more polygons. The more polygons, the smoother the curve - this can slow your computer down.

In the cube below, there are eight vertices, 12 edges and six faces.

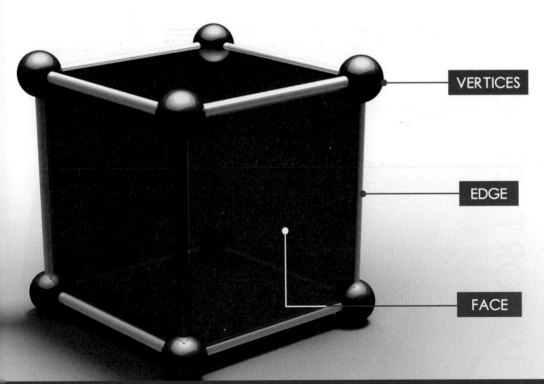

VERTICES

EDGE

FACE

3D VIEW TYPES

All CAD packages can display 3D models using a range of views. Knowing how to control the views within your CAD software can make your life far easier when it comes to creating, editing or analysing a 3D model.

You will be expected to know about different view types for your exam. Shown below is a list of the views all CAD packages can show - some software packages will have a lot more options.

WIREFRAME

SOLID

SHADED

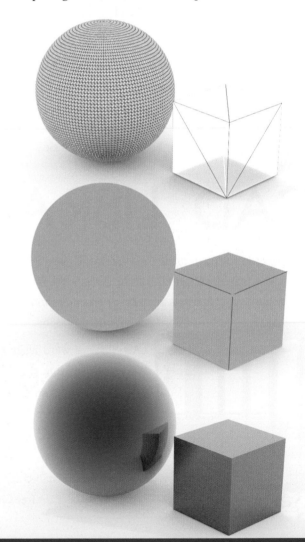

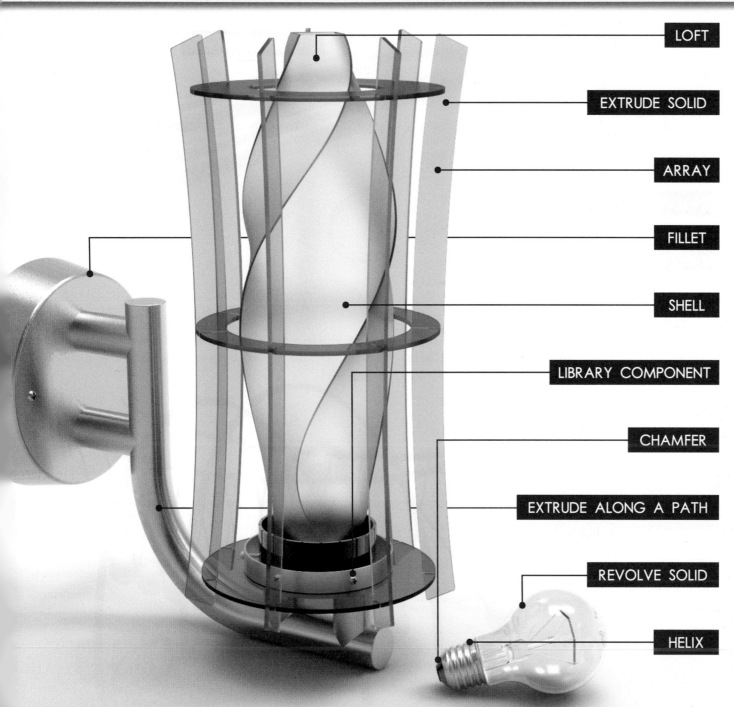

LOFT

EXTRUDE SOLID

ARRAY

FILLET

SHELL

LIBRARY COMPONENT

CHAMFER

EXTRUDE ALONG A PATH

REVOLVE SOLID

HELIX

FEATURES

CAD is an important aspect of graphic communication and you will be expected to understand and use CAD within the course.

You need to become familiar with the official CAD terms and how CAD features can be used and edited to create a range of 3D models.

The CAD illustration here highlights the range of features and techniques that you should study.

Different software platforms may use different titles for the features - this is normal, as software companies like to distinguish their packages. However, they mean the same thing. For your course assignment and exam, ensure you use the terms shown in this book.

Ensure you are confident with the features on this page and you can improve your grade in your exam.

SWEEP

WHAT IS IT?

Sweep, more commonly known as 'extrude along a path', is a useful method of making a profile follow a route to create one continuous feature.

This can be used to make long components that have a consistent cross-section for instance, a straw, paperclip, pipes or handles are good examples.

Extrude along a path is a powerful tool, practice using it and you will be able to create complex items that have long, smooth shapes.

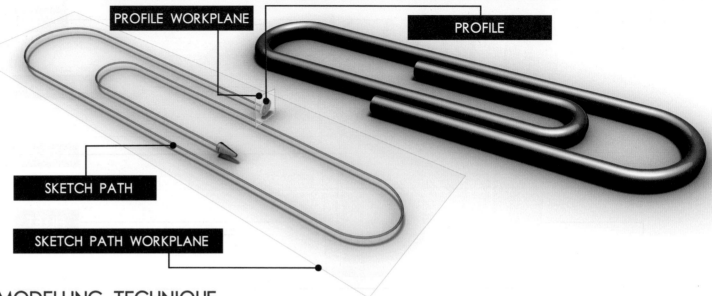

PROFILE WORKPLANE

PROFILE

SKETCH PATH

SKETCH PATH WORKPLANE

MODELLING TECHNIQUE

You require two sketches to create a sweep; a **profile** that is the cross-section of the item and a **path** that you want the profile to follow. The profile will need to be perpendicular to the path; you will be working on two different work planes.

How sweeps work can depend upon your CAD application. Some will require the profile to be intersecting the path, whilst others will not.

EXAM PREP

Sweep is a very useful tool for creating long, flowing shapes.

In an exam, you may be asked about creating the path, including critical sizes and the profile.

Remember, sweeps can be used to add or subtract material and you can be asked about either scenario.

Make your answers very clear - ensure you use sketches to explain the path and/or profile.

Using multiple sweeps can allow you to create frame structures.

CAN YOU MODEL THIS?

A simple coat-hanger that is modelled using a sweep is shown below.

This is your opportunity to show that you are comfortable using the sweep command. You will need to create the path and the profile in the sizes shown.

Creating the path can be the most challenging aspect of using the sweep command. You will likely want to start with that.

Depending on your 3D CAD application, you may need to position the profile sketch intersecting - sitting through - the path. You will need to experiment with this to find out more.

Keep a record of the processes you go through. You could do this as a series of screenshots or a sketched modelling plan. You should practice creating a production drawing from the 3D CAD model you create. Can you think of a clear way of presenting the profile (cross-section) shape of the model?

SKETCH PATH

R30

30 30°

R30

MIRRORED TO LEFT SIDE
LENGTH CAN BE CHOSEN

R25

120

200

400

ELEVATION

PROFILE

2.5   5   2.5

2.5

5

2.5

ELEVATION

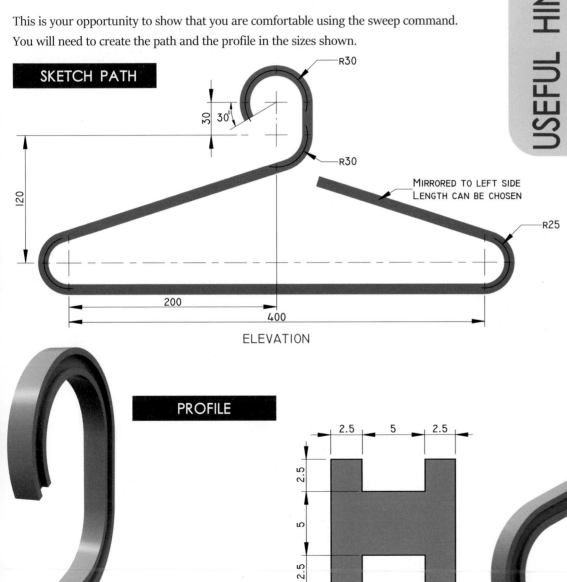

TASK

A task not to get hung up on...
(sorry about the pun)

WHAT IS IT?

A loft is a clever way of making one shape gradually turn into another shape over a set distance. The technical term for this is 'transition piece'.

Transition pieces in industry have typically been used to join one pipe shape to another, and were formed from sheet metal.

Using 3D CAD, transitions are used for a wider range of product features.

MODELLING TECHNIQUE

Lofting requires a minimum of a profile on each of two workplanes that are offset - or separated - from each other. You can use lots of workplanes to create more complex models.

Depending on your CAD software, you may be able to angle workplanes too.

With some software you will be able to select which vertices will connect across the profile.

LOFT

In your exam you are likely to be asked questions about lofting. In most cases you will need to describe three distinct areas:

- The profiles - their shape and size - the distance between workplanes.
- Which corners or 'vertices' are connecting.
- Are any of the workplanes angled?

EXAM PREP

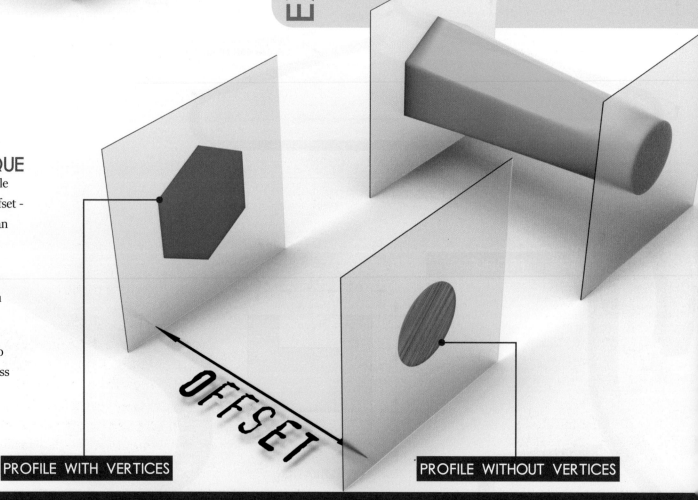

OFFSET

PROFILE WITH VERTICES

PROFILE WITHOUT VERTICES

CAN YOU MODEL THIS?

A small trinket box is to be made. It has two components; a box and a lid.

The box is in the form of a twisted hexagon and has a hexagonal prism to provide a neck to locate the lid at the top.

The lid is a hexagonal prism with a transition to a circle at the top. No sizes are provided for the lid; use your problem-solving skills to work out the details.

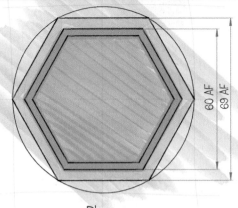

ORTHOGRAPHIC VIEWS

Note: The loft is vertex to vertex. Can you work it out yourself on your 3D CAD software?

Some software may require you to use 'rails' which guide the loft between vertices.

60 AF
69 AF

EXAM PREP

If your school has a 3D printer your teacher may show you how to print a physical model of the trinket box.

Answer the following questions:

Q1. *What type of file is used when 3D printing?*

Q2. *What are the benefits of 3D printing a new design?*

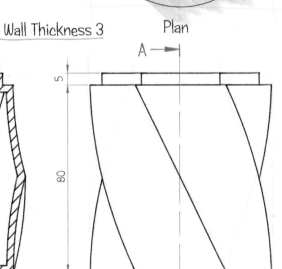

Wall Thickness 3

Plan

A →

5

80

A →

Elevation

TASK

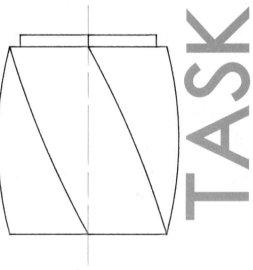

End Elevation

USEFUL HINTS

Analyse the box	**Analyse the lid**
Study the drawings and work out:	*Study the drawings and work out:*
Where can you source the hexagonal sketch?	How to top-down model the lid?
How many workplanes will you need?	How will you create the pyramid effect?
How far apart (offset) the workplanes be?	How many workplanes are required?
How will you put the twist in?	What will the offset be?
How can you add the lip at the top?	Whether the lid should be hollow or solid?
How will you make it hollow?	What tolerances should be applied?

HELIX

WHAT IS IT?

A helix is often described as a spring or coil. Put simply, it is a profile that revolves around an axis. With every full revolution it rises or drops a set distance; this distance is called the 'pitch'.

A helix can be used for more than just springs or coils. You can create other features, including aesthetic details on items such as bottles.

The most common use of the helix feature is to add a customised thread to an item. The thread is described as customised as it will not be conforming to any British or international standards for screw threads (yes, designers and engineers have agreed standards for threads).

If done correctly, you will be able to create a customised thread that will actually work. If you have access to a 3D printer, give it a try!

RADIUS

PITCH

AXIS

PROFILE

MODELLING TECHNIQUE

You need to specify four things when creating a helix. All of them will seem pretty obvious when you think about it.

- **Profile**

  What shape do you want the helix (coil) to be?

- **Axis**

  The length which the coil will be and the centre which the profile will 'revolve' around.

- **Pitch**

  The distance the profile will travel along the axis for each revolution.

- **Radius**

  The distance between the axis and the centre of the profile. Each full revolution of the axis creates a diameter.

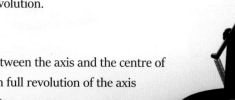

Springs are another favourite application of the helix tool.

Check whether a spring is stretched or compressed in an exam question.

CAN YOU MODEL THIS?

This is an "eggcelent" task to prove your 3D CAD skills.

A simple egg cup is shown to the right. It uses helices and two revolves, all using the same size and shape profile.

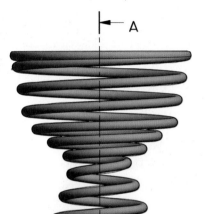

ELEVATION

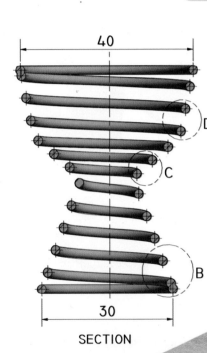

40

30

SECTION

5 ‖ TAPER 12°

DETAIL D

3 ‖ TAPER 50°

DETAIL C

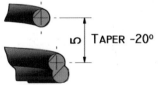

5 ‖ TAPER -20°

DETAIL B

What technique was used at the very top and very bottom of the egg cup? Can you do this to your 3D model?

TASK

What modelling techniques have been used in this breakfast scene? Could you recreate this render?

EXTRUDE

WHAT IS IT?

Extrude is the most basic command in 3D CAD and one you should be very familiar with from National 5 Graphic Communication.

Extrude is the command feature for making a 2D profile into 3D geometry by 'pulling' the shape above or below a workplane. This creates a **solid** 3D model.

Many features can be extruded, however it can sometimes be a very inefficient way of modelling products - sometimes a revolve or extrude along a path can be a better option in the long run.

MODELS CAN BE CREATED AS SOLID MODELS OR SURFACE MODELS

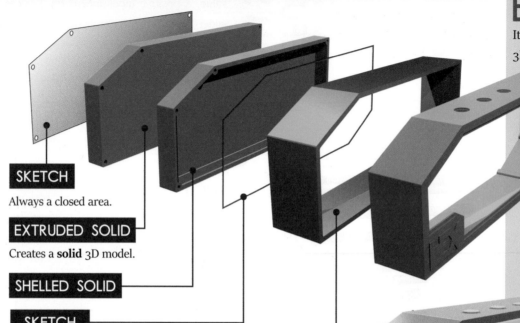

SOLID MODEL

SKETCH

Always a closed area.

EXTRUDED SOLID

Creates a **solid** 3D model.

SHELLED SOLID

SURFACE MODEL

SKETCH

Can be a closed shape or an open line.

EXTRUDED SURFACES

The line is given a thickness to create a **surface** model.

EXAM PREP

It may be the most simple technique in 3D modelling software, but the questions you may face in an exam will really test your knowledge.

Questions that require an extrude will likely need the following four pieces of information:

- The size and shape of the profile to be extruded.
- The position of the workplane.
  - The distance the extrusion will go.
  - Whether you are adding or subtracting material.
  - Whether you require a solid or a surface model.

Be careful to check that it is an extrude command that the marker is expecting and not something more complex such as a loft or revolve...

EXTRUDE ABOVE WORKPLANE

EXTRUDE BELOW WORKPLANE

EXTRUDE SYMMETRIC ABOUT WORKPLANE

CAN YOU MODEL THIS?

A sketch for a whistle is shown right. If you are accurate in your 3D modelling and have access to a 3D printer, this whistle will actually work! However, you must be very precise if you are to be successful when you draw and extrude the profiles.

Partial Enlargement A

12°

CAD IN ACTION

If you have access to a 3D Printer, print the whistle. Does it work?

Try printing the whistle at different scales: 1:2, 2:1, 5:1

Does the whistle still work? What is the difference?

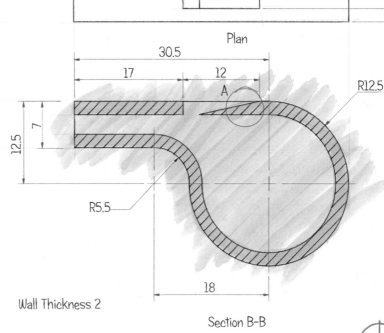

Plan

B   B

16   20

30.5

17   12

A

R12.5

12.5   7

R5.5

18

Wall Thickness 2

Section B-B

TASK

USEFUL HINTS

Extrudes may seem simple enough, but achieving the profile you want can be tricky. When you have models with multiple surfaces things can get really hard.

Look for flat shapes that can be extruded. Remember, only one part can be extruded at a time, so draw the simplest shape you can but carefully and accurately and extrude it. It can be very useful to sketch your modelling method down first and plan what you are going to do before sitting in front of the computer.

REVOLVE

WHAT IS IT?

Revolve is another modelling technique that you should be familiar with from National 5 Graphic Communication.

It is a fantastic tool for creating rounded features and one of the most commonly used commands in industry.

You can create components in one command that would take several extrude features to model. This tool can take some practice, but stick with it.

EXAM PREP

Revolving profiles are also part of the National 5 Graphic Communication course, but questions will be much tougher at Higher.

Questions are more likely to include subtraction of solids or use of a removed or offset axis.

Look out for sizes of profiles and lines that may be part of an axis. Critically, look for any revolved component that is revolved less than 360°.

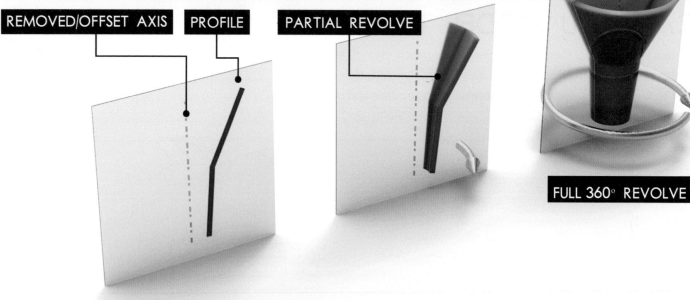

REMOVED/OFFSET AXIS PROFILE PARTIAL REVOLVE

FULL 360° REVOLVE

MODELLING TECHNIQUE

The profile is drawn accurately and the axis created. Accuracy is so important in 3D modelling. Use dimensions to ensure accuracy and to constrain your profile.

The profile can be revolved partially by specifying the angle of revolution. Choosing the most efficient modelling technique is important.

This part was revolved using a **single sketch** and a **single revolve** command. How many sketches and extrude commands would it take to create this model?

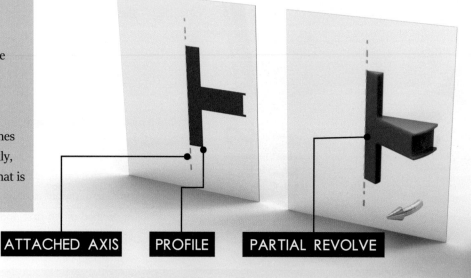

ATTACHED AXIS PROFILE PARTIAL REVOLVE

CAN YOU MODEL THIS?

This passive speaker is a single component and can be 3D printed in your school.

Modelling techniques: This modelling task should test your skills in revolving, extruding and extrude along a path.

Dimensions: Not all the dimensions are shown. Use your judgement and measurements from your own music device to work out sizes that are missing.

Features: While the product is made as a single component it has features such as the slot and the hollow 'sound pipe'. The dimensions of the slot should be made to suit your own music device. The sound pipe should exit in the centre of the sphere and, while the exact curvature of the sound pipe is not critical it should start in line with the speaker on your device.

60

Plan

Elevation

USEFUL HINTS

Have a close look at the sketches to understand how the speaker works.

Sketch a modelling plan: You should plan the modelling techniques you will use and plan the order in which you will tackle the model. Begin modelling with a revolve.

PASSIVE SPEAKER	ALL SIZES IN mm	NTS	
3D PRINTED	MATERIAL: ABS	WALL THICKNESS 2mm	

TASK

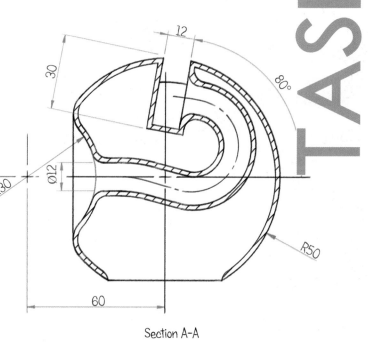

12
30
80°
R30
Ø12
R50
60

Section A-A

ARRAY

WHAT IS IT?

An array is the process of creating a pattern of 2D shapes or 3D features. The pattern can be either linear, rectangular or radial.

A rectangular pattern is called a box-array. A circular pattern is known as a radial array. Your software may use different names for this process.

A box array requires that the pitch (spacing), number of rows and the number of repeated shapes are specified. A circular array needs the number of shapes and the included angle specified.

ARRAYING 3D FEATURES

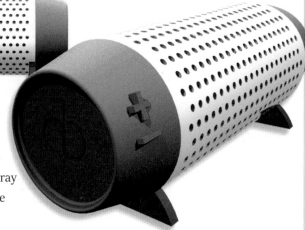

Features (extrusions and subtractions) can also be arrayed. The holes in the speaker were created as two rows of circles in a linear array and then subtracted from the cylinder. Each row of holes (features) was arrayed in a pattern around the cylinder. Try adding perforations to a hollow cylinder. Keep it simple and create your own sizes.

EXAM PREP

Models that feature an array could crop up in your course exam. You will be expected to recognise this and describe how you would model them.

Look for features that have a pattern. Does the pattern fit a circular or a rectangular design?

Describe the process including the spacing of the pattern, number of shapes and angle of the array if it is circular.

RADIAL ARRAY

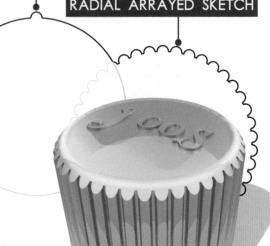

ORIGINAL SKETCH

RADIAL ARRAYED SKETCH

BOX ARRAY

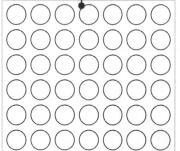

ORIGINAL SKETCH

BOX ARRAYED SKETCH

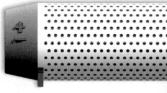

Shell is a very useful command when an object needs hollowed out. You have the ability to set a 'wall thickness' to the model and the computer will subtract all the other material.

Sounds simple, but you need to make sure that the walls are not too thin, especially if your CAD model is to be manufactured.

The shell tool can also be used to 'delete faces'. This is useful if you are modelling cases or bottles.

PROFILE DETAIL

The neck of this bottle has a thread and a lip that are too small to shell.

SHELL TO BE APPLIED

The top face is selected and the shell fails.

SOLUTION

Shell the bottle before adding the screw thread and lip.

SMALL DETAILS ADDED

The screw thread and lip can now be added without causing shelling issues.

FLUTES

WHAT IS IT?

The shell command is used when a solid model needs hollowed. It gives the model a uniform wall thickness.

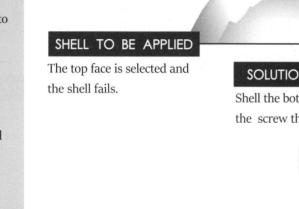

SHELL

Features ▼
⊞ ⬭ revolve 1
⊞ 🌀 helix 1
⊞
⊞ 🧊 shell 1
➡ update
🏁 finish

The incomplete modelling tree, left, applies to the bottle above. Examine the modelling tree and the bottle and answer the questions below.

Q1. *Describe one repositioning move in the modelling tree that would allow the shell to work.*

Q2. *Describe the missing CAD feature that is required to complete the neck details shown in the solution above.*

Q3. *The bottle below the neck is fluted to improve grip. State one CAD technique or feature that was required to create the ring of flutes.*

TOP DOWN MODELLING

WHAT IS IT?

Most everyday products include more than one component. It is the CAD engineer's job to ensure that components fit in the assembly correctly. A **top down** modelling approach helps to ensure components fit together at the modelling stage. Top down modelling is an efficient process and speeds up CAD modelling. It's an especially helpful method when complex parts are involved. Essentially, top down modelling means using one part to help model the next part. There are several different methods of top down modelling. Here are two:

Projected Modelling: copying or mirroring 3D parts or features.

Projected Geometry: using geometry (lines and shapes) from one part to create another part.

PROJECTED MODELLING

SYMMETRICAL OBJECTS
One half is modelled as normal and a mating surface is identified.

MIRROR
The part (feature) is mirrored to create the opposing half.

DELETE ORIGINAL
The original is deleted and the new part saved...

ASSEMBLY
.... before assembling the two parts as normal.

PROJECTED GEOMETRY

BOTTOM PART
One part is modelled as normal and **opened in an assembly file.**

SELECT GEOMETRY
Geometry is selected; in this case the mating face. Note: additional curves have been selected. A new sketch is created on the mating face.

PROJECT THE GEOMETRY
The geometry is projected onto the new sketch. The additional curves and bosses can be de-activated until required.

MODEL THE NEW PART
The model is created from the projected geometry.

BUILD UP THE MODEL
Geometry for other details is activated and projected to create new features.

DELETE THE ORIGINAL PART
Complete the other features and delete the original part. Save the new part separately.

ASSEMBLY
Additional parts are top-down modelled and assembled as normal.

WHAT IS IT?

In manufacturing, parts are normally made separately before being assembled into a functioning product. Similarly, CAD models can be built separately and assembled at the end of the modelling process.

These CAD parts are often built using dimensions from preliminary sketches. If errors are made they may not be spotted until the assembly is put together. Errors can prove costly and time consuming and need to be avoided.

The CAD modelling of the portable speaker below is inaccurate and the front and back panels have bosses that don't line up properly. It is a costly mistake and re-modelling has to be done to correct the error.

In bottom up modelling each part (component) is made separately before being brought together for assembly.

There are risks with this approach because the geometry (sketches and dimensions) that parts are built from is not transferred from one part to the next. It means that absolute accuracy is required when each part is built and the use of detailed preliminary design work is vital.

Often the parts are built from information (dimensions and details) shown in preliminary design sketches. Errors made in these preliminary sketches will cause errors when parts are modelled. These errors may not be noticed until the parts are assembled and fail to fit together accurately. It can be time consuming and expensive to identify and correct these errors.

PRELIMINARY SKETCHES

80
56
76
155
R14
Ø4
R17
61
73
35
Ø2

FAULTY MODELLING

BOSSES MISALIGNED

BOTTOM UP MODELLING - PARTS

REDUCING ERROR

It is very easy to make mistakes with functional sizes when modelling.

One way to improve accuracy is to use **top down modelling** instead of bottom up modelling. See page 100.

BOTTOM UP MODELLING

EDGE EDITS

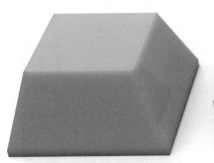

IRREGULAR

An irregular chamfer will remove the corner of a model, but will 'cut' into one face further than another. This can be a quick technique for creating parts with long, gentle slopes.

These slopes are often referred to as 'draft' angles as they allow parts to be removed from a mould when they are manufactured.

REGULAR

A regular chamfer is a commonly used method of removing a corner of an item to create a uniform slope. This is a quick and easy method of removing sharp corners.

Sharp corners are usually not wanted on products. Apart from the obvious safety aspect, corners are often very brittle and prone to snapping - especially if the product is made from wood or plastic.

Chamfers are fairly easy to dimension in production drawings.

NO EDGE EDITS

3D CAD models are intended to represent real products that will be manufactured.

Most products will try to avoid sharp corners for safety, aesthetic, comfort and production reasons.

To achieve this, designers and engineers will remove corners by applying a chamfer or a fillet. On this page, you learn more about these techniques.

REGULAR

A regular fillet will radius all the edges with a constant value.

You can select either an edge or a face to create a radius.

This is the most common form of edge edit and is applied to most edges in production models.

Be careful however - choosing a radius of a really peculiar size will make your production drawings difficult to dimension.

IRREGULAR

Irregular fillets change the radius of the curve along the length of the edge.

This can be used to create interesting curved shapes.

Every CAD package will have a different technique for applying an irregular fillet, but most will require you to set the radius at different points along the edge.

These features can be difficult to dimension in production drawings.

SIMULATION

CAD models can be used for more than just developing design ideas and creating production drawings.

CAD companies have been developing more sophisticated means of testing designs by using the computer to assign material characteristics to CAD models. This is called **Finite Element Analysis** (FEA). It can provide useful information to a designer or engineer when improving design ideas. CAD simulations can determine the potential heat loss from a building or the flow of air through the building. This is called **Computational Fluid Dynamics** (CFD).

CAD simulation is a huge field of study and is evolving all the time. However, you only need to know about some of the different forms of simulation in common use.

In industry, **training**, **testing** and **predicting** are three areas supported by CAD simulation. You should be aware of the benefits of each of these specialised simulation technologies. Check out online videos of each of the processes described on this page.

PREDICTING

Computer graphics are routinely used to predict things like weather patterns, the likely success of a medical procedure or how effective a complex electronic circuit will be.

Computer simulations involve animations to make the data visual while giving valuable feedback to users. The predicted movement of weather systems across the country provides data about temperature rainfall and wind speed and direction and is easy to interpret.

TESTING

Finite element analysis (FEA) tests the strength of an engineered component by assigning the properties of a material, say, 'steel' to it. When the CAD model is put under load the colours show where most and least stresses occur. The computer will also calculate the weight, strength and centre of gravity of the 3D model (along with a whole host of other things). The benefits of FEA of testing are:

TRAINING

CAD models are often used to train people to learn skills that would be too dangerous or expensive to practice in real situations, using real equipment. Pilots, race car drivers and surgeons are good examples - pilots will learn how to fly different models of aircraft from the comfort and safety of a flight simulator and race car drivers can perfect their racing technique before they get to the circuit. Surgeons are trained using simulations so that patients are not put at risk.

Using 3D CAD models for training is an expensive business and will rely on a range of other technologies and computer power to make complex calculations.

- *It identifies design faults.*
- *It minimises the cost of materials.*
- *It assesses performance prior to manufacture.*
- *It reduces development costs.*
- *It speeds up the time taken to get to market.*

MANUFACTURE

3D PRINTING

3D printing is an exciting technique for converting CAD data into a physical **prototype** that can be handled. This can help designers and engineers to identify design or assembly problems before preparing a CAD file for manufacturing.

Historically, 3D printing was very expensive and time consuming. Now, 3D printers are becoming more affordable to buy and run. You may have one in school or even at home.

You do not have to use 3D printing in the course, but it can be a great way to see your 3D CAD models turned into something real. If you get a chance to 3D print, go for it!

CNC TECHNICIAN

The CNC technician will have skills to plan the machining operation and have a knowledge of drawings, CAD modelling, materials, tooling and CNC machinery. The technician will program the CNC machine, prepare CAD/CAM data, set up tool paths, apply tolerances and run simulations before machining the part. CNC manufacture may produce one-off parts, a batch of parts or a mass-production of parts and products.

CNC machining creates identical parts accurately and quickly. Precision engineering relies on CNC technology and CNC technicians will be valued and academically qualified, normally to HND standard.

CNC MACHINING

We often forget that an important role of CAD models and CAD files is to enable manufacture. CNC (computer numerical control) machines produce parts in metal, plastics or wood that are machined (cut and shaped) to match a 3D CAD model or a 2D CAD file. This is precision engineering and is highly technical. CNC machines are now an integral part of our manufacturing landscape can be used for small, medium and high volume manufacturing.

The benefits of CNC production are that:

- It produces parts very accurately.
- Consistency improves and parts are identical.
- Software can be updated.
- Speed of production increases.
- Operator safety improves.
- Simulations test the process before manufacture.

EXAM PREP

Check online videos of any three of the CNC applications listed and note down the role of CAD in each process, including the file types used.

Applying manufacturing tolerances is an important feature of CAD modelling and prototyping. Describe three benefits of applying manufacturing tolerances to drawings.

- Milling
- 3D Printing
- Laser Cutting
- CNC Welding
- CNC Lathe
- CNC Router
- Plasma Cutting
- Plotters & Cutters

CAD ILLUSTRATION
MAKING THE UNREAL REAL

Inside every CAD engineer or designer is a budding artist, just waiting to get out.

Most 3D CAD software will come with rendering and illustration features that can be used to add realism to a model. These are powerful enough to achieve a top grade in Graphic Communication.

However, if you want to create some really stunning visuals, you may want to download a stand-alone rendering application.

Either way, the techniques and process detailed in this chapter will help you create a new, custom-made reality...

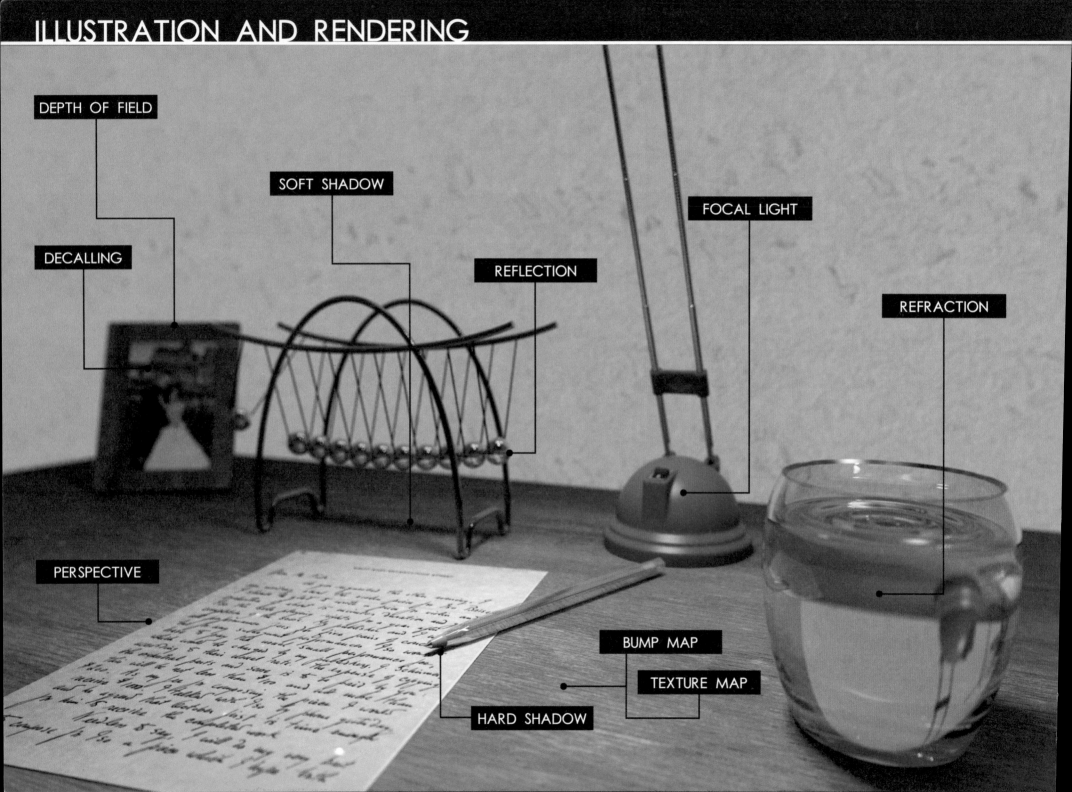

Creating scenes that put 3D CAD models in context are important. You will be assessed on your ability to create a realistic environment, so it is good to practice the techniques to demonstrate your skills whenever you can. Here we detail four key stages required when making a scene.

There are five things to consider when assembling a scene, these are **Scale**, **Position**, **Association**, **Contact** and **Exhibition** (SPACE).

POPULATE

Populating your scene effectively is important.

Scale: The scale of models relative to each other is vital. Making something too big or small can shatter the illusion of realism.

Position: Position items in a realistic manner. Positioning items close together can allow light and reflections to bounce around the scene.

Association: Put models together that you would expect to see together, such as the pen and paper above.

Contact: Make sure items aren't floating, or intersecting each other.

Exhibition: Decide what you want to draw attention to.

TEXTURE MAP

Applying base textures will begin to achieve realism. You need to consider what materials would be used in real life, however don't be limited by them.

Using a different material may actually achieve the realism you want. In the example on the previous page, the water in the glass is set as 'crystal' and the rear wall is set as 'cotton balls'. It can be surprising to see what works, so experiment with textures. If you are struggling, you can always make your own texture map using a camera, hand scanner or illustration software.

Remember, to scale your texture mapping effecitvely to achieve realism.

AMBIENT LIGHT

It is likely that your illustration software will have the ambient or 'global' light already turned on, allowing shadows and highlights to show as you are working.

As your scene becomes more complicated - especially if you have reflective or transparent items - your computer may become very slow and unresponsive. Turning off the ambient light can help you by making it easier and quicker for the computer to process items as you set them up. When you are happy, you can turn the light back on.

Most software will allow you to change the brightness and colour of the light. Play around with these settings to see what effects you can get.

FOCAL LIGHT

Adding focal lights can make a dramatic impact on a scene and allows you to focus attention on an item you are exhibiting.

When you are using additional lights it can be worthwhile lowering or removing the ambient light.

Focal lights will significantly slow down the rendering of your final scene, so it is worth making a series of lower resolution renders to make sure you are happy with the lighting.

Tip! Do not waste your time including models that you will not see and that won't have an impact on lighting or reflection.

TEXTURES

Textures change 3D CAD models from simple forms on the screen to representations of how these objects would look if they were real.

3D CAD and illustration software will have a range of preset library textures for you to choose from and many of these can be edited to suit a specific purpose.

Textures fall into different groups, usually depending on the levels of detail, reflection and transparency. Typically these are woods, metals, plastics, glass and fabrics, although your software may have more. Texture can normally be edited in a variety of ways, including scale, brightness, reflection, colour and contrast.

Some textures will also allow you to edit how rough it appears - a process called 'Bump Mapping'.

Selecting textures is an important stage in creating your scene and it is worth spending some time experimenting with different effects to showcase your work to best effect.

You will be graded on your scene in your Course Assignment and your choice of materials will have an impact on your final mark.

If you are not happy with the textures options available it is worthwhile learning how to create your own or how to download others from the internet.

Remember that textures are subject to the same copyright as photographs, so if you eventually create your own commercial work, make sure you have permission to use the texture files you download.

FEEL IT - BUMP MAPS

Texture will often have a roughness that you can not only see, but looks like you could feel if you touched it.

It is possible to model a rough or bumpy texture onto a 3D CAD model, however this is exceptionally time consuming and will slow down your computer as more edges, faces and vertices are introduced (check out the 3D CAD chapter for more). However, we can introduce a rough looking surface by using a process called Bump Mapping.

Bump mapping allows you to import an image and the illustration software will make the image appear to stick 'in' or 'out', giving the illusion of a rough, textured, bumpy surface.

GETTING WHAT YOU WANT

It can be challenging getting the right textures for a particular environment and if you have a specific look in mind, it can be all the more frustrating.

One method of capturing realistic textures is to use either a camera or a hand scanner. This allows you to capture photo realistic images of materials, however you will not be able to 'tessellate', or repeat the texture seamlessly in order to cover a larger area than the image covers. Scanners and cameras save images as a .JPG file which is used by all illustration and CAD packages for texture mapping.

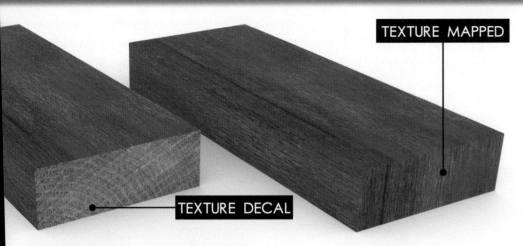

TEXTURE MAPPED

TEXTURE DECAL

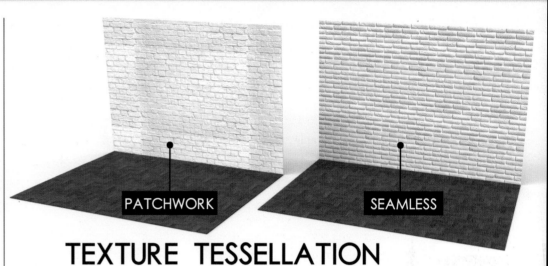

PATCHWORK

SEAMLESS

DETAILS MATTER

All materials have different features and characteristics and this can be difficult to represent on some CAD applications.

Wood is a good example of a material with unique characteristics. The 'grain' of the wood will follow the direction of growth. Cut across this grain and you will reveal 'rings' showing the cylindrical nature of the tree. CAD software will not show this 'end-grain', and instead will use the linear wood texture. This will look poor and shatter the illusion of realism. To overcome this, use your software to apply a 'decal' .jpg over the affected area.

SCALE MAKES A DIFFERENCE

A simple way of changing the apparent size of a 3D CAD model is to play with the scale of the texture applied. It is important that all the models and textures in your scene are scaled appropriately to each other. This can have a big impact on your grade.

TEXTURE TESSELLATION

Tessellation is the mathematical term used to describe a shape or pattern that can be repeated indefinitely without a seam or gap.

This is an effective way to use textures for large objects such as wall or floors.

Many of the pre-installed textures in your CAD or illustration software will be designed to tessellate.

It can be difficult to find tessellating textures online and it is almost impossible to capture one with a scanner or camera (at least, without some intensive modification in a photo editing application).

If you can't find a tessellating texture, you can try to put the 'seams' out of camera shot or hide them with other models.

You can create your own tessellating texture in a vector drawing or photo editing programme. Key to creating perfect tessellation requires an image where the top and bottom edges are identical with each other and the left and right edges are identical with one another. This allows one small image to cover a huge area.

LIGHTS

GLOBAL

Global or 'ambient' lighting is the standard illumination used in the scene. If you are lucky, this will be perfect for you and you won't need to do any editing. You can however choose the brightness and colour of the lighting to suit a particular look.

FOCAL

A focal light will be either conical, with the light spreading out in an arc, or cylindrical with the light not spreading out, but focused as a beam.

Focal light is used to highlight specific features and creates some bright sections, with deep shadows surrounding.

RADIAL

Radial lights are softer than focal lights and allow you to introduce a general brightening of a particular area.

You can often use radial lights to create soft shadows in the locations that you want.

SHOW ME THE LIGHT

Lighting is one of the most dramatic and powerful tools for the illustrator or designer. When used properly, lighting can change the entire mood of a scene and make ordinary, or even boring, compositions look exciting.

Adding lights is easy; almost all CAD applications will allow you to control lights and it is definitely something you will find in rendering software. However (you knew there would be a problem), adding different lights will significantly slow down your computer, especially the rendering times. The more detailed or complex the lighting, the longer it will take to get a result.

Don't worry however, there are a few tricks you can use in this chapter to help you get the most from lighting your renders.

You do not need to use additional lighting to achieve a top mark - just make sure your global lighting is working to your advantage.

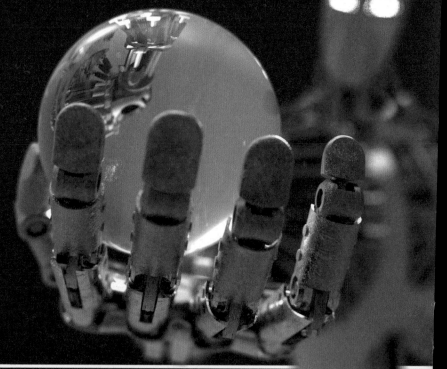

VOLUMETRIC LIGHTING

Volumetric - sometimes called emissive - lighting is an advanced technique used to show a ray of light emanating from a source. This can make scenes appear more realistic and dramatic. It is also a good technique for focusing attention on a specific item.

Volumetric lighting will seriously slow down your computer and make rendering times far longer. You are best saving volumetric lights for your final render...

SEE THROUGH MATERIALS

Reflection and refraction are two terms you may learn from studying physics and having an understanding of them can help you to create realistic renderings. Reflection describes the amount of light that will bounce off a given surface, whilst refraction - often called transmission - is the light that will pass through a surface. Materials such as water or glass will have a ratio of reflection and transmission. The precise amount is determined by the 'Fresnel effect', an option your rendering software may well have.

LIGHT, BUT WITHOUT THE HASSLE

If you are creating your own fake volumetric lighting effect, you will likely be using a radial or focal light in your scene. Create your render as normal and import it to an illustration package.

Draw the 'ray' of light that you want as a closed shape within your illustration package. Fill this with colour of light ray that you want, in this case white. Try to think how the light will spread from the light source.

Use the transparency tools to soften your shape. Using some of the elliptical or radial transparency settings will likely give a better effect. Don't be afraid to use multiple 'rays' to build up the effect you want.

REFLECTION

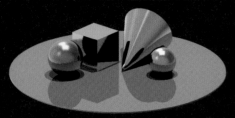
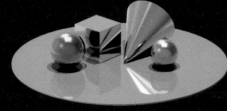
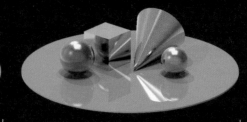
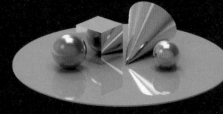

1 REFLECTION

Okay, this is an extreme example of low reflection count. No software will have this as a default option and few packages will allow you to reduce the settings by this much.

However, this is an example of why reflection count matters. Surfaces where light should bounce will appear dark or even black, reducing realism.

2 REFLECTIONS

Waiting for your computer to render your scene can be frustrating and is not very productive use of your time.

Your illustration software will have an option for reducing the number of reflections or allowing a 'draft' or 'low quality' mode. Make use of this feature as you develop your scene. You don't need all the details to understand how it will finally look.

10 REFLECTIONS

The default level for many CAD rendering packages will be between 10 and 30 reflections of light. This is suitable for most mirrored, chrome or metallic surfaces.

This is a good balance between speed and quality of render and would be suitable for any assignment submission.

256 REFLECTIONS

The higher reflection count can appear to have little benefit, especially considering the extra time it can take to render. However, look closely and you will notice an improvement in the quality of the shadows. This is because the computer has increased the number of bounces calculated and carried the shadow into smoother sections.

You have to decide if it is worth the wait...

JOIN THE DARK SIDE

All CAD and illustration software will have a default global or ambient lighting that is useful for basic presentations.

It is typical for most amateur illustrators to increase the default light level to highlight all the details, textures and CAD models. However it can be more dramatic to actually reduce or eliminate the ambient lighting and rely purely on focal or radial lights. This can make for more dramatic and impressive scenes that can draw the attention of your intended audience onto a specific feature. Materials and colours will often become deeper and shadows more pronounced.

Be careful that your printer will cope with dark areas of your render. If it doesn't, you may need to increase the contrast level of your rendering through a photo-editing application.

IMAGE BASED LIGHTING

REFLECTION

Creating a 3D environment can be a time consuming task; you may require dozens of 3D CAD models, hundreds of textures and multiple lights, just to get the look you want.

A professional method of creating the illusion of full, realistic environments is to use Image Based Lighting (IBL).

IBL uses photographs in any model that has reflective surfaces and will also 'bounce' light off the photograph to affect colours, hues and shadows.

IBL maps can either wrap round an entire scene or be applied as a single plane behind the camera and in front of your 3D models.

WITHOUT IBL

Without Image Based Lighting only the brick wall, wooden table and global light source are reflected within the sphere. The scene feels 'empty', flat and less interesting.

If your software does not use IBL, it may be worthwhile creating a fuller scene with more CAD models - this just takes longer to create.

WITH IBL

With IBL enabled there will be a change in the colour, brightness and hue of the materials you have assigned to objects. This is because the 'light' is carrying the colours of the photograph and these are interacting with colours, textures and bump maps of the 3D models. In this example, the colour of the wall is more vibrant, the wood more realistic and there appears to be a room reflected in the sphere.

CREATE YOUR OWN HDRI MAP

High Dynamic Range Imagery (HDRI) make the most effective IBL maps. This is because all the colour values are represented with adequate light.

Most photo-editing packages will allow you to merge images of different exposures and save them as an HDRI (.hdr) image. These can then be loaded into your illustration software.

HIGH EXPOSURE   MID EXPOSURE   LOW EXPOSURE

HDRI IMAGE

The human eye rapidly adjusts to take in various amounts of light and our brains stitch these images together. Cameras aren't as smart, so need to take multiple photographs and different exposures and combine them. The more levels of exposure, the more detail HDRI images have. As a minimum, you will need three exposures. You will learn more about this in the photography chapter.

CAMERAS

Camera angles are built adjustable in most illustration packages and are used to set how you will view your scene. If your CAD or illustration package can create animations, you will also be able to change the position and focus of these cameras during a set time.

Most CAD applications will have a range of camera settings that you will need to experiment with. One of the most useful features you may have is the option to save multiple camera views, so you do not need to manually move the camera between each render you would like to make.

WHERE TO LOOK?

You have spent a long time inserting your 3D models, downloaded and applied textures, corrected scale and applied lights... Don't spoil your work by taking a render from a boring angle.

Experiment with the position of the camera to try different angles. For example, from a low or a high angle. Spend time getting the position of your camera just right.

CAMERA SETUP

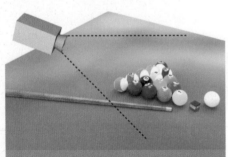

Setting your camera up is an important task. You may have options such as angle and focal length as these control how much of the scene you will focus on within the render. Experiment with the tools available to you, you may be surprised what you create.

ORTHOGRAPHIC...

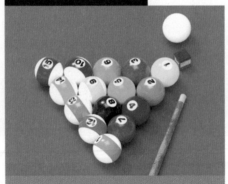

An orthographical render can make the scene appear boring and lifeless.

Orthographic renders are simple and useful for explaining how objects fit together or are related to one another. They are not however, good for creating realistic renders.

TOO MUCH...

Far too much perspective has been added to this scene, exaggerating the scale of the foreground and distorting the shape of each pool ball.

Extreme perspectives can sometimes be useful, such as suggesting something moving fast, but not here...

JUST RIGHT.

Good use of two point perspective can make scenes appear realistic and dynamic. It's all about experimenting with camera positions and training your own eye to spot what works and what doesn't.

DEPTH OF FIELD

Depth of Field (DoF) is a photography technique that is increasingly used in CAD renderings to focus a viewer onto a specific area of the render.

DoF creates a sharp, focused part of an image, whilst the rest of the foreground and background is blurred. The further away or closer to the focal point, the more blurred the image will become.

Many CAD applications will allow you to create DoF renders. However, the computer will need to do more processing work and this will mean a longer render time, so be sure you are happy with your setup before committing.

You do not need to use DoF to achieve a top mark, but it will make your visuals more impressive if you can do it.

MIXING REALITIES

A mixture of a photograph and a CAD render is called a 'mediated reality'. Live action video and computer graphics are called 'augmented reality' and graphics that require a headset are called 'virtual reality'.

Mediated reality is a quick way of inserting a CAD model into a realistic environment, simply by over layering your render onto the photograph. However there a number of things to consider before you render your 3D model.

Shadows: Make sure that you have set the lighting in your render to the same in the photograph. Having shadows fall in the wrong direction can shatter the illusion.

Perspective: Render your model in the same direction and perspective required by the photograph.

ORIGINAL PHOTOGRAPH

CAD RENDER

RENDER YOUR IMAGE

COPY RENDER AND BLUR

ADD TRANSPARENCY

MERGE BOTH IMAGES

DIY:DOF

If your CAD package does not have a Depth-of-Field option or you simply don't have the time for the computer to render one, fear not, there is a simple solution that simulates the effect.

Render your image as you normally would. In this case, we have used a mediated reality image.

Make a copy of your render and open this in a photo-editing application. (Some DTP software will do this trick too.) Use the 'blur' tool to distort the image. The more you use the blur tool, the deeper the DoF effect will be. Save this new, blurred image.

Insert both the original render and the new blurred render into your photo-editing software and align both images, with the blurred image on top.

Use the transparency tool to make the blurred image reveal the non-blurred render beneath.

MAKE A SCENE

A well created scene should be close to photo realistic. Careful placement of your 3D CAD models and a good selection of textures will help you achieve this. Try to position things in a realistic manner; small details, such as the coffee cup and books above help achieve this.

Don't be afraid to play with different lighting levels and the transparency of certain materials that light can shine through. Lighting can make a huge impact on the realism of the scene. Multiple small, softer lights are often better than one really bright light.

TIME TO COMMIT...

Creating the perfect render can take time, experimentation and a great number of drafts.

Once you are ready to render, be prepared for the computer to take a long time to produce the final result. This may mean leaving the computer to process for several hours and in extreme cases, over night to finalise things. It will depend on the quality settings you have selected and the power of the computer you have available.

Be sure you are happy with your environment before committing the time to a full render - maybe creating one more small, draft render just to be sure, is a good move...

WHAT YOU SEE IS WHAT YOU GET

Things look great on screen, right? Well we have some bad news - your monitor will either be showing an image at 72dpi, 96dpi or if you are very lucky, 120dpi. Printers however will produce images at 300dpi (and sometimes more). This means if you try to expand a screen image to print size you are likely to get extreme pixelation. Pixelation will lose you marks in your assignment. Render at a resolution to match your paper size. For reference, here are some resolutions for different paper sizes:

A5	Paper size= 21.0 x 14.8 cm	Render Size = 2480 x 1748
A4	Paper size = 29.7 x 21.0 cm	Render size = 3508 x 2480
A3	Paper size = 42.0 x 29.7 cm	Render size = 4961 x 3605

DESKTOP PUBLISHING
A
GRAPHIC DESIGN TOOL

Desktop publishing (DTP) is the part of the publishing industry where all types of publications are designed, created and prepared for printing. Publications from leaflets and business cards to monthly magazines, newspapers and billboards are created by graphic designers and printed by the publisher.

Publishing however, is nearly always a team effort and many specialists are employed in the publishing industry. This chapter looks at the DTP features that you will use in your course work and the creative skills that can make a real difference when you design your own promotional layouts.

INTRODUCTION

The term desktop publishing is derived from the desktop computer used in the process. These computers can be stand-alone PCs or Apple Mackintosh machines or networked computers such as those used in major publishing firms.

Desktop publishing (DTP) is the process of designing newspapers, magazines, books, leaflets, booklets, and reports on a desktop computer.

The industry that produces these items is the **publishing industry**. Designing the structure and format of the publication and the layout of each page is the job of the **graphic designer**, while the process of creating the publication on paper is **printing**.

You will tackle several DTP projects in your course and use specialised DTP software to create exciting promotional publications.

BENEFITS OF DTP TO INDUSTRY AND SOCIETY

DTP is now the norm when it comes to producing magazines, leaflets, flyers and newspapers. There are a number of advantages of using DTP:

- There is more control over the way text is arranged and formatted.
- Modifications are quick and easy to make.
- DTP can be used to bring lots of different files together in the same document.
- Images and graphics can be imported into a DTP document from a scanner, from a drawing package, frames from a video camera and text from a word processor.
- It speeds up the process of graphic design.
- It links directly to the printing process, the publication can be prepared for printing on the same computer.

DTP DESIGN TEAM

The graphic designer usually works as part of a larger publishing team. Team structures depend on the size of a company and the type of publications they produce. The publications team often comprises:

- Creative Managing Director – responsibility for overall creative direction.
- Publishers – responsible for working with authors to produce manuscripts.
- Graphic design team – responsible for creative layout and design work.
- Editorial or copy-writing team – preparing text for books or magazines, or pulling together text for advertising campaigns.
- Production team – responsible for pre-press work, print preparation, print buying and other aspects of production.
- Illustrators – creating 2D or 3D images.
- Sales and Marketing Team – responsible for marketing and selling the published work, may include selling advertising space and dealing with customer contracts.

In small companies employees might perform multiple roles, while in big companies there might be separate web and print publishing teams.

Increasingly in the publishing industry, many functions are outsourced to specialist companies or to self-employed individuals. For example, a freelance designer or specialist design studio may design the concept for a book and a typesetter may lay out the pages according to the design template. Editors or designers may be contracted to edit or create a publication on a one-off basis.

TOOLS OF THE TRADE

The hardware below is standard in a DTP system.

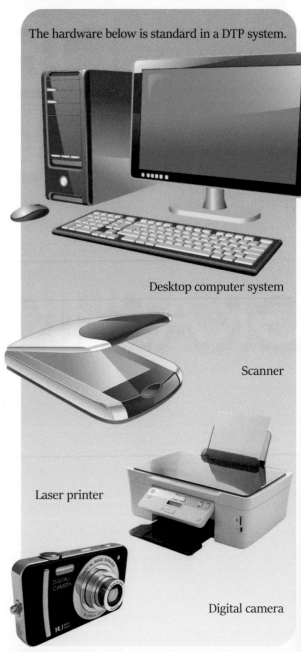

Desktop computer system

Scanner

Laser printer

Digital camera

LAYERS AND MASTER PAGE

Description and Benefits

Using layers as you build up a layout allows you to separate the contents of the layout into parts. This is important in a complex, multi-page publication like a magazine because each layer can be worked on separately without disturbing the others. Layers can be visible or hidden to de-clutter the layout while working. Layers can be locked so they can't be altered by accident.

LAYERS DIALOGUE BOX

All DTP software uses layers. When you start a new publication your software automatically creates your work on a layer. It may even create two layers automatically.

The first layer is called the **Master Page**. The second is the first page of your publication.

The layers tab or dialogue box will look something like the one here.

When you add items to your layout you can select a new layer using the 'add layer' command. The icons in the layer tab are common across DTP. The 'Eye' icon shows that the layer is visible on-screen. The contents of a layer can be locked and can be made printable or non-printing. Here layer 4 holds the images and it is visible, printable and locked.

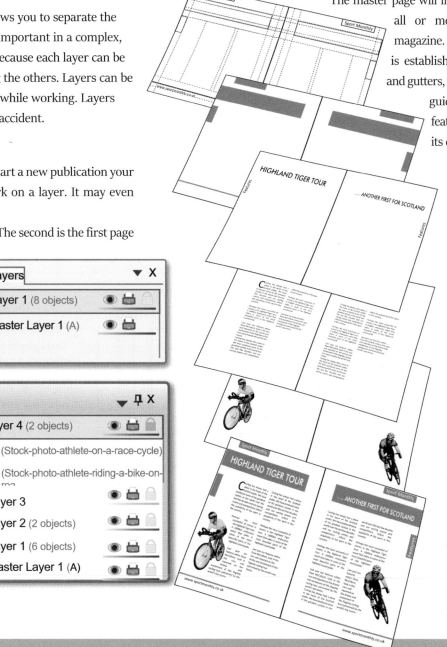

TYPICAL LAYER SPECIFICATION

The **Master page** is where the template for the publication is stored. The master page will include items that appear on all or most of the pages in the magazine. The structure of the layout is established with columns, margins and gutters, headers and footers, borders, guidelines and logos. These features help give the publication its distinctive identity.

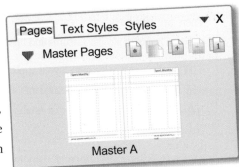

Layer 1 has the colour fills around the headline and section tab. The colours will change from section to section.

Layer 2 stores the headings, sub-headings and section names.

Layer 3 stores the body text. This will be imported from word processing software and can be edited at any time without disturbing the other layers. This is easily managed when the layer is active and the other layers are fixed.

Layer 4 stores the images which have been imported from photo-editing and can be active for editing without interfering with other layers.

The **final page layout** will have all the layers visible. Any item that requires editing can be selected via its layer. It is a simple and effective method of managing complex layouts. You will use layers in your promotional DTP work.

DTP FEATURES

There are several types of software each designed for a different purpose but with similar features and functions. These include:

• **DTP software** this is a page layout application for assembling text and images into finished documents ready for printing. DTP software has many features that enable the graphic designer to create exciting page layouts.

• **Photo editing applications** for manipulating digital photographs and scanned artwork.

• **Vector drawing applications** for producing high quality line-based drawings and illustrations.

Graphic designers use all of these packages and there are software packages that include features from each of them. We will focus on DTP software in this section.

DESKTOP PUBLISHING - DTP

The DTP features and techniques described on this and the next 27 pages are commonly used in all types of publications. You will need to know these DTP features for two reasons:

1. To be prepared for questions in the course exam and unit assessments.

2. So that you can make good use of them in your creative promotional layouts.

The trick when you are using DTP features in your layouts is to make them subtle. Each feature should improve the layout without being noticed itself and certainly without dominating the layout.

TEXT ALIGNMENT - LEFT ALIGNED

Good graphic design relies on the graphic designer knowing what makes a layout work. The graphic designer breaks the layout down into smaller parts and works with each part in turn. These smaller parts are called design elements and design principles. You need to understand design elements and principles and be able to speak about them in the course exam.

Description and Benefits:

Left-aligned text creates a visually strong line on the left hand edge and can make a document look sophisticated. It is the most commonly used style. It looks less formal than right alignment. In the USA it is known as 'Ragged Right'.

TEXT ALIGNMENT - RIGHT ALIGNED

Good graphic design relies on the graphic designer knowing what makes a layout work. The graphic designer breaks the layout down into smaller parts and works with each part in turn. These smaller parts are called design elements and design principles. You need to understand design elements and principles and be able to speak about them in the course exam.

Description and Benefits:

Right-aligned text creates a visually strong line on the right edge. It is often useful for captions and sub-headings. It can also provide alignment with a photo or the right-hand edge of a page. It is not a good style for body text because it is difficult to return your eyes to the start of the next line which is staggered (ragged left).

TEXT ALIGNMENT - JUSTIFIED

Good graphic design relies on the graphic designer knowing what makes a layout work. The graphic designer breaks the layout down into smaller parts and works with each part in turn. These smaller parts are called design elements and design principles. You need to understand design elements and principles and be able to speak about them in the course exam.

Description and Benefits:

Justified text creates clean vertical lines on both sides. It gives text a strong visual shape and saves space. News papers like this style because it looks neat and can save space but it can create unwanted hyphenation and exaggerated word spacing.

TEXT ALIGNMENT - CENTRE ALIGNED

Good graphic design relies on the graphic designer knowing what makes a layout work. The graphic designer breaks the layout down into smaller parts and works with each part in turn.
These smaller parts are called design elements and design principles. You need to understand design elements and principles and be able to speak about them in the course exam.

Description and Benefits:

Centred text creates symmetry but should be used sparingly. It is difficult to read and lacks a strong visual line. Aligning centred text with other content such as pictures is difficult. It is most commonly used for the text inside greetings cards and should only be used for short paragraph of body text in symmetrical layouts.

COLUMNS

Description and Benefits:

Text is often displayed in a vertical, rectangular structure known as a column. Column structure is carefully planned at the start of the design process.

Multiple columns are used in publications for a number of reasons:

- If a single full width column is used, when the reader gets to the end of a line it can be difficult to find the start of the next line. Reducing the length of the line by creating columns **reduces the reader's eye movement** and **makes it easier to find the start of the next line**.

- Multiple columns help to give the page a structure. Having an obvious column structure **helps the reader navigate through the layout**.

- A multi-column structure creates visual interest by breaking up a large block of text into columns. It can create **visual rhythm.**

- A multi-column structure **reduces the impact** of reading a large, unbroken block of text by breaking it up into smaller, less daunting columns. Paragraph spacing also achieves this benefit.

Single column structure

When extended text or body copy appears in a document it is often arranged in columns. The orientation of a page can can make a difference to the impact layout.
The orientation of a page can make a difference to the impact layout. Sometimes the format or orientation is specified in the brief from the client because the layout needs to fit a particular space. There are two formats; portrait and landscape.

The orientation of a page can make a difference to the impact layout. Sometimes the format or orientation is specified in the brief from the client because the layout needs to fit a particular space. There are two formats; portrait and landscape.

The orientation of a page can make a difference to the impact layout. Sometimes the format or orientation is specified in the brief from the client because the layout needs to fit a particular space. There are two formats; portrait and landscape.

Sometimes the format or orientation is specified in the brief from the client because the layout needs to fit a particular space. The orientation of a page can can make a difference to the impact layout. The orientation of a page can make a difference to the impact layout.

Three column structure

When extended text or body copy appears in a document it is often arranged in columns.

The orientation of a page can make a difference to the impact layout. Sometimes the format or orientation is specified in the brief from the client because the layout needs to fit a particular space. There are two formats; portrait and landscape.

The orientation of a page can make a difference to the impact layout.

Sometimes the format or orientation is specified in the brief from the client because the layout needs to fit a particular space. There are two formats; portrait and landscape.

The orientation of a page can make a difference to the impact layout. Sometimes the format or orientation is specified in the brief from the client because the layout needs to fit a particular space. There are two formats; portrait and landscape.

These columns make the text easier to read by shortening the length of each line of text. Columns also help make the layout more visually pleasing. When a text box is created it can be easily split into columns.

LEADING

Standard leading	Good layout design is important. The graphic designer knows this.
Reduced leading	Good layout design is important. The graphic designer knows this.
Increased leading	Good layout design is important. The graphic designer knows this.

Description and Benefits:

Leading (pronounced Led-ing) is the vertical space between lines of text. Careful leading makes body text easier to read. Reducing the leading can help to fit body text into a limited space.

KERNING

Headline with no kerning — **YOU WAVE**

Headline with Kerning applied — **YOU WAVE**

Description and Benefits:

Kerning is used to reduce space between letters with sloping uprights and overhangs; like WAV or Yo. The space between those letters can look unsightly and reduce impact; kerning corrects this problem. Kerning is used on **headings** and **titles** to create a **bolder heading** with more **visual impact**. Kerning is also used to **fit text into limited space.**

TRACKING

WAVE RAVE -40 tracking

WAVE RAVE 0 tracking

WAVE RAVE +80 tracking

Description and Benefits:

Tracking **alters the spacing between letters uniformly**. Tighter tracking (top) can help to increase the mass or impact of a heading, while looser tracking (bottom) might be used to expand a line of text to fit the width of a text frame.

DTP FEATURES

DROP CAPITAL (DROP CAP)

Good graphic design relies on the graphic designer knowing what makes a layout work. The graphic designer breaks the layout down into smaller parts and works with each part in turn.

These smaller parts are called design elements and design principles. You need to understand design elements and principles and be able to speak about them in the course exam. You will also use them in your own promotional layouts.

Having an understanding of design elements and principles will allow you to apply this knowledge in your unit work and your assignment. It will help you improve layouts whether they are manually done or produced on the computer.

Description and Benefits:

Enlarging the first letter in an article **emphasises** the start of the article and creates a **contrast** in size. Commonly used in magazine and newspaper layouts.

HANGING INDENT

Good graphic design relies on the graphic designer knowing what makes a layout work. The graphic designer breaks the layout down into smaller parts and works with each part in turn.

These smaller parts are called design elements and design principles. You need to understand design elements and principles and be able to speak about them in the course exam.

Having an understanding of design elements and principles will allow you to apply this knowledge in your unit work and your assignment. It will help you improve layouts whether they are manually done or produced on the computer.

Description and Benefits:

Drop cap is left **'hanging'** above a widened margin (indent). It creates white space and even more emphasis at the start of the article.

INDENT

Good graphic design relies on the graphic designer knowing what makes a layout work. The graphic designer breaks the layout down into smaller parts and works with each part in turn.

These smaller parts are called design elements and design principles. You need to understand design elements and principles and be able to speak about them in the course exam. You will also use them in your own promotional layouts.

PARAGRAPH BREAK

Good graphic design relies on the graphic designer knowing what makes a layout work. The graphic designer breaks the layout down into smaller parts and works with each part in turn.

These smaller parts are called design elements and design principles. You need to understand design elements and principles and be able to speak about them in the course exam. You will also use them in your own promotional layouts.

Description and Benefits:

An **indented first line** creates a visual start to a new paragraph. A **paragraph break** (spacing between paragraphs) chops a large body of text into smaller paragraphs; it makes the body text less daunting to read.

RULE

SUBTLETY IN LAYOUTS

Good graphic design relies on the graphic designer knowing what makes a layout work. The graphic designer breaks the layout down into smaller parts and works with each part in turn.

These smaller parts are called design elements and design principles. You need to understand design elements and principles and be able to speak about them in the course exam.

You will also use them in your own promotional layouts.
Having an understanding of design elements and principles will allow you to apply this knowledge in your unit work and your assignment. It will help you improve layouts whether they are manually done or produced on the computer.

Description and Benefit

A **vertical rule or column rule,** set between columns adds a visual separation and a crisp, clean sharpness to the columns especially when the text is left aligned and leaves a ragged right edge. A **horizontal rule** can **separate** or **emphasise** items and can lead the eye across the layout.

PULL QUOTE

Good graphic design relies on the graphic designer knowing what makes a layout work. The graphic designer breaks the layout down into smaller parts and works with each part in turn.

These smaller parts are called **design elements** and **design principles**. You need to understand design elements and principles and be able to speak about them in the course exam. You will also use them to improve your own promotional layouts.

... understanding elements and principles will help improve your layouts.

Having an understanding of design elements and principles will allow you to apply this knowledge in your unit work and your assignment. It will help you improve layouts whether they are manually done or produced on the computer.

Description and Benefits:

A pull quote is normally a short extract from the body text. It is always in a **bigger font size** and **different typeface** than the body text.

A pull quote is often, but not always, a **controversial** extract. This will be read before the article and it can grab the reader's attention.

A pull quote is used to **draw readers into** the article or advert and is often combined with **text wrap** to connect it closely with the article.

Good graphic design relies on the graphic designer knowing what makes a layout work. The graphic designer breaks the layout down into smaller parts and works with each part in turn.

These smaller parts are called design elements and design principles. You need to understand design elements and principles and be able to speak about them in the course exam. You will also use them in your own promotional layouts.

... understanding elements and principles will help improve your layouts.

Having an understanding of design elements and principles will allow you to apply this knowledge in your unit work and your assignment. It will help you improve layouts whether they are manually done or produced on the computer.

CAPTION

Description and Benefits:

A caption is text that describes an image, often a photograph.

A caption is normally discrete and descriptive but it can be made more visual if required.

Sunset on the Forth

BULLET POINTS

- Bikes are cheap
- Trains are safe.
- Planes are quick.
- Boats are an experience.

Description and Benefits:

Bullet points are visual aids and are used when **listing** facts or items. Bulleted lists can help create **visual rhythm**.

TEXT WRAP

Practice and improve. Persevere and succeed. These are the options and opportunities you have to create something from nothing. To work at your craft and hone your skills is a privilege that we each have. Seize it and reach for the stars.

Description and Benefits:

Wrapping text enables it to follow the shape of an object or image. It creates a **link** (unity) between image and text. It **changes** the rectangular text box into a curvy or angular **shape** and it can **save space** in a busy layout.

FLOW TEXT

Slipstream Off-Road Bikes

Description and Benefits:

Flowing text along a path adds **eye-catching contrast.** Flow text can **suggest movement**. It can also create soft curves from a line of straight text and can **lead the reader's eye** through a layout.

FLOATING ITEMS

Description and Benefits:

A floating item is normally a picture or a pull quote that is placed outwith the structure of the page; it does not fit into the normal column structure.

Floating items are more **obvious** and **emphasised** and create eye-catching **contrast** in a layout. A floating item can make a layout **less formal.** The three layouts here each include a floating item.

EXAM PREP

Q1. Describe the other DTP features, used in the three layouts on the right, that make the floating items even more eye-catching.

Good graphic design relies on the graphic designer knowing what makes a layout work. The graphic designer breaks the layout down into smaller parts and works with each part in turn.

These smaller parts are called **design elements** and **design principles**. You need to understand design elements and principles and be able to speak about them in the course exam. You will also use them in your own promotional layouts.

Having an understanding of design elements and principles will allow you to apply this knowledge in your unit work and your assignment. It will help you improve layouts whether they are manually done or produced on the computer.

These smaller parts are called **design elements** and **design principles**. You need to understand design elements and principles and be able to speak about them in the course exam. You will also use them in your own promotional layouts.

Having an understanding of design elements and principles will allow you to apply this knowledge in your unit work and your assignment. It will help you improve layouts

These smaller parts are called **design elements** and **design principles**. You need to understand design elements and principles and be able to speak about them in the course exam. You will also use them in your own promotional layouts.

Good graphic design relies on the graphic designer knowing what makes a layout work. The graphic designer breaks the layout down into smaller parts and works with each part in turn.

These smaller parts are called **design elements** and **design principles**. You need to understand design elements and principles and be able to speak about them in the course exam. You will also use them in your own promotional layouts.

Having an understanding of design elements and principles will allow you to apply this knowledge in your unit work and your assignment. It will help you improve layouts whether they are manually done or produced on the computer.

These smaller parts are called **design elements** and **design principles**.

You need to understand design elements and principles and be able to speak about them in the course exam. You will also use them in your own promotional layouts.

Having an understanding of design elements and principles will allow you to apply this knowledge in your unit work and your assignment.

These smaller parts are called **design elements** and **design principles**. You need to understand design elements and principles and be able to speak about them in the course exam.

You will also use them in your own 2D layouts. Perhaps the best way to build your own design skills.

Good graphic design relies on the graphic designer knowing what makes a layout work. The graphic designer breaks the layout down into smaller parts and works with each part in turn.

These smaller parts are called design elements and design principles. You need to understand design elements and principles and be able to speak about them in the course exam. You will also use them in your own layouts.

Having an understanding of design elements and principles will allow you to apply this knowledge in your unit work and your assignment. It will help you improve layouts

These smaller parts are called design elements and design principles. You need to understand design elements and principles and be able to speak about them in the course exam. You will also use them in your own layouts.

DTP FEATURES

SQUARE CROP

The crop tool looks like this and can be used to pull the frame handles inwards to square crop the image, removing parts of the image, usually unwanted background.

Description and Benefits:
Square cropping reduces the image in size. It can remove unwanted background and provide a focus on a particular item or part of the image.

FULL CROP

Description and Benefits:
A full crop removes the entire background from the image leaving only the part required for the layout. It removes the rectangular box shape and leaves the outline of the main image, creating a focal point and a visually interesting shape in the layout.

It enables a more suitable background to be used in place of the old one. It also saves space and puts greater emphasis on the remaining image.

CROP TO SHAPE

Description and Benefits:
Cropping to any given shape can be achieved:

1. Select a shape or text
2. Remove the fill and add an outline.
3. Select an image.
4. Place the outline on top of the image.
5. Apply the crop to shape feature.

This technique can help create visual interest in a layout and **visual impact** in a title or heading.

BLEED

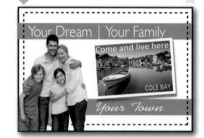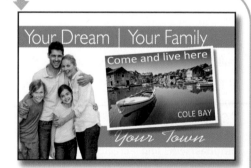

Without a bleed each item is contained within the frame of the page. It is formal, framed and confined inside the margins.

A bleed is made by setting the bleed margin on your DTP software; normally between 3mm and 5mm. The images can overlap this bleed margin.

After printing the paper is trimmed to leave the images running over the edge of the paper.

Description and Benefits:
Printers cannot print to the edge of paper. A bleed allows edge to edge printing. It requires printing on oversized (OS) paper.

The bleed creates a more expansive layout that is not confined by a margin. It is modern and suggests there is more happening beyond the boundaries of the page.

DROP SHADOW

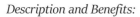

Subtle Subtle

Description and Benefits:

A drop shadow casts a shadow behind an image or text. The shadow takes the shape of the image and gives the impression that there is a surface below or behind the image. It creates a **3D effect** and suggests **depth** in the layout.

The position, colour and intensity of the shadow can be controlled. A drop shadow can be used to emphasise an image or text and make it stand out. It can also add the illusion of 3D realism to an image. It is a subtle effect that can improve a layout while hardly being noticed itself.

REVERSE

Description and Benefits:

A reverse is created when text (normally black) is made white.

A reverse can aid legibility if the text is on a dark background.

It can also lighten a layout by reducing the impact of dark tones and increasing the value (brightness) of the text.

Join us at Breaker Surfing Club

TRANSPARENCY

The "Adventure Trails" sub-head is difficult to read.

A colour fill placed behind it improves legibility but obscures part of the cyclist.

A transparency effect on the colour fill allows the image to be seen and the text to be read.

Description and Benefits:

A transparency is a means of making an image or colour-fill see through.

It is often used on top of an image to make text legible. The effect is also subtle; it can improve a layout without being noticed.

A transparency is easily controlled and manipulated. It can work on simple fills as well as JPEG images.

DTP FEATURES

DRAWING TOOLS

Many publications and websites need original artwork, which can range from simple boxes with colour fills to very complex drawings. Drawing tools enable these graphics to be produced and integrated into page layouts.

Drawing tools include: Line, Rectangle, Circle, Ellipse and a variety of useful shapes.

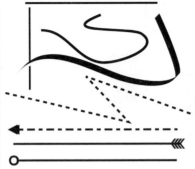

DRAWING TOOLS | LINE

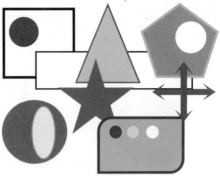

Description and Benefits:

Lines can be straight, curved, angled, zig-zagging and freeform. A variety of useful styles including solid, broken and chain can be set to almost any width. Line end shapes can be chosen from a library of styles.

DRAWING TOOLS | SHAPES

Description and Benefits:

Shapes can range from geometric and symmetrical to organic and abstract. Colour fills can be controlled to create bold or subtle images. Shapes can be created or chosen from a library of styles.

DRAWING TOOLS | BEZIER CURVE

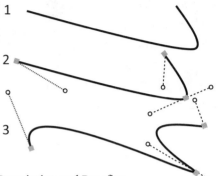

Description and Benefits:

Lines can be controlled using 'nodes 'and 'bezier' points. Nodes break the line into segments and the 'bezier' control handles allow precise adjustment. Nodes can be added as required and complex curves and shapes can be drawn.

COLOUR PALLETS AND MIXERS

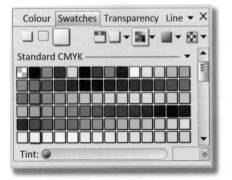

Description and Benefits:

DTP software comes with extensive pallets of pre-mixed colours, often called 'swatches'. These are invaluable to a designer. It can make choosing colour combinations easier. These ready-mixed options help provide the designer with many colour options.

COLOUR MIXING

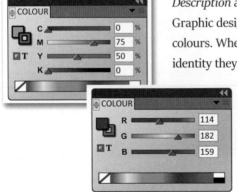

PANTONE® COLOURS

CMYK AND RGB

Description and Benefits:

Graphic designers need to be able to mix their own colours. When a company has its own corporate identity they need their colours to be reproduced accurately on products and promotional materials. The graphic designer can mix the pallet using an RGB or CMYK colour matching system like the ones shown here.

The common colour mixing standards are:

RGB - creating colours using mixes of **red**, **green** and **blue.** This colouring system is used to create **on-screen colours** and **colours for web-sites.**

CMYK - Creating colours by mixing **cyan**, **magenta, yellow** and **black** (known as the key colour). **CMYK** mixes are used when a layout is to be **printed**. It is the common commercial printing format. Inside your laser printer there will be four CMYK cartridges.

Description and Benefits:

Pantone® colours are ready mixed colours, sometimes called **'Spot colours'.** There is a vast range of colours, tints, shades and tones. These are used in pre-mixed inks for printing special colours (gold & silver etc) and in the marker pens you will use in your Graph' Comm' class. Pantone® colours come in a vast range of colours, tints, tones and shades.

COLOUR MATCHING

Description and Benefits:

The colour matching tool is sometimes called the **colour picker** or colour sampler. It is a vital part of the graphic designer's toolbox. It can identify a colour used in one part of a layout so that it can be copied exactly, in another part.

The colour picker tool speeds up the colour mixing process because it is automatic. Matching colours across a layout helps to **create unity**. The yellow in the football shirt was sampled and used in the text and the line to create a layout unified through colour.

MESHES & WARPS

Description and Benefits:

The warp or mesh tool enables shapes to be re-shaped or distorted.

Selecting the image (right) reveals control nodes and bezier points which are used to twist and pull the shape (see 'bezier curve' on the previous page).

The mesh feature can create contrast and visual interest by creating curved shapes in a rectangular layout. It also creates shapes that can look 3D.

WIDOWS AND ORPHANS

Description and Benefits:

A **'widow'** is a typographical error in which the last word (or words) in a sentence or paragraph has found its way to the top of the next column.

An **'orphan'** is the opposite. When a word is left behind at the foot of a column it is known as an orphan.

These are errors that proof readers check for before a publication is printed. Look out for them in your own publications.

Good graphic design relies on the graphic designer knowing what makes a layout work. The graphic designer breaks the layout down into smaller parts and works with each part in turn.

These smaller parts are called design elements and design principles. You need to understand design elements and principles and be able to speak about them in the course exam. ← **WIDOW**

You will also use them in your own promotional layouts.

Having an understanding of design elements and principles will allow you to apply this knowledge in your unit work and your assignment. It will help you improve layouts whether they are manually done or produced on the computer.

Good graphic design relies on the graphic designer knowing what makes a layout work. The graphic designer breaks the layout down into smaller parts and works with each part in turn.

These smaller parts are called design elements and design principles. You need to understand design elements and principles and be able to speak about them in the course exam.

will also use them in your own promotional layouts.

Having an understanding of design elements and principles will allow you to apply this knowledge in your unit work and your assignment. It will help you improve layouts whether they are manually done or produced on the computer.

You ← **ORPHAN**

DTP FEATURES

3D EFFECTS AND TEXTURES

Description and Benefits:

DTP software has a huge variety of colour options including a range of pre-set colours and fill styles. These give the designer many creative options. Colour fills can be applied when a closed shape is to be filled.

Careful choice of colour fills can create the correct moods and visual impact in a layout. The designer needs to have an eye for colour and a feel for dominance and depth to use colour fills effectively.

COMMON FILL EFFECTS

Plain fill with outline

Plain fill outline removed

Gradient fill vertical

Gradient fill horizontal

Two colour gradient

COMMON FILL EFFECTS AND MATERIALS

Description and Benefits:

Preset fills can create 3D effects or represent materials in a similar way to those applied in 3D illustration packages. They can be useful as long as the effect does not dominate a layout; be careful and selective when you use them.

COMBINING FILL EFFECTS

Description and Benefits:

Using different fill styles together can create some interesting and useful effects. Experimenting with fill effects is a good way of learning to use the graphics part of the software.

USING COLOUR FILLS IN LAYOUTS

A promotional poster is required for a cycle race. It needs to be simple and striking with a minimum of information. The image of a cyclist has been selected. The cyclist is a strong image but the original background (below) is too busy.

So the background is cropped and the cyclist positioned in a layout made entirely of fill styles and text.

The result is a simple but bold advertising poster.

REFLECTIONS / MIRROR

A second poster (below) shows how a mirror or reflection effect can be used to provide a subtle texture that improves the layout without dominating it.

WHAT IS TYPOGRAPHY?

The style, character and appearance of text on a page or screen is known as typography. It is a vital part of communication. Type can influence the mood of a layout and can be chosen to appeal to a particular target audience. Type can be sleek, heavy, light, modern, traditional, slim, masculine, feminine, chunky or elegant.

The choice and use of typeface in layouts will be covered in detail in this chapter but it is useful to have a look at the structure of typeface and understand some of the terms applied to its shape and design. There are many more terms applied to the design features of letters, those shown here are the main features associated with typeface.

EXAM PREP

The italic text in the question Q1 has been formatted.

Q1. State which feature of paragraph text has been adjusted in this question. Explain what this adjustment does to the text and how it might affect the appearance and legibility of a longer paragraph of text.

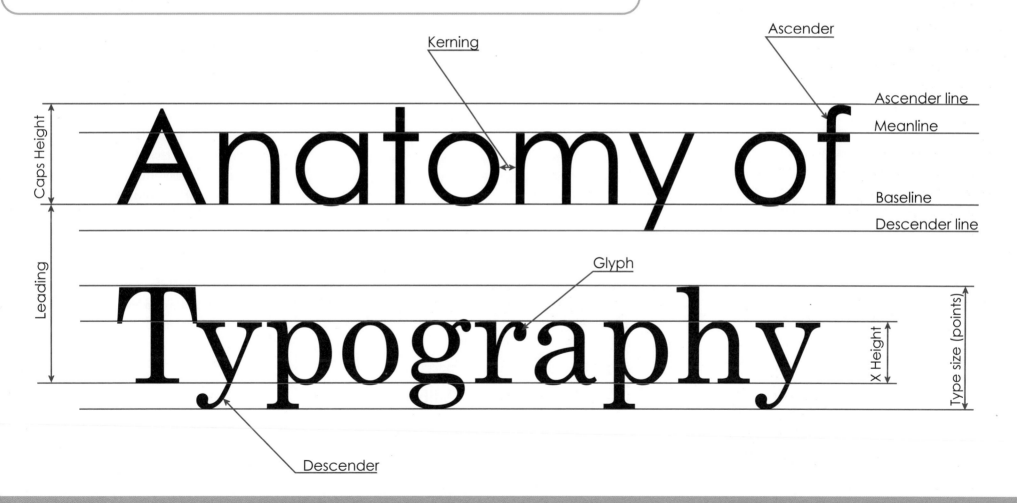

TYPEFACE AND FONTS

The choice and style of typeface plays an important part in any promotional publication. We read text every day and it communicates instantly that a promotional layout is either serious or fun, friendly or forceful, modern or traditional, relaxed or emotive. The mood created is supported by the choice of typeface.

In the consumer's eyes, the value of the product being promoted is carried by the typeface. The choice of typeface can make or break a design, it must connect with the target market and communicate the appropriate mood. The next four pages will help you make decisions about your choice of typeface.

DEFINITION

A **typeface** is a font family while a **font** is a member of that family.

Arial is a **typeface** family.

Arial Narrow, Arial Black and Arial Rounded are **font** members of the Arial typeface.

Typeface is split into several groups. The two main groups are **Serif** and **Sans Serif** fonts:

SERIF FONTS

Serif
└─ Glyphs or Serifs

Description and Benefits:
Serif fonts are so called because they have decorative flicks or serifs on the ends of strokes. At one time all fonts were serif fonts.

Serif fonts have a **formal or traditional** look because they are based on very old font styles. The flicks or serifs can make these fonts very readable because they lead the eye from one letter to another when they are used in blocks or columns of text. Serif fonts are often used in magazines and newspapers for the body text.

Popular Serif fonts include:

Accord	BruceOldStyle
Baskerville Old Face	Goudita SF
Bookman Old Style	Tennessee Light SF
Sitka Banner	Times New Roman

SANS SERIF FONTS

Sans Serif

Description and Benefits:
These fonts do not have flicks on the ends of strokes: **sans** means **without** in French.

Sans serif fonts are **modern** in style and were designed in the 1950's specifically for advertising modern products. Chunkier sans fonts are used in headings and titles to create impact but are also used in body copy when a simple, modern or elegant look is required.

There are hundreds of sans serif styles to choose from. They can be useful when making a connection with a younger target market or when promoting a modern product. Choose carefully, you can select one to connect with a particular age group, gender and interest range.

Popular Sans Serif fonts include:

Arial	Calibri
Century Gothic	Lucida Sans
Gill Sans	Verdana

DISPLAY AND SLAB FONTS

DISPLAY FONT

Description and Benefits:
Slab fonts (once called Slab Serifs because they were originally all serif fonts) were developed to produce fonts that were bold and chunky and had enough impact to be used on posters and billboards. They were designed to be **noticed in advertising campaigns.**

Display fonts are also designed to look good in larger sizes. They are not easy to read in body text but their use in headings, headlines and titles can help to draw the reader into the article. **Do not use in body text, only use in titles and headings.**

Popular Slab Serif & Display fonts

Accord	Adamsky
Bodini	Eras Bold
GOUDY	Gill Sans ultra bold

MORE ABOUT FONTS .....

Though serif and sans serif are the two main families there are several other typeface groups in common use today.

It is important to know the names and to be able to identify the features of these font styles but it is also important to understand their uses.

When are they appropriate in promotional layouts?

Which target audiences do these font styles connect with?

You will choose typeface for each of your promotional layouts, it is part of the design process. So it is important to make the right choices.

Typography is one of the most important components of a promotion, it is said that typography can make or break a design. Develop your knowledge here and add each choice of typeface to your own experience of creative layout design.

...OTHER TYPEFACE GROUPS

FONT WEIGHT **Heavy** or Light?

Description and Benefits:

Fonts come in thick, chunky or **heavy** styles that are good for adding impact to a title or heading in a display. Fonts also come in slimmer styles that appear **lighter**. These are good when a more elegant or sophisticated feel is required.

SCRIPT FONTS

Script Fonts

Description and Benefits:

Script fonts are designed to imitate handwriting. Some, like the script style shown above, have strokes that extend to link letters together. This helps the letters flow. However, script fonts can be **difficult to read** when they are used in blocks of body text. They are normally used in small quantities as a decorative addition and can be used in promotions for brand names, captions and tag lines when the promotion needs a **feminine**, **personal**, **warm** or **friendly** typeface.

Popular script style fonts include:

Tropicali Script	*Gelfing SF*
Cold spaggetti BTN	*Kunstler Script*
Ancestory SF	*Galeforce BTN*
Embassy BT	*Undercurrent BTN*

FUN FONTS

Fun Fonts

Description and Benefits:

Fun fonts are so called because they convey humour through their shape, style or pattern.

Fun fonts have a very **informal** look and should be used sparingly in captions, tag-lines and occasionally headings. They are not generally suited for use in body text because they can be difficult to read in blocks. When a promotional layout requires humour or is aimed at a young or very young target audience a fun style can make a useful connection.

Popular fun fonts include:

CRAZY LOOT	ROCK SALT
Fluffy Slacks	Giggles BTN
Snap	Troutkings
Chiller	Youngsook

MODERN OR FUTURISTIC FONTS

Futurist Fonts

Description and Benefits:

Not really a typeface group but these modern font styles are part of our printed world. They are used in logos, brand names, product names, magazines and comic strips and have been designed for a particular purpose and to connect with particular target audiences.

The moods, feelings and impressions they generate can include: excitement, youthfulness, graffiti, grungy, modernism, space age, movement, speed, technological and mechanistic.

Popular futurist fonts include:

CHUB GOTHIC	MAXIMUS BT
Bolts SF	OCTIN SPRAYPAINT
Platinum Beat	Ultra Serif SF
Greyhound SF	SONIC XBD BT

HOW TO CHOOSE A TYPEFACE

CHOOSING TYPEFACE TO ENHANCE YOUR LAYOUT - TEN RULES

Read through the ten rules on this page before you select a typeface.

We know that rules are made to be broken but if you apply the advice on this page you will not go far wrong when you choose fonts for your own layouts.

There is a limitless choice of fonts but you may be restricted to those on your computer system in school. Don't worry about this, there will be more than enough to choose from. Read this page, choose wisely and have fun.

When selecting a typeface you must consider what purpose it is going to be put to. There are many purposes that text has in a layout:

- Headings
- Sub-heads
- Body text
- Pull quotes
- Slogans or sound bites
- And Logos

You could probably choose a different typeface for each purpose but that would introduce too many different font styles and could be distracting for the reader.

1. Make legibility the priority, fonts must be readable.

2. Know your target audience and choose a font style to connect with them: male, female, young, old etc?

3. Judge the mood required. Your typeface should reflect this: light and airy when appropriate, heavy when needed and rough or grungy when required.

Natural goodness in every bite. Fresh fruit everyday delivered to your home no matter where you live.

4. Limit the number of fonts in a layout to two, three max. Too many and the the layout becomes messy or confusing. A single font can look bland.

5. Create a Hierarchy of dominance. Use larger font sizes for headings and smaller sizes for body text. Sub-headings, pull quotes and slogans can be sized in between. See pages 140 - 142.

6. Choose contrasting fonts for your headline and body text. Make the differences (contrasts) obvious.

Try Aberdeen's new board retailer. Our boards are fun, stylish, and can be customised to meet your own spec'. We hope you find our young staff friendly, knowledgeable and eager to help.
"A truly fantastic boarding experience"
Joe Sebratto

7. Use colour carefully. Colour can help create the right mood but it can also affect readability.

8. Choose the most appropriate weight for typeface. Heavy fonts are chunky and bold while lighter fonts are thin and elegant.

9. Consider the location of the promotion. A poster on a billboard may need different fonts from those in a magazine.

10. Consider the product you are promoting; does it suggest robustness, strength and durability or lightness, fragility and delicacy? Your typeface should reflect this.

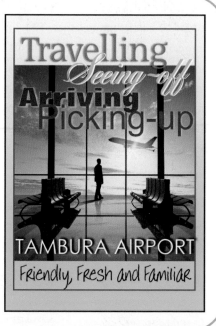

CREATIVE TYPEFACE TIPS

Using typeface creatively can help give your layouts visual impact. The title, heading or product name is normally the **second** most important item in a promotional layout, next to the main image. But a company name or product name can be the most important item in a layout.

Typeface should:

- Support the message
- Connect with the target audience
- Set the correct tone or mood
- Draw the reader into the layout

These two pages will give some ideas to help you make creative use of typeface in titles and headings.

- Add a drop shadow behind the text to make it stand out.
- Use uppercase and lower case together to create contrast.

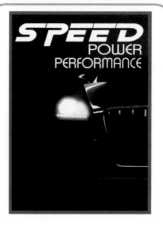

- Reverse the text on a dark background.
- Combine two very different fonts.

- Copy and flip text to make a reflection.
- Adding a fade or transparency on the reflected text completes the illusion.
- The result adds a glossy texture to the layout.

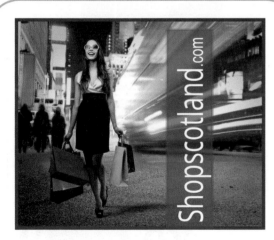

- A heading positioned vertically can increase visual impact.
- When the background is busy, text can get lost. a transparent colour fill aids readability on the busy background.

- Flow text adds a quirky, inventive appeal to the slogan. Suitable for a younger target market.
- The sans serif fonts in the product name and business name are very different from one another; useful for creating eye-catching contrast.

- Using multiple fonts and sizes can work but needs careful choice of fonts, colours and layout.
- The text layout is intended to look random and modern to appeal to a young target audience.
- Note the two key words, the product name and the business name are larger to create impact and emphasis.

USING FONT EFFECTS IN LOGOS & LAYOUTS

Using typeface in logos, company names and product names is an opportunity to experiment. Remember, type is simply a shape with a colour fill and an outline. The shape of the typeface in itself can bring a striking visual component to a layout. It can be textured and coloured and built into a new creation that can sell an idea, a product or a belief. Typeface is a powerful visual tool. Graphic designers know this and make full use of it.

The four examples here show the original raw material and the finished result after some creative DTP input. Study the four ideas and come up with your own when the opportunity arises, it is your chance to develop your own style.

A slab font and a grungy, textured background combine to make a striking poster. There is contrast between the clean, smooth fonts and the textured backdrop.

JUMP STOP

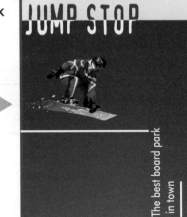

A poster to promote the Jump Stop board park is required. Can you work out how the two-tone text was created?

The best board park in town.

Ever Present designs require a logo.

Colour the letters and add an outline. The image is cropped to a circular shape. A transparency allows the background to show through the letters. The letters are layered on the image to create depth and visual interest.

Blue Water Gym

A logo for a gym is required from three words and an image. Making use of the square shape of the image allows the words to be sized and flipped. A blue border completes a simple but effective logo.

EXAM PREP

Each of the layouts on this page make use of DTP editing features that were explained earlier in this chapter.

Q1. Describe one DTP editing feature used in each of the layouts (a different one in each layout) and the impact the DTP edit has on the layout.

The promotional layouts below all use the same typeface in the heading, 'Papyrus'. This font is not a good choice of typeface for any of the four layouts. There is a different font to suit each headline in the list on the far right of this page.

Your task is to study each layout and the information on each promotion. Match a suitable typeface from the list to each layout and explain (giving 2 reasons) why the chosen typeface is suited to the headline in each advert.

Layout 'A'

Promotion: An advert for a new cooking magazine; Eat Well, Live Well.

Target market: Mothers of young children in middle to high income families.

Message: to encourage mothers to cook healthy and enjoyable meals for their families.

Layout 'B'

Promotion: An advert for a Skateboarding magazine.

Target market: Teenage and young adult males. Low and irregular incomes

Message: To reveal the exciting world of boarders, and the excitement of the sport and teenage attitudes to it.

Layout 'C'

Promotion: An advert for a modern and Hi-Tech communication product.

Target market: Younger career males with income at the upper end of the scale and with a passion for technology.

Message: Our technology is modern, reliable, essential and stylish.

Layout 'D'

Promotion: An advert for a business advice centre.

Target market: Aimed at directors of new and established companies

Message: Our advice is reliable and vital if you want your business to succeed.

EXAM PREP

Each of the layouts on this page requires a replacement typeface for the heading. Consider the options below and answer the questions at the foot of this column.

1. TIMES NEW ROMAN

2. 28 DAYS LATER

3. RAVIE

4. CINZEL

5. DISTANT GALAXY

EXAM PREP

Q1. Choose the most suitable typeface from the list above for the heading in each layout.

Q2. Explain why, for each layout, your chosen typeface works best.

You have not selected the leftover typeface.

Q3. Explain why you found the leftover typeface unsuitable.

TEXT HIERARCHY

Text is a vital component of most promotional layouts. In promotional publications, including your own layouts, text is governed by a hierarchy that ranks the importance of each line and paragraph of text. The order of importance indicates the order in which the layout is read and helps to lead the reader through the page.

The ways in which this ranking is achieved is something you will learn about.

TEXT WITHOUT HIERARCHY

The layout, right, is being prepared for publishing. The text is imported from a word file and all the text is the same size and the same typeface.

There is no hierarchy of importance. The image is the dominant item in the layout and the text is informative but visually bland.

The layout requires editing and the first part of the process is to establish an order of importance (hierarchy) in the text. *See the next page.*

Cover Story

Kelly Green speaks out

Exclusive interview about her great new album and new career

"Make no mistake, I'm ready for solo success".

There are few women who embody celebrity as perfectly as Kelly Green. She had hits all around the world; "Rock - Rockin'" as the leading lady of Dark Love, and then we fell "Crazy in Love" when she embarked on her solo career with success shortly thereafter. The songstress delighted beauty editors and fans alike early last year with the launch of her first album 'Heat and Dust' to critical aclaim. We got the chance to ask Miss Green a couple of questions about her newest record, career moves, body image, and the lovely Rob Ford! You were selected as the celebrity with the Best Body Image by High Chic! readers in 2014. Do you have any words of wisdom for girls who struggle with their image? The thing to strive for is to have the healthiest body you can have. It's really not about being skinny or being curvy.

3   *www.rockstar.com*

DESIGN SPECIFICATION

The target market that the Kelly Green article (left) is intended for is:

1. **Age**:
   16 - 30 years.

2. **Gender**:
   Male and Female but predominantly female.

3. **Marital or family status**:
   Mainly single but includes couples.

4. **Education level**:
   High school to College & University Student.

5. **Location**:
   Europe, USA, Japan & Korea.

6. **Income**:
   Variable range (pocket money to 30K).

7. **Interests**:
   Reality TV, Fashion, Music, Celebrities.

8. **Ethnic background**:
   All backgrounds.

9. **Magazine the article is to be published in.**
   'Rock Star' magazine.

SIZE IS EVERYTHING

How do I achieve hierarchy?

With text, the obvious way to achieve levels of importance is by **Size**; big text is more noticeable than small text.

IMPROVEMENTS

The layout now has a better flow because of the text sizing. The reader is led through the layout and can navigate the page more easily. The title now competes with the image for dominance. There is no doubting what or who the content is about and, reading a little further, we know it's an interview and that she is happy to have gone solo (see the pull quote) and that she has a new album to promote (see the sub-heading).

All this information and the reader has only glanced at the layout for a few seconds. The larger text gives us this information instantly.

The body text gives us detail. Using the text hierarchy wisely is all about grabbing the reader's attention and enticing them to read more.

Cover Story

Kelly Green speaks out

Exclusive interview about ....
...her great new album and new career

"Make no mistake, I'm ready for solo success".

There are few women who embody celebrity as perfectly as Kelly Green. She had hits all around the world; "Rock - Rockin" as the leading lady of *Dark Love*, and then we fell "Crazy in Love" when she embarked on her solo career with success shortly thereafter. The songstress delighted beauty editors and fans alike early last year with the launch of her first album 'Heat and Dust' to critical aclaim. We got the chance to ask Miss Green a couple of questions about her newest record, career moves, body image, and the lovely Rob Ford!

You were selected as the celebrity with the *Best Body Image* by High Chic! readers in 2014. Do you have any words of wisdom for girls who struggle with their image?

The thing to strive for is to have the healthiest body you can have. It's really not about being skinny or being curvy.

3   www.rockstar.com

TEXT HIERARCHY RULE OF THUMB

The table below describes the rules for establishing text sizing to indicate the levels of importance of the text in a layout. As always, rules are made to be broken.

Largest fonts
- Headline or Title
- Sub-Heads
- Pull Quotes
- Body text
- Captions
- Headers and footers

Smallest fonts

The improved layout, left, has a clear text hierarchy...

...but it still doesn't have the right feel to connect with a young target audience!

TEXT HIERARCHY: CREATING IMPACT

...THEN AGAIN, WHAT IF...
...SIZE ISN'T EVERYTHING?

There are many ways, other than text size, to establish a text hierarchy in a layout. The finished layout, here, uses a number of techniques:

Weight - emboldening text makes it heavy enough to stand out more.

Typeface - some fonts are bolder and more noticeable than others while some stand out because they are different or quirky, like the heading here.

Emphasis - using an **underline** or **italics** can make text more obvious and more dominant.

Colour - Applying a **colour fill** or texture behind text can also create emphasis and add visual impact. Applying a colour to the text itself has a similarly emphasising effect, as long as you select your colours carefully.

Drop caps - A drop cap emphasises the start of the body text and creates contrast in size.

Reverse - reversing the text colour creates emphasis and can improve legibility.

Tilting or rotating - Applying a tilt to a block or line of text can create a subtle, eye-catching emphasis, as long as you don't overdo it.

CONFIRMING THE HIERARCHY WORKS...

The final layout demonstrates a variety of ways to emphasise the hierarchy and create a flow through the layout.

The improved layout, left, has a clear text hierarchy but also includes features (listed opposite) that work together to create a dynamic layout that appeals to the young target audience.

All of these effects are achieved using DTP features and techniques explained earlier in this chapter. Use them and learn how they work together to improve a layout. It will improve your own layouts and prepare you for the course exam.

Ray Eames

THE KELLY GREEN DOUBLE PAGE LAYOUT BEFORE IT IS EDITED AND IMPROVED FOR PRINTING AND PUBLISHING

Cover Story

Kelly Green speaks out

Exclusive interview about ....

...her great new album and new career

"Make no mistake, I'm ready for solo success".

here are few women who embody celebrity as perfectly as Kelly Green. She had hits all around the world; "Rock - Rockin'" as the leading lady of Dark Love, and then we fell "Crazy in Love" when she embarked on her solo career with success shortly thereafter. The songstress delighted beauty editors and fans alike early last year with the launch of her first album 'Heat and Dust' to critical aclaim. We got the chance to ask Miss Green a couple of questions about her newest record, career moves, body image, and the lovely Rob Ford!

You were selected as the celebrity with the Best Body Image by High Chic! readers in 2014. Do you have any words of wisdom for girls who struggle with their image?

The thing to strive for is to have the healthiest body you can have. It's really not about being skinny or being curvy. It's really all about you and your own outlook.

The new album

How has working with producer Bob Styles helped your performance?

I love music and I love getting my songs heard by a young audience. I love to perform and I love being a girl and being feminine and putting on my favorite stilettos. But I learned a long time ago from my mother that beauty is from within. To feel confident and secure...... is important.

What are your favorite tracks on the new album?
There are rockers like 'Down and out' and 'Last Chance' that I love to perform but there are balads that I prefer when I'm relaxing; 'Tomorrow will Arrive' is one.

You just released 'Tomorrow will Arrive' as your first solo single, why that particular choice?
We felt that it says a lot about me as a person and me and my manager thought it would connect with the fans and, hopefully, attract some new ones.

Which fragrance would Kelly Green be more likely wear - Hotter or Viva?

I love Hotter more because it is a fiery fragrance.

Kelly has distinguised herself as an actress, too, with acclaimed roles in Cadillac Racers and Rouigh Girls. Will we be seeing you on the screen again soon?

Hopefully soon.
We are looking at a script right now. Can't say more than that.

Rob rocks up for the album launch in a casual look before a night out at the movies!

Kelly at the Mercury awards at Earls Court in June.

Cover Story

Kelly's Passions

MY GREEN BAG

MY TOP SHOP SCARF

MY GREEN LES PAUL

AND, OF COURSE, MY NEW ALBUM

"The band was great. Rob led us well and the harmonies were tight."

The Kelly Green article is a double-page magazine layout.

The layout here includes all of the items chosen for the double page spread. Careful alignment helps to organise it and give it structure.

However, the layout is bland. It lacks visual impact and certainly would not appeal to the intended target audience.

The graphic designer will use their knowledge of both DTP features and Design Elements and Principles to edit the layout and ensure it appeals to the target audience.

These techniques are the same as those that you will apply in your own promotional layouts.

Read the next page and answer the **Exam Prep** questions on the subsequent pages.

BREATHE LIFE INTO YOUR DTP LAYOUT

The final layout is much more vibrant and demonstrates creative layout skills. While the designer's creative eye is vital, the use of DTP editing features allows him to create his vision easily and quickly.

If you learn to use your DTP software and understand it's role in communicating with a target market you will create layouts that are exciting, appropriate and connect with your target audience.

CREATIVE LAYOUT TIPS

- **Bold** text creates a thicker or chunkier font that stands out beside non-emboldened text.

- *Italics* creates a more subtle emphasis that stands out if it is used sparingly.

- <u>Underline</u> is another method of demonstrating importance.

- **Colour** can be used to establish dominance or create an accent in a layout.

- **Reversing** text on a dark background will create contrast and therefore emphasis.

- **Floating** an item in a space (outwith the structure of the layout) will make it stand out.

- **Tilting** an image or text can draw attention and create emphasis.

- Using a colour fill **behind the text** can make the text stand out.

- **Textures** can be introduced to create a 'feel' or a 'mood'.

Cover Story

Kelly Green speaks out
Exclusive interview about ...

... new solo career and her great new album

Here are few women who embody celebrity as perfectly as Kelly Green. She had hearts all around the world "Rock - Rockin" as the leading lady of *Dark Love*, and then we fell 'Crazy in Love" when she embarked on her solo career, with success shortly thereafter.

We got the chance to ask Miss Green a couple of questions about her newest record, career moves, body image, and the lovely Rob Ford! You were selected as the celebrity with the *Best Body Image* by High Chic! readers in 2014. Do you have any words of wisdom for girls who struggle with their image?

Make no mistake, I'm ready for solo success.

The songstress delighted beauty editors and fans alike early last year with the launch of her first album ' Heat and Dust' to critical acclaim.

The thing to strive for is to have the healthiest body you can have. It's really not about being skinny or being curvy. It's really all about you and your own outlook.

The new album

How has working with producer Bob Styles helped your performance?

I love music and I love getting my songs heard by a young audience. I love to perform and I love being a girl and being feminine and putting on my favorite stilettos. But I learned a long time ago from my mother that beauty is from within. To feel confident and secure... is important.

What are your favorite tracks on the new album? *There are rockers like 'Down and out' and 'Last Chance' that I love to perform but there are balads that I prefer when I'm relaxing; 'Tomorrow will Arrive' is one.*

You just released 'Tomorrow will Arrive' as your first solo single, why that particular choice? *We felt that it says a lot about me as a person and me and my manager thought it would connect with the fans and, hopefully, attract some new ones.*

Which fragrance would Kelly Green be more likely wear - Hotter or Viva?

I love 'Hotter 'more because it is a fiery Fragrance.

Kelly has distinguised herself as an actress, too, with acclaimed roles in Cadillac Racers and Rough Girls. Will we be seeing you on the screen again soon? *Hopefully soon. We are looking at a script right now. Can't say any more than that!*

Cover Story

Kelly's Passions

What does Kelly enjoy spending her hard earned cash on?

MY LITTLE GREEN BAG

MY COZY SILK SCARF

MY GREEN LES PAUL

AND, OF COURSE, PROMOTING MY NEW ALBUM

"The band was great. Rob led us well and the harmonies were tight."

Snapshots

Rob rocks up for the album launch in a casual look before a night out at the movies!

Kelly at the Mercury awards at Earls Court in June.

3   www.rockstar.com

www.rockstar.com   4

DESIGN SPECIFICATION

The target market that the Kelly Green article is aiming at is defined as follows:

1. **Age**:
   16 - 25 years

2. **Gender**:
   Male and Female but predominantly female.

3. **Marital or family status**:
   Mainly single but includes couples.

4. **Education level**:
   High school to College & University student

5. **Location**:
   Europe, USA, Japan & Korea

6. **Income**:
   Variable (pocket money to 30K)

7. **Interests**:
   Reality TV, Fashion, Music, Celebrities.

8. **Ethnic background**:
   All backgrounds

9. **Magazine the article is to be published in** 'Rock Star' magazine.

EXAM PREP

The final double page layout (previous page) shows the Kelly Green layout ready for inclusion in the magazine. Study this double page layout and answer the questions below:

The graphic designer worked hard to create unity between the two pages.

Q1. Describe four DTP features he used to help create unity between the page layouts.

A transparency has been incorporated in the layout.

Q2. Explain two reasons for the transparency.

Layering has been used to good effect in the layout.

Q3. Explain how layering improves the layout.

Emphasis has an important role in the layout.

Q4. Describe four DTP features that have been used to achieve emphasis in the layout.

Texture is a feature of the layout.

Q5. Explain how the use of texture improves the layout.

EXAM PREP

The improvements to each of the items in the layout involves the use of common DTP editing features. Your task is to answer the following questions:

Column structure has been carefully prepared in the layout.

Q6. Explain how column structure improves the reader's experience.

The font styles (typefaces) were chosen very carefully.

Q7. Select two and explain why the designer chose them.

The article is designed to appeal to a young target market.

Q8. Describe two ways in which the designer has used DTP editing features to create a youthful feel.

The colour scheme was built around the main close-up image of Kelly Green.

Q9. Explain how the restricted pallet of colours helps to make this layout work.

The layout is busy, the article deals with three main aspects of Kelly Green: her solo career, her new album and things she is passionate about. It would be easy to lose control of the content and create a confusing layout.

Q10. Describe how the designer separated each aspect of the article while maintaining visual unity.

GRID STRUCTURE - THE FRAMEWORK FOR LAYOUT

Publishers and graphic designers spend a great deal of time establishing a page structure that gives their publication a distinct, stylish and unified look.

The work that is done in setting up a page, before any of the content is added, is a vital stage in the DTP process.

Features that determine the structure of a page are carefully sized and positioned to give the publication identity.

These features include:

- Column structure.
- Gutter width.
- Margins, Left & Right.
- Header space.
- Footer space.
- Headline size & position.
- Bleed margins
- Other features such as section tabs etc

MASTER PAGE

Description and Benefits:

DTP software enables us to set up a master page at the start of a publication. The master page is where the designer creates the layout structure and features that will be repeated throughout a publication. The colour fills at the top and bottom in this book are examples of such features. You should set out a master page for your own publications.

GRID

Description and Benefits:

A square grid is used to help establish the structure of a layout. The grid is non-printing and can be visible or hidden. The **'snap to grid'** feature ensures that items on the page jump to grid spacing and can be positioned quickly and accurately. The grid and 'snap to grid' features also help to achieve **accurate alignment** in a layout.

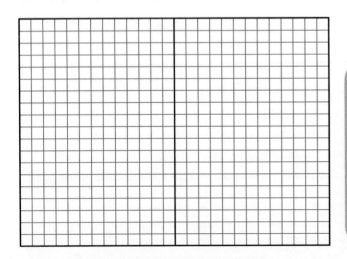

NOTE

The grid and guidelines can be switched on or off so that the layout can be viewed clean; as it would appear on paper..

IMPORTANT

The principle of having each page with exactly the same layout no longer applies to most commercial magazines. The graphic designer wants to maintain reader interest and does this by varying the layouts from article to article. The master page however, establishes a structure which is flexible and can be altered from page to page.

GUIDELINES

Description and Benefits:

Guidelines are pulled onto the page from the top and left hand rules. They are vertical and horizontal but can be angled easily. Guidelines can be positioned accurately and text frames placed on top. Guidelines are non-printing. The 'snap to guidelines' feature enables accurate alignment of columns and images etc. The grid and guideline structure may be carried through the entire publication to ensure consistency.

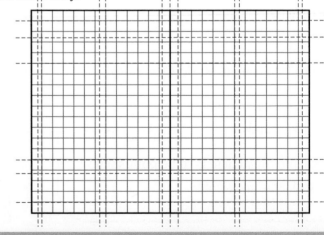

SETTING UP A MASTER PAGE

1. TEXT FRAMES

Text frames are added on top of the guidelines. Each text frame can be split into columns. The space between the columns is called the gutter space. This can be increased or reduced as required. A grid (not shown) helps this process.

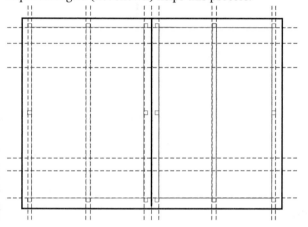

2. COLUMNS

The graphic designer will try different column structures before selecting the one that works best in a layout.

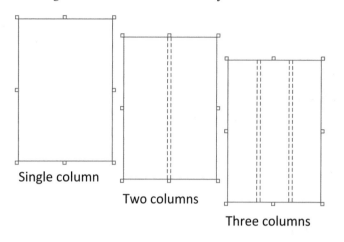

Single column

Two columns

Three columns

3. FLEXIBLE COLUMN STRUCTURE

The graphic designer wants to build flexibility into the master page to allow creative options when developing a layout. The use of a very narrow column structure with multiple columns achieves this. The structure below is the master template used for the 'Kelly Green' layout.

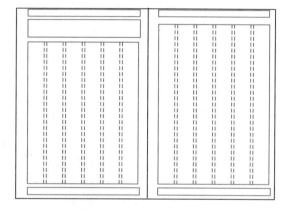

4. FLEXIBILITY

Changing the column structure from page to page or even within the same page can add visual interest to a publication. The example below shows how changes to the column structure between the top and bottom of the page can help create visual interest.

5. ASYMMETRIC STRUCTURE

Asymmetric layouts can also create visual impact. Asymmetry helps the layout look more **modern** and **less formal**. An asymmetric layout begins with an asymmetric structure as the structure below demonstrates.

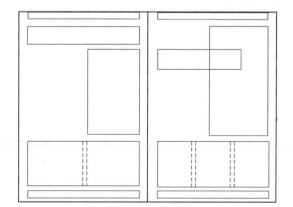

6. FINAL MASTER PAGE

The master page for the Kelly Green article is set up to include the text frames for Title, Sub-heads, body text, header and footer. The structure of the Kelly Green layout is asymmetric and has been adapted from the master template above.

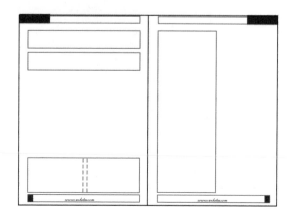

ANATOMY OF A PAGE

These are page layout features that you need to know for your assessments.
They are all described in more detail earlier in this chapter.

White space · Single Column · Colour fill · Header · Header Space

Heading, Headline or Title

Rule

Sub-heading

Image

Two Columns

Drop Capital

Gutter

Pull quote

Hanging indent

Reverse text · Tilt or rotate · Caption · Drop Shadow · White space · Fully cropped · Footer space

Cover Story

Kelly Green speaks out
Exclusive interview about ...

... new solo career and her great new album

The new album

How has working with producer Bob Styles helped your performance?

I love music and I love getting my songs heard by a young audience. I love to perform and I love being a girl and being feminine and putting on my favorite stilettos. But I learned a long time ago from my mother that beauty is from within. To feel confident and secure... is important.

What are your favorite tracks on the new album?
There are rockers like 'Down and out' and 'Last Chance' that I love to perform but there are balads that I prefer when I'm relaxing; 'Tomorrow will Arrive' is one.

You just released 'Tomorrow will Arrive' as your first solo single, why that particular choice?
We felt that it says a lot about me as a person and me and my manager thought it would connect with the fans and, hopefully, attract some new ones.

Which fragrance would Kelly Green be more likely wear - Hotter or Viva?
I love Hotter more because it is a fiery Fragrance.

Kelly has distinguised herself as an actress, too, with acclaimed roles in Cadillac Racers and Rough Girls. Will we be seeing you on the screen again soon?
Hopefully soon. We are looking at a script right now. Can't say any more than that!

Kelly's Passions

What does Kelly enjoy spending her hard earned cash on?

MY LITTLE GREEN BAG

MY COZY SILK SCARF

MY GREEN LES PAUL

AND, OF COURSE, PROMOTING MY NEW ALBUM

"The band was great. Rob led us well and the harmonies were tight."

Here are few women who embody celebrity as perfectly as Kelly Green. She had hearts all around the world "Rock - Rockin" as the leading lady of *Dark Love*, and then we fell 'Crazy in Love' when she embarked on her solo career, with success shortly thereafter.

Make no mistake, I'm ready for solo success.

The songstress delighted beauty editors and fans alike early last year with the launch of her first album " Heat and Dust" to critical acclaim.

We got the chance to ask Miss Green a couple of questions about her newest record, career moves, body image, and the lovely Rob Ford! You were selected as the celebrity with the *Best Body Image* by High Chic! readers in 2014. Do you have any words of wisdom for girls who struggle with image. The thing to strive for is to have the healthiest body you can have and not worry about your body image.

Snapshots

Rob rocks up for the album launch in a casual look before a night out at the movies!

Kelly at the Mercury awards at Earls Court in June.

www.rockstar.com

Cover Story

3 · 4

Left margin · Folio or Footer · Column rule · Text wrap · Footer · Bleed · Right margin

PREPARING YOUR DOCUMENT FOR COMMERCIAL PRINTING IS CALLED PRE-FLIGHT

Commercial printing is done on off-set lithography (off-set litho) printing machines. They apply four colours of ink. Each colour is applied separately from a printing plate wrapped around a roller. The plates each apply one of: Cyan, Magenta, Yellow and Black (the **key** colour). This is called CMYK or 4 colour Printing.

The printing plates need to be lined up carefully so that each colour is applied in exactly the correct position. The preflight features shown here enable the printer to check the colours are applied accurately and guide the trimming of the over-sized paper to the finished publication size. Off-set litho printing is high quality but is only economical for large print runs.

Your laser printer in school can be used commercially for small runs of leaflets and posters etc. The choice of printing method depends on a number of factors including; the size of the print run (is it thousands or hundreds?), the budget available and the material being printed on (paper, cardboard or polythene etc).

OFF-SET LITHO PRINTING PRESS

PRINTING TERMS

OS paper: Oversized paper is required because printing does not go right to the edge. To achieve a bleed the publication is printed on bigger, OS, paper and cropped to size after printing.

Crop marks: these indicate the lines along which the OS paper is to be cropped (trimmed) to size after printing.

Bleed size: This indicates the area outside the publication size that is printed on. It is usually 3 mm or 5 mm.

Registration marks: There are 4 registration marks. They should be sharp and black if the printing plates are lined up correctly. These are checked with a magnifying glass to ensure the plates are correctly aligned.

Colour bar and densitometer bar: Used to check for an accurate colour match at printing. The printer compares the colours against an accurate swatch card. These are printed on the OS margin but will be trimmed off during cropping.

Spot Colours: Printing colours that are pre-mixed e.g silver or gold are added as spot colours. Often used when corporate-specific colours are required. Pantone colours are also spot colours.

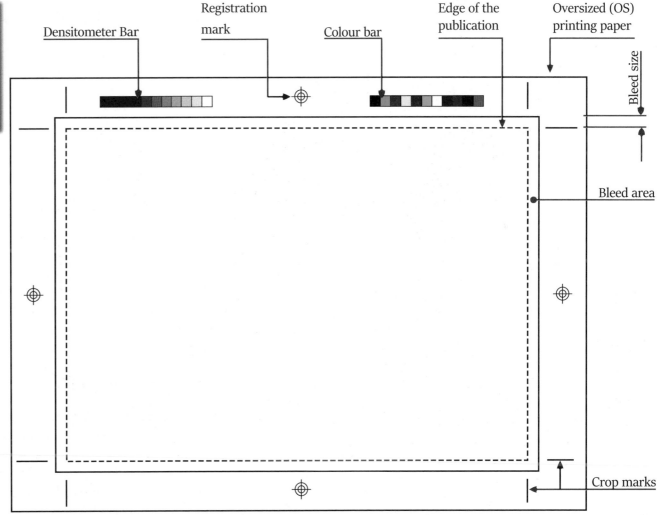

Densitometer Bar — Registration mark — Colour bar — Edge of the publication — Oversized (OS) printing paper — Bleed size — Bleed area — Crop marks

FILE TYPES AND PRINTING FOR A GREENER PLANET

PROFESSIONAL DTP PRINTING

PDF or *Portable Document Format* is the most common industrial format used for printing. It can contain both raster and vector graphics, be configured with colour information such as RGB, CMYK and spot-colours and have preflight information imbedded; crop mark, bleed, registration etc.

RESOLUTION FOR PRINTING

It may be obvious, but make sure you use high resolution images - at least 300 dpi at their original width and height. Remember, you can make an image smaller and maintain quality but you can't make it bigger without losing quality. Make sure your preflight PDF is not compressing your images.

UNCOMPRESSED

COMPRESSED

DTP AND THE PAPERLESS OFFICE

Although it is not the norm yet, the advantages of businesses operating entirely without paper are significant: It reduces the amount of paper we use; it takes up no physical space; storing large files can now be done using cloud storage; scanning can electronically copy any paper document.

Online business is much easier and can be done when banks and businesses are closed. Electronic documents can be located quickly through a file search. Electronic documents are shared electronically via email or on web sites - which streamlines document workflow. Security is much more enforceable with electronic documents than it is with paper.

PRINTING AND THE ENVIRONMENT

Printing on paper has been costly to the environment. Currently 40% of the world's logged timber is used to make paper and this figure is projected to increase *(source: Friends of the Earth)*. Paper manufacturing is also costly in energy and water.

PRINTING INKS

The printing industry world-wide uses very large quantities of oil based inks every year. As oil runs out so will the option of using ink made from this source. Already, vegetable based inks are being introduced to manage the industry in a more sustainable, eco-friendly way. Using vegetable inks also makes the recycling process easier, cheaper and less polluting.

DIGITAL PUBLICATIONS

Newspapers and magazines were once only available in paper form. This put a strain on our natural timber resources because paper is made from timber. Now newspapers and magazines are available in an electronic format. Online subscriptions mean that readers can enjoy publications on their computer or mobile phone which reduces the impact on our natural resources.

RECYCLED PAPER

Many publications are now reducing their impact on the environment by using recycled papers. Recycling once produced only low quality paper but modern recycling methods produce excellent quality printing paper. The process of recycling also uses 70% less energy and water than making virgin paper from timber. Recycling paper is easier when vegetable inks are used on the original publication. Remember also, that paper which is not recycled becomes landfill waste.

PHOTOGRAPHY

Photography is a powerful tool for a graphic designer. A good photograph can make the rest of the creative process more successful.

Photographs are also becoming increasingly popular when rendering aspects of a 3D environment - you learn more about this in the CAD illustration chapter - so learning about photography and photo-editing is worthwhile.

You don't need to take your own photographs for any of your assignment work in Graphic Communication, but you may find it useful to capture the exact image you want, rather than trawling the internet for hours hunting for something that 'will do'.

You will need to know about owning photographs and watermarks and file types for your exam, so study these sections closely.

PIXEL PERFECTION

Digital cameras use a light sensitive sensor to take a photograph. The light coming through the camera lens will fall onto a small part of this sensor and this is recorded as a 'Picture Element' or pixel. The more pixels a sensor can handle, the sharper and better quality the picture.

Cameras use sensors which can record over a million pixels, or "a megapixel". The higher the megapixel count, the better the quality the photograph.

YOU OWN IT

If you take a photograph, you own it. It is that simple. Even if you take a photograph of someone else, you are the owner of the image, not them.

Photographs and graphics are all big business and you will find dozens of companies online that sell a range of professionally made images. Companies watermark their graphics so they cannot be stolen or used without permission.

You cannot use a photograph, graphic or logo professionally without having

official permission from the licence holder. If you use an image without permission you may be taken to court.

However, it's OK to download images from the internet if you are using them for educational purposes only.

CHOOSE YOUR CAMERA

We are surrounded by devices that will take images, from drones to tablet computers, photography is always at our finger tips. The most common methods of taking photographs are digital cameras, such as DSLR, point-and-shoot and mobile phones. Digital Single Lens Reflex (DSLR) are the most expensive, most adaptable cameras available. They are excellent for zooming in on objects, due to the quality of the lenses. Point-and-shoot cameras are incredibly affordable and come with a range options to help guide you to taking a good image.

Camera phones are good for taking quick shots, but struggle with low light or distant items.

SETTING THE SCENE

Don't worry about the quality of your camera until you have developed your instinct for taking a really good photograph!

It takes a well trained eye to identify what would make a great photograph; we constantly take in pictures with our eyes and it can be difficult to exclude the clutter to focus on the ideal shot.

It can be worthwhile focusing on taking photographs that fulfil a simple description such as, 'texture', 'light', 'movement'.

The image below of a cobbled street could be anywhere. A bar, some shops and litter may not seem like an exciting or inspiring photograph. However, focusing the camera on the cobbled streets, their colour, shape, texture and reflection is different.

The image of the cobbled stones may be useful for a future DTP layout...

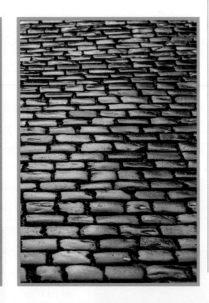

Digital cameras come with a huge range of settings. Most novice photographers will often opt for 'automatic' mode and let the camera choose the settings. For those brave enough to experiment with settings, the effort is worth it!

Nature can be one of the most interesting and exciting things to take photographs of. If you are planning to grow your own library of stock images, learning how to take photographs of plants and wildlife is a great place to start.

Taking 'macro' images can reveal a whole different side to nature. Macro is the term used to describe close-up images and every camera has this function. It is usually represented by a small flower symbol (🌷).

The cameras in mobile phones are often excellent at taking macro shots.

KEEPING SAFE

You must be very careful when taking pictures. Do not ever risk your life or the lives of others by trying to take a photograph. Stay well clear of trains, automobiles or any other moving vehicle. It is far too easy to get distracted by your camera when taking a photograph and accidents can happen. It is also advisable to stay well back from high drops or fast moving water, especially if you are on your own.

Be aware that many countries have very strict laws about what and who may be photographed. If you are in any doubt, always seek permission from someone with the authority to allow you to take images.

Whilst not always illegal, it is very rude to take photographs of people or their property without their permission.

If you are going out to take photographs, make sure someone knows where you are going and what time you will return - it may sound overcautious, but it is better to be safe than sorry.

Photo-editing software comes with a huge range of features and effects that can transform even the dullest of images into something stunning.

It's impossible to cover every single technique - you would need several books to cover everything - but we can highlight some of the most commonly used and important tools.

There are many free and paid-for photo-editing applications available; starting with free software is a good way to learn many of the tools and features than can improve your images.

You don't need to do any photo-editing to achieve a high mark in assessments, however it may help you improve your work.

ORIGINAL

HANDY HINT

You are not limited to using photo-editing software on just photographs. If you have created a CAD render that can do with some manipulation or improvement, then do it! You will not lose any marks in your assignment for improving your render further; it can help you improve your grade if it makes some of the environment details clearer or more realistic.

CONTRAST

Contrast can increase or decrease the difference between the light and dark areas of in image.

Increasing the contrast will make any differences in brightness more pronounced.

BRIGHTNESS

Brightness increases the amount of white (or the amount of black, if you are darkening an image).

Brightness is used to make dull images stand out more, or over-exposed images less bright. Brightness is often used in conjunction with contrast.

HUE + SATURATION

Hue is the amount a colour in an image, whilst saturation is the amount of grey.

A lower saturation value means more grey (until the image becomes entirely grey-scale)

SHARPEN + BLUR

The sharpen tool will remove any anti-alaising (blurring between pixels) to create a harder, grainier image, whilst the blur tool will soften any edges by increasing the anti-alaising.

MONOCHROME

Taking a colour photograph and removing all the colour information may seem a bit odd, but monochromatic images have a certain appeal and style useful in DTP. Using monochrome also allows you to keep colour in just one feature to add a focal point.

INVERT

The invert tool will take the colours and swap them for those on the opposite side of the colour wheel (see page 156).

This effect can be excellent for creating dramatic effects. Sometimes small details you didn't see can also appear...

MISTAKES BEGONE!

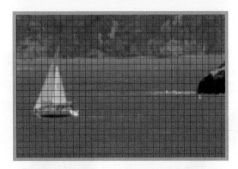

ORIGINAL

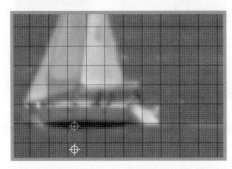

EDITED

You thought you had the perfect photograph for your promotional work - you may have travelled far or waited a long time to get the image you wanted, only to get home and realise that there is something in the image you don't want. Don't panic!

'Air brushing' is a common tool used to remove parts of an image that are undesirable. In this case, the small yacht next to Alcatraz needs to be removed. A 'clone' tool is used to copy pixels in one area and overlay them in another.

To use the clone tool, open your image in a photo-editing application. You will need to zoom into the image to see individual pixels. Tell your clone tool what pixels to copy - try and stay close to those you want rid off - and simply paint away the feature you want rid off.

Very quickly, you will be able to return the original magnification and you are unlikely to see any traces of the offending part. You can now export this file, ready to be used in your DTP layout or CAD illustration.

EXPORTING IMAGES

JPG

JPG (Joint Photography Expert Group) is the most commonly used image file format. It is used for both electronic displays and printed media, benefiting from a low file size that can be further compressed, it can also support the CMYK colour palette. The more compressed, the lower quality it will be.

✓ CMYK Capable?
✗ Alpha Channel?
✓ Compression?
✗ Websafe Colours?

BMP

Bitmaps are often referred to as the loss-less format. It is perfect for retaining all the colour and image information. However, file sizes can be huge! Bitmaps cannot be compressed, do not support transparency, cannot be processed as CMYK and are not great for websites.

✗ CMYK Capable?
✗ Alpha Channel?
✗ Compression?
✗ Websafe Colours?

PNG

Portable Network Graphic is the format of choice for electronic displays. PNG is rapidly becoming the image file used for all websites, mobile phone and tablet graphics. The file sizes are small, while maintaining a clean, sharp image. They also handle transparency.

✗ CMYK Capable?
✓ Alpha Channel?
✓ Compression?
✓ Websafe Colours

TIFF

Tagged Image File Format is the industry standard for images in books, posters, packaging and magazines. TIFF images are almost loss-less and allow for CMYK and transparency. TIFF can also have 'meta' information, such as who took the photograph and where it was shot.

✓ CMYK Capable?
✓ Alpha Channel?
✓ Compression?
✗ Websafe Colours

DTP GLOSSARY

ARTISTIC TEXT/WORD ART
Easily edited, stretched and shrunk text. Can be pulled into size using handles. Used in headings

BITMAP
Image made of pixels. Large files and loss of quality when scaled.

BLEED
An image or colour fill that extends beyond the edge of a page.

BODY TEXT
The main columns of reading text.

CAPTION
Text explaining a graphic.

CLIP-ART
Purpose-made images from a library; usually vector images.

CMYK
Cyan, Magenta, Yellow & Black (Key colour) used in laser and off-set litho printing (the 4 colour process).

COLOUR PICKER
Tool that selects and matches colours exactly.

COLOUR SWATCH
Ready-made colour chart used for checking printed colours.

COLUMN
Vertical, rectangular form that body text is contained in.

COLUMN RULE
Vertical line separating columns.

CROP MARKS
Marks in the print margins of a publication that show the printer where to trim the page.

CROPPING
Removing all or part of an image's background.

DROP CAP
A large first letter in an article that emphasises the start.

DROP SHADOW
Shadow placed behind an image to create emphasis or suggest depth.

DTP
Desk-top publishing. Creating publications on a computer.

FLOATING ITEM
Graphic item that is not constrained by the layout structure.

FLOW TEXT
A line of text that follows a line or curve.

FOOTER/FOLIO
Text in the footer space at the bottom of a page.

FRAMES
Re-sizable, non-printing boxes that contain text or images.

GRID & SNAP
Square grid that the snap function attaches to. Improves accuracy and speed of production.

GUIDELINES
Non-printing lines pulled onto page to support layout construction.

GUTTER
Narrow space separating columns.

HANDLES
Means of re-shaping and re-sizing frames.

HEADER
Text in the header space at the top of the page.

HEADLINE/HEADING/TITLE
Large text that introduces the publication or article.

HIERARCHY
Order of importance of text in a layout or publication.

IMPORT/EXPORT
To transfer files to and from software.

INDENT
When the paragraph starts further in than the margin.

JPEG
File type commonly used for storing digital photographs.

KERNING
Narrowing or widening the space between letters to create impact or to save space in body text.

LAYERS
The arrangement of items in levels, one on top of the other, in a layout.

LEADING
The vertical spacing between lines of text.

OFFSET LITHOGRAPHY
The main commercial mass production printing method.

OS PAPER
Oversized paper that is trimmed to size after printing.

PANTONE®
Colour system used to categorise pre-mixed inks; used in marker pens and spot colour printing.

PDF
Portable Document File used for commercial printing and digital documents.

PNG
Image file that comes with a transparent background.

PULL QUOTE
Catchy or controversial comment pulled from the body text and enlarged. Draws the reader in.

PRE-FLIGHT
Preparations for setting up a document ready for a print-run.

REGISTRATION MARKS
Marks on the printing margins of a publication that help line up the printing plates and printing colours.

REVERSE
Converting black text to white.

RGB
Red, Green & Blue. Used to create colours on-screen.

ROTATING
Turning or tilting an item in a layout, normally to create emphasis.

SANS SERIF & SERIF
Two main types of typeface. Serif letters have flicks while sans serif letters do not. This text is serif, the sub-heads are sans serif.

SPOT COLOURS
Pre-mixed colours used in printing. e.g Silver, Gold and shades of colours.

STRAP LINE/TAG LINE
Catchy or memorable sub-heading used to draw the reader's attention.

SUB-HEADING
Larger than body text, smaller than the heading. Catchy lead in to the body text.

TEXT JUSTIFICATION
How the text is aligned in a frame; left, right, centred or fully justified.

TEXT WRAP
Text wraps around the outline shape of an image.

TIFF
Tagged Image File Format. Industrial format used in commercial printing.

TRACKING
Adjusting the spacing between letters to fit a space.

TRANSPARENCY
See-through colour fills or images.

TYPEFACE AND FONTS
Different families and styles of text.

UNDERLINE
Underlining text for emphasis.

VECTOR GRAPHIC
Scalable computer generated graphic made of lines, shapes and colour fills.

WHITE SPACE
Blank spaces left in a layout to rest the eye and aid composition.

WIDOW/ORPHAN
Word at the top of a column that should be at the foot of the previous column / Word at the foot of a column that should be at the top of the next column.

DESIGN
ELEMENTS &
PRINCIPLES

CREATIVE
LAYOUT SKILLS

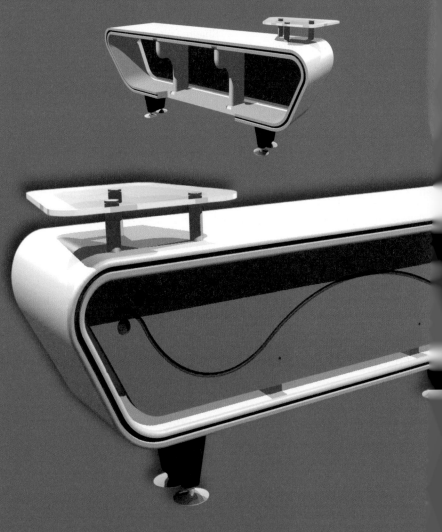

Being good at Graphic design is a bit like playing football; you either have it or you don't.

NOT TRUE!

Creativity does not always come naturally, it is learned. Designing a layout so that it appeals to a specific audience is a creative skill. Even the most talented designers have worked hard to learn their creative skills.

Creative skill is actually multiple skills and knowledge which come together on the page or screen to present the message concisely, clearly and effectively. This chapter will show you how to apply layout skills that you can practice and refine during your course. You will learn the psychology of graphic design and how best to communicate an idea.

DESIGN ELEMENTS AND PRINCIPLES

WHAT ARE THEY?

Designers use their knowledge of layout elements and design principles to create exciting graphical layouts.

Layouts are comprised of graphics (images, drawings, photographs and illustrations) and text (titles, headings, sub-headings and body text). It is the understanding of design elements & principles (Es & Ps) that enables the graphic designer to create a layout by structuring, editing, combining and positioning the content of the layout to best effect.

Your knowledge of design elements & principles will help you secure a good pass in your Higher course by enabling you to create exciting layouts and ensure you are prepared for your course exam which will test your knowledge of Es and Ps.

WHAT DO I NEED TO LEARN?

The list of design Elements & Principles below are what you need to understand and answer questions on.
These are:

Alignment, Balance, Colour, Contrast, Depth, Dominance, Emphasis, Line, Mass/Weight, Proportion, Repetition, Rhythm, Shape, Texture, Unity/Proximity, Value, White space.

Several elements and principles are closely related:

- **Mass, weight and value.**
- **Unity and proximity.**
- **Dominance and emphasis.**

These all have close connections and can be difficult to separate. Learn the simpler elements & principles first; alignment, colour, contrast, line, shape & white space and use them in layouts. Then answer the **EXAM PREP** questions on each page in this chapter.

COMBINING DTP WITH ELEMENTS AND PRINCIPLES

It is vital that you think of **Elements & Principles** in conjunction with **DTP** features.

- Elements & Principles are part of the process of creating an exciting layout.
- DTP Features are the tools with which you can carry out this creative process.

EXAM PREP

The exam can feel very long and you may be tempted to rush some answers. Don't! Use all the time available wisely .

While there are no drawings to create, there is a lot to read, analyse, interpret, understand and visualise. You should spend more time doing these things than actually writing answers.

It is vital that you slow yourself down when you are answering elements & principles and DTP questions. You need to study each layout carefully.

It's important to get into the mindset of the designer and the viewpoint of the target audience.

Each item in the layout is there for a reason. It's your task to work out why the designer made important decisions about the layout and how they went about it. You need to determine which DTP features and Es & Ps have been combined to create a successful layout and explain how and why.

The checklist below will allow you to keep track of the Es & Ps that you have used in your own design work and the Es & Ps that you have learned about in preparation for your prelim and final course exam.

CHECKLIST

ELEMENTS AND PRINCIPLES

DESIGN ELEMENTS AND PRINCIPLES	USED IN A LAYOUT	REVISED FOR MY EXAM
Alignment		
Balance		
Colour		
Contrast		
Depth		
Dominance		
Emphasis		
Line		
Mass/weight		
Proportion		
Repetition		
Rhythm		
Shape		
Texture		
Unity/proximity		
Value		
White space		

ALIGNMENT

WHAT IS IT?

Alignment is the process of lining up items in a layout. Alignment creates a **neat, organised** and **structured layout** and helps to make a layout **easier to follow**. Alignment also creates a **visual connection between the aligned items** helping to establish **unity**.

DTP software has features that make accurate alignment easier to achieve; **grids, guidelines** and **snap to grid** and **guidelines** are standard alignment tools in DTP. Alignment often goes unnoticed but can be the most important design feature in a layout.

> **Alignment:** *Orderly arrangement or positioning in relation to something else, linear positioning for proper performance.*

CASE STUDY - WITHOUT ALIGNMENT

The draft layout below, has been put together without considering alignment. The reader can't pick out a structure. It looks and feels as if the content was scattered in a random fashion. The result is a layout that lacks both organisation and structure and can be difficult to follow. Careful alignment can improve this layout.

DRAFT LAYOUT

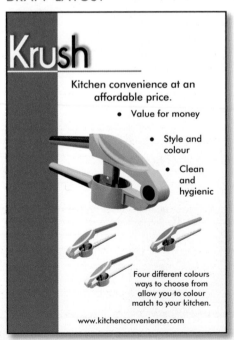

WITH ACCURATE ALIGNMENT

The final layout benefits from the use of *snap to grid* and *snap to guidelines*. These DTP features have been used to line up items accurately. The visual impression is that the layout now has a structure and is easier to follow and read.

WHAT ABOUT THE ITEMS WHICH ARE NOT ALIGNED?

Because most of the items in the layout are carefully aligned, the items which are not aligned (the main image and the quote) stand out. These items have been placed out-with the structure of the layout and are known as **floating items.** They create dominance and visual tension in an organised layout.

HOW OFTEN SHOULD I USE ALIGNMENT?

You should consider alignment in every layout you create. Even if only two of the items are aligned, an organised structure is implied. It is simple to achieve and is the most important feature in many layouts.

FINAL LAYOUT

> Tip: The square colour-fills help to align small cropped images. It makes alignment easier to achieve and more obvious.

WHAT IS IT?

There are three main forms of balance: **Symmetrical**, **Asymmetric** and **Radial balance**. Balance can help create a traditional, formal layout or a dynamic modern layout. The type you choose depends on the content of the layout and the feel you wish to create. All three are shown here.

SYMMETRICAL BALANCE

All of the main features (text and the main image) are centred. A symmetrical layout tends to look formal; too formal for this modern furniture. It can also look static, safe and dull.

Another issue is that it leaves two spaces, one either side of the main item, which can be difficult or awkward to fill. This example looks clumsy.

The symmetrical layout is not a good choice for promoting this modern product.

ASYMMETRIC BALANCE

The main item is positioned off-centre and on or close to a **'rule of thirds'** focal point (see page 163). The space beside the main item is easier to fill and the asymmetric layout creates a modern feel. The layout flows from the main image, across to the company logo. In this layout the designer makes good use of contrast and depth and space. The layout looks co...

The asymmetry also creates vis... the modern feel.

An asymmetric layout is the mo... product.

The other two forms of balance... different content.

> **Balance:** Equilibrium, poise, steadiness, A state in which various parts form a satisfying and harmonious whole and nothing is out of proportion or unduly emphasized at the expense of the rest.

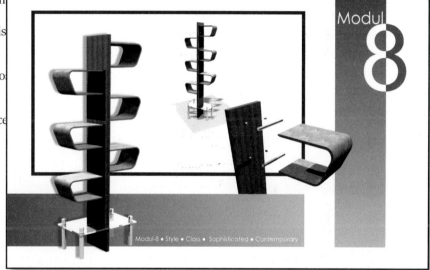

RADIAL BALANCE

There is a centred focal point and other items are arrayed around the focal point.

In this case the layout looks cluttered. Other items over-power the main image and it doesn't flow.

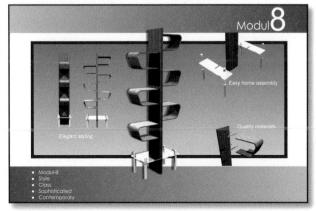

EXAM PREP

*Q1. Describe two ways in which the designer creates **contrast** in the asymmetric layout, above.*

*Q2. Explain **why** contrast can be important in a layout.*

Q3. Describe two ways in which the designer created depth in the asymmetric layout, above.

The use of alignment in the above layout is not obvious but it helps organise it.

Q4. Describe where alignment occurs in the above layout.

*Q5. Choose one **DTP technique** from: full cropping or colour fill that has been used in the above layout and explain why the designer chose to use it.*

COLOUR

WHAT IS IT?

In design, colour is not an after-thought or an add-on, it is integral to the design of products and how we communicate graphically. It is our response to colour that makes it so vital in the design of our environments and the products we use.

COLOUR AND THE MOODS THEY CREATE

When you choose colours for a layout, it is useful to understand how we react and respond to colour. You can energize with colour or create calm with colour. Careful choice of colours can produce elegance or harshness or convey youthfulness. Colour can draw attention to a product or appeal to a specific group of people. Colour can be a powerful design tool if you learn to use it effectively.

RED — Advancing - Warm - Exciting Passionate - Courageous - Active - Vibrant - Revolutionary

ORANGE — Advancing - Warm - Cheerful - Energetic - Approachable - Informal - Appetising

Yellow — Advancing - Warm - Happy - Energetic - Sunny - Cheerful - Glowing - Upbeat - Lively

VIOLET — Advancing - Warm - Dreamy Fantasy - Playful - Impulsive Solitary

BLUE — Receding - Cool - Elegant Formal - Relaxing - Soothing - Classy - Distant - Spiritual

ADVANCING AND RECEDING

Cool colours are also known as **receding** colours because they appear more distant. This is especially true if a pale tone is used.
Warm colours are known as **advancing** because they appear to come forward in a colour scheme. This is especially true if a strong, saturated tone is used.

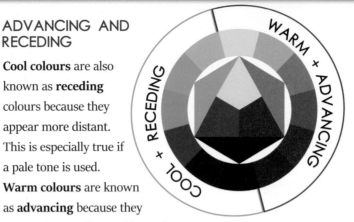

GREEN — Receding - Cool - Natural - Fresh - Soothing - Calm - Healing Tranquil - Restful - Quiet

PURPLE — Receding - Cool - Royal - Rich - Creative - Luxurious - Self-important - Wealthy

BROWN — Advancing - Warm - Natural Reliable - Earthy - Safe - Good - Reassuring

GREY — Advancing - Warm grey (added red) Receding - Cool Grey (added blue) - Neutral - Calm - Restful - Dignified

BLACK & WHITE — White - Receding - Innocent - Pure Black - Advancing - Formal - Mysterious - Elegant - Stylish

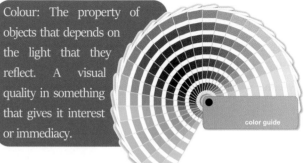

Colour: The property of objects that depends on the light that they reflect. A visual quality in something that gives it interest or immediacy.

TINTS AND SHADES

TINT = A colour with added white

SHADE = A colour with added grey

Your DTP software will enable you to create your own tints and shades. Designers often use marker pens that contain **PANTONE COLOURS** and have hundreds of **pre-mixed** tints and shades.

EXAM PREP

Q1. Which of the two colours below appears closest to the viewer. Explain why.

| Pale blue | Red |

Designers often use different colouring media at different stages of the design process.

*Q2. Explain why designers often find that using a **pantone** colouring medium is convenient when they are at the preliminary stage of a design project.*

COLOUR

Colour is an integral part of promoting and selling products and a promotional layout needs the colour choice to be considered carefully. The images of this product show small areas of strong, low value tone and areas of bright, high value tone. Always try both strong and weaker tones in the backdrop when you are creating a layout - you may be surprised at what works best.

CHOOSING BACKGROUND COLOURS

The product you are promoting will have its own colours. The product may have a colour pallet that is harmonised or one that is contrasting.

Test 1

Test 5

Test 2

Test 6

Test 3

Test 7

Test 4

Test 8

HOW MANY COLOURS SHOULD I USE?

Because this product image includes two strong colours the rest of the layout colours should be restricted. One layout colour can be matched to a part of the product.

TRY OUT COLOUR SCHEMES

This can be done quickly on-screen. The product has primary colours; red, yellow and blue, that create contrast. It can be difficult to narrow down the best colours to use in the background.

These need to be chosen carefully or the promotional message can become confusing.

In this test some background colours clash with the product; tests 3, 4 & 6. While 1, 2 & 8 overpower the product. This leaves tests 5 and 7 to experiment with.

Colour 5 was selected. The colour chosen is a mix of red and blue and helps unify the primary colours in the product.

WHAT IS THE FUNCTION OF THE PRODUCT AND WHO IS THE LAYOUT AIMED AT?

Important factors to consider when choosing layout colours are the **age** and **gender** of the target market and the **function** of the product. These factors will also influence choice of **typeface** and the **style** of the layout. Think carefully about these factors when choosing colours.

TONES, TINTS & SHADES

Remember, editing the tone, tint or shade of a colour can have a dramatic effect on the layout. Colour fill styles also have an impact. In the final layout only one new colour, purple, has been added. This is a mix of red and blue colours that both appear in the product. The red line is colour-matched to the red component in the product.

The result is a colour scheme that helps unify the strong contrast in the product. The background colour does what is expected of it. It enhances the product without dominating the layout.

DESK architecture

REFRESH YOUR DESK WITH OUR FUNKY PRODUCT RANGE

EXAM PREP

The layout is has been created using several **separate items.**

*Q1. Explain how the designer created **unifying** connections in the layout other than with colour.*

*Q2. Describe how the random **angled lines** improve the layout.*

CONTRAST

WHAT IS IT?

Contrast is about creating eye-catching visual interest by using opposites. These opposites can be **colours**, **tones**, **values**, **shapes**, **sizes**, **styles**, **genders**, **fonts**, **distances** (near & far) or **orientations** (vertical & horizontal). Pretty much anything you introduce to a layout will have an opposite that can be used to create contrast.

Understanding contrast and learning how it can be used to improve a promotional layout is one of the most important design skills you will acquire. Contrast can grab the attention of readers and draw them in.

CASE STUDY

Evaluate the draft layout below? The layout is neat and organised but it lacks visual impact. The items in the layout appear scattered and, other than careful alignment, there is nothing connecting the items. The layout needs a focal point and a sense of depth. The use of contrast can achieve both.

DRAFT LAYOUT

WHAT TYPES OF CONTRAST CAN BE ADDED TO A LAYOUT?

When contrast is introduced to this simple layout below the effect is striking and immediate. Just how many different forms of contrast do we find in the final layout?

Colour - Blue and orange.

Tone -   Dark shadows and bright highlights.

Depth - Near and far (foreground and background) the smaller chair looks distant.

Shape - Rectangles and circles.

Font style - Serif and sans serif.

Typeface - Formal and informal.

Text styles - Italic and non-italic text. Uppercase and lowercase.

Orientation - Vertical and horizontal features.

The result is a layout that has much more visual impact. This comes from the contrast in the layout, especially the illusion of depth. It has a foreground and a background and the items in the layout are layered and visually connected.

FINAL LAYOUT

Contrast: Difference, opposites, distinctiveness, divergence, a noticeable difference in something.

EXAM PREP

Unity (creating connections between items, see page 167) is important in the final layout.

Q1. Describe four ways in which the designer creates **unity** *in the final layout, left.*

Unusually, four different **typefaces** are used in the final layout.

Q2. Justify the choices of typeface for the heading and the body text.

Colour plays an important role in this layout.

Q3. Identify where a cool colour has been used and explain the effect it has on the layout.

Justified paragraph text is used in the body text.

Q4. Explain why justified text is used in this layout.

Depth: Three-dimensional space or thing,
Distance between front and back or top and bottom.

DEPTH

WHAT IS IT?

Graphic layouts are flat, 2D compositions printed on paper or displayed on a screen. Graphic designers realised a long time ago that creating a layout that appears to show depth or distance can make a better job of presenting a product to the audience.

Depth is a staple feature in the advertising industry. It can make a promotional image appear more real and it can help push the product to the front of a layout and make it catch the eye of the target audience.

CASE STUDY

The draft layout includes the same content as the final layout but does not have the same visual impact. *Why not?*

Let's analyse it:

Background:

The background colour-fill sits fully behind everything. When you surround an item with a background fill, there is no opportunity for the items to break forward and create depth.

Space:

Every item occupies it's own space. There is no physical connection between items.

Layering:

The layout appears flat with all seven items sitting above the background fill.

DRAFT LAYOUT

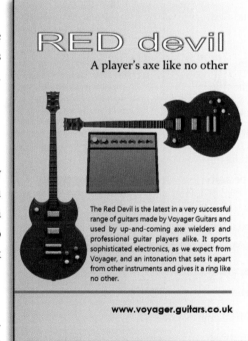

Scale:

The guitars are the same size; an opportunity to create depth through scale is lost.

2D or 3D:

Both guitars are 2D images and look flat.

HOW TO ACHIEVE DEPTH

The final layout includes the same content as the draft layout but has much more visual impact. *Why?*

Let's analyse it:

Background:

The colour-fill in the background sits behind the top of the guitars but does not surround them. When part of an image breaks across the edge of a background it creates depth in the layout.

Space:

Some items are brought closer together and overlap. It gives the impression of a mini 3D scene and suggests depth.

Layering:

Guitars overlap text at the top and the line at the foot of the layout. This creates depth as well as connections between the guitars, the heading and the blue line; it also creates unity.

Scale:

The guitars have been scaled, one to look big and close-up and the other to look smaller and more distant.

2D or 3D:

Both guitars are shown in a pictorial style, reinforcing the 3D look.

FINAL LAYOUT

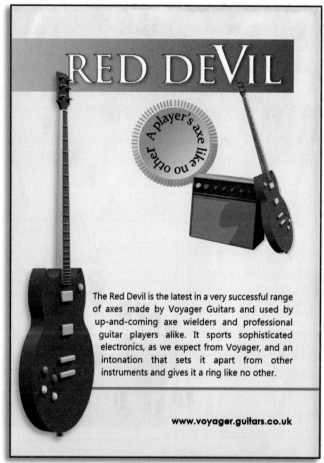

EXAM PREP

The colours of the guitar and amplifier are fixed and cannot be changed. Other colours have been introduced.

Q1. Explain the designer's choice of introduced colours.

DOMINANCE + EMPHASIS

WHAT ARE THEY?

Dominance and emphasis are closely linked. Dominance is essential in order to create a focal point and establish a hierarchy of importance in the layout.

A layout without clear dominance can be confusing because the items in the layout fight for prominence. Carefully planned dominance will lead the reader's eyes through the layout and help make the message clear.

Emphasis is the method designers use to create levels of importance, to make features stand out from other items in the layout.

CASE STUDY

The draft layout lacks proper dominance or emphasis. The layout is read from the top left down to the bottom right and that is normal. But the layout is 'flat' and without obvious focal points.

The product image and the text both need edited so that the layout has two or three focal points. Also, the background colour fill surrounds the image which gets lost in the layout.

DRAFT LAYOUT

DARK EYES DESIGN

The importance of having well designed and well crafted furniture in your home can't be overstated. Value for money comes from paying a fair price for a product that, in durability and style, will last a life-time. This is the aim of Dark Eyes design. Our commitment to using quality materials and employing skilled craftsmen is our pledge to you. We will honour our pledge to provide a product for your home that you can be proud of.

Style and affordability meets great design.
If you want to make a statement and the vision is modern, then look no further than our website. We offer work from top designers to set the tone inside your home. you want to make a statement and the vision is modern, then look no further than our website. We offer work from top designers to set the tone inside your home.

Dominance: Supremacy, power, authority, control, prime importance, effectiveness, or prominence.

Emphasis: Importance, prominence, special importance, significance, or stress.

FINAL LAYOUT - WHAT HAS CHANGED AND WHAT HAS BEEN ACHIEVED?

- The title has greater **mass** (it's much bigger) and will be noticed and read first.

- The title is positioned with **white space** around it to create more **emphasis**.

- The **underline** also **emphasises** the title.

- The product image is bigger creating more **mass** and a **dominant focal point**.

- The image has been **cropped** from its background, **emphasising** its shape and creating **dominance**.

- The product image is positioned on a **'rule of thirds' focal point**.

- The product **faces into the layout**; always have the product facing into the page.

- The body text has a **drop cap** emphasising the start of the text and creating contrast.

- The second paragraph is **reversed** and set in front of a blue colour fill, creating emphasis.

- The blue colour fill behind the credit is **tilted** to create **emphasis**.

FINAL LAYOUT

DARK eyes DESIGN

The importance of having well designed and well crafted furniture in your home can't be overstated. Value for money comes from paying a fair price for a product that, in durability and style, will last a life-time. This is the aim of Dark Eyes design. Our commitment to using quality materials and employing skilled craftsmen is our pledge to you. We will honour our pledge to provide a product for your home that you can be proud of.

If you want to make a statement and the vision is modern, then look no further than our website. We offer work from top designers to set the tone inside your home.

'U' shelf *by Siggurson*

EXAM PREP

The designer has implied connections (unity) between items in the layout.

Q1. Describe four ways in which the designer establishes unifying connections between items in the layout.

LINE

WHAT IS IT?

Line has several functions in a promotional layout but should be used carefully. Remember, line is a feature that you have introduced into the layout. It may not need to be there and it certainly should not dominate a layout.

Line can:

- Connect items in a layout.
- Separate items in a layout.
- Lead the eye across or down a layout.
- Give structure to a layout.
- Create depth in a layout.

DRAFT LAYOUT

CASE STUDY

A LAYOUT WITHOUT LINE

This layout is proportionally long and narrow and the content is spread down the layout. The product, a child's desk and stool, is quite angular and makes the layout look busy.

The layout lacks structure, there is no depth in the layout and there is nothing connecting the items together. This leaves the items floating.

The trick is to improve this layout without overdoing it.

Line: A long narrow mark or stroke. A row of people or things. A path or direction of movement.

LAYOUT 1 IMPROVEMENTS

The four lines introduced to layout 1 offer a number improvements:

The top horizontal line
Underlines and emphasises the title and creates a more interesting asymmetric layout.

The vertical line
This leads the eye down the layout and creates depth by sitting behind the desk. It also suggests structure by defining a margin and it connects the top of the layout with the bottom.

The two lower horizontal lines
These lead the eye across the layout and separate the images from the body text achieving a more organised structure.

LAYOUT 2 IMPROVEMENTS

The lines here include boxed outlines. These perform the same function as lines in the layout. The boxes suggest structure by defining margins. They create depth by sitting behind images and they connect the images by sitting behind both sets of images.

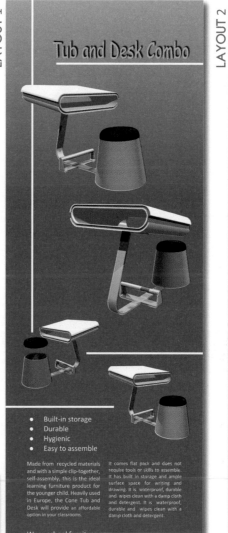

LAYOUT 1

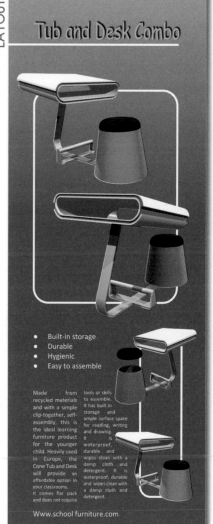

LAYOUT 2

EXAM PREP

The tonal value of the background in the layouts is mid-value.

Q1. Explain why a mid-value background was chosen for this layout.

MASS/WEIGHT

WHAT ARE THEY?

Mass is equivalent to size: The bigger the item, the more mass it has in the layout. Mass has a bearing on dominance. The bigger the item, the more dominant it is likely to be in the layout.

Weight is also related to size; the bigger an item is, the heavier it will be. But it is also influenced by value. A dark, dense item will have a heavier weight than a light, airy item. The see-saw diagrams will help explain the principles.

MASS & WEIGHT

Equal sized items have the same mass.

Smaller items have less mass and are less dominant.

Achieving a visual balance using mass can sometimes be done by moving the largest mass closer to the centre of a layout and keeping the smaller items further out.

Different tonal and colour values have different weights. Darker, saturated tones appear heavier than pale, light tones.

Mass: *Size, the amount of matter it contains, and its influence in a gravitational field.*
Weight: *Influence: heaviness, load, power.*

MASS IN VISUAL TERMS

Larger mass

Bigger size = Larger mass

Smaller mass

Smaller size = smaller mass

Lighter weight

Lighter font = less weight.

Paragraph breaks also reduce the weight.

The first among equals, our new initialed pick is possibly the finest pick in music today.

The innovative textured grip and personal design makes its on-stage use much more practical for the pro musician and amateur alike.

The colour range is limitless, just specify your choice.

Heavier weight

Heavy font = more weight

The first among equals, our new initialed pick is possibly the finest of its type in music today. The innovative textured grip and personal design makes its on-stage use much more practical for the pro musician and amateur alike. The colour range is limitless, just specify your choice.

Heavier weight

Strong tone/strong colour = More weight

Lighter weight

Lighter tone or colour = Less weight

CASE STUDY

Layout 1 is nicely balanced with the emphasis on the photograph because of its large mass. The red pick has less emphasis because of its smaller mass. The light font of the body text means this has less weight in the layout.

In Layout 2 the photograph has been reduced in size and therefore mass, while the red pick is scaled-up (increasing its mass). The focus changes from the photograph of the band to the red pick. The red pick now dominates the layout.

In layout 3 the photograph is grey scale only. This reduces its weight in the layout. A heavier typeface is used for the body text and this gives it more (too much) emphasis in the layout.

LAYOUT 1

LAYOUT 2

LAYOUT 3

EXAM PREP The layouts all make use of an asymmetric style of balance.

Q1. Explain, giving two reasons, why an asymmetric balance was chosen.

WHAT IS IT?

There are two ways of looking at proportion.

1. Proportion is relative. Two items exactly the same size occupy different proportions when they are in publications that are different sizes; one A4 and the other A5.

2. Proportion is the comparative mass (size) of items in the same layout.

DRAFT 1

This smaller sized layout, draft 1, looks busier and the image dominates but the layout feels congested.

DRAFT 2

The larger format of the layout, draft 2, allows more space for the image which now has room to breath. The lines help create a visual link between the image and the text.

DRAFT 3

Text is also a visual item that influences the proportions of a layout. In the layout, right, the column of text dominates the layout which also lacks a focal point. The proportions of text and images fight against each other.

DRAFT 4

When two images are used together they can't both dominate a layout. Here, right, the proportions of the images are similar, they vie for dominance and neither wins. Again, the layout lacks a suitable focal point.

FINAL LAYOUT

Changing the proportions of the images can create dominance in the larger image. Large and small proportions can also create depth. Dominance of the larger image is strengthened by its position on a focal point and by placing it in front of a line. It brings pleasing proportions, a clear focal point and a hierarchy of dominance that helps us make sense of the layout.

Proportion: Share, percentage fraction, ratio, a quantity of something that is part of a whole.

RULE OF THIRDS

Photographers use the technique of dividing a layout into thirds. The red lines are focal points and the crosses, impact points. Placing key items on or close to these points can make them more prominent in a layout.

RHYTHM AND REPETITION

WHAT ARE THEY?

Rhythm is achieved by repeating features in a layout in order to help the layout flow, make a layout easier on the eye or lead the eye through a layout.

CASE STUDY

Q: When do we need rhythm?

A: When we need to create a flow through a layout. The layout, right, is an article promoting a new range of office furniture. The intention is to create a modern, minimalist look. It looks fine and is certainly modern. Alignment is accurate and helps organise the layout.

However, the layout does not flow easily from top left to bottom right, the one large block of body text is daunting and difficult to read and the white space in the centre of the layout creates a gap that the reader needs to bridge. The text needs broken into manageable chunks to make it visually less daunting. Introducing rhythm would be a good way to start.

Q: How do we create rhythm?

A: *By introducing repetition.*

When the layout includes a large block of body text your first task might be to try a **multiple column structure**. This creates repetition and encourages the eyes to flow down one column and up and across to the top of the next column. Using **paragraph breaks** also creates a visual punctuation that breaks up the body text into smaller, more manageable blocks.

Repeating features such as **bullet points, lines, shapes**, **columns** and **sub-heads,** can also be used to create repetition. This makes the layout more manageable and leads the reader's eye through the article.

DRAFT LAYOUT

FINAL LAYOUT

EXAM PREP

The final layout has a formal column structure. The designer needed to create a modern feel and she decided to use **'floating items'** in the layout.

Q1. Explain what is meant by 'floating items' and how this creates a modern feel in the final layout.

Emphasis plays an important role in the final layout.

Q2. Describe three techniques the designer has used to create emphasis in the final layout.

WHAT IS IT?

Your default shape is the rectangle. The page or screen are rectangular, columns of text are rectangles and so are photographs. Looking for new shapes became part of the challenge for graphic designers looking for ways to liven up a layout. Using different shapes in a layout can bring movement and contrast to the design and help set a mood.

CASE STUDY

A compliments slip is required by an upmarket indoor lighting manufacturer. An image has been sent to the designer along with the content and draft layout of the compliments slip. How can the designer use shape to improve the layout?

DRAFT LAYOUT

LUMA Lighting

With compliments from the team at Luma

www.lumalighting.co.uk

WHICH SHAPES TO USE?

Shapes can be defined as hard and soft shapes and light and heavy shapes:

Circles are soft, light and moving while squares are hard, heavy and static. Shapes can also be classified as geometric, organic or abstract.

Your choice of shape in a layout will depend on the purpose of the layout and who will read or view it. The lamp in the draft layout is modern and has a curved outline. It would be wise to start trying out simple geometric shapes.

MEETING THE CHALLENGE

Applying a full crop to an image is enough to change the rectangular shape and create a more interesting, irregular shape.

The next step is to try opposite shapes. Circles and curved shapes will create contrast against the rectangular layout.

It can be useful to try a range of shapes in your own layouts. The layouts below each benefit from the inclusion of different shapes. The shapes may be regular and used in a pattern to create rhythm. Or they can appear random for use in an abstract style backdrop.

LAYOUT 1

LAYOUT 2

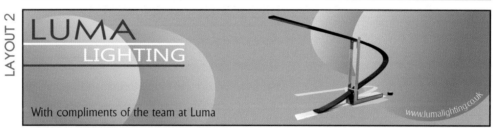

LAYOUT 3

LAYOUT 4

> **Shape:** *Silhouette, figure, profile, contour, the outline of something's form.*

EXAM PREP

The lamp is most prominent in layout 1

Q1. Explain why the lamp stands out most in layout 1.

Layout 1 uses patterns of circles.

Q2. Explain what the patterns of circles bring to the layout.

All of the layouts make use of unity.

Q3. Describe two ways the designer achieved a unified look in layout 2.

Each layout makes use of eye-catching contrast.

Q4. Other than by colour, describe two ways in which contrast has been achieved in layout 3.

TEXTURE

WHAT IS IT?

There are two ways to use texture in graphic design. There is physical texture and visual texture. The physical texture of the printing paper can be thick, thin. smooth, rough, bumpy, matt, satin or glossy. Visual texture comes from the use of images to replicate texture. These visual textures can establish a mood or style. Different textures appeal to different target audiences. Designing promotional graphics requires consideration of the target audience and the product being promoted.

CASE STUDY

The Scottish indie band 'Dante' require a flyer to promote their tour. Dante's music is somewhere between indie and folk and they write their own material. The graphic artist has been sent files, shown below, to be included in the flier. She was asked to create a layout that reflects the 'take us as you find us', youthful, indie style of their music that would reflect the band's 'on the road' style.

Material to be included in the tour flyer.

Band Name: Dante

Quote: "Folk-flecked indie gems"- The Skinny

2015 Tour Dates:

			Images
March	19	Stan's bar, Edinburgh	
March	26	Blue Room, Perth	
April	3	Perch Inn, Ullapool	
April	9	Cafe Diamond, Aberdeen	
April	11	Electric Rooms, Edinburgh	
May	12	Smith Hall, Kirkcaldy	
May	18	Green Hotel, Kinross	
May	21	Apple Tree, Aberdeen	

> **Texture:** *The feel and appearance of a surface, especially how rough or smooth it is.*

DRAFT LAYOUT

DRAFT LAYOUT

The draft layout above, is organised and informative but lacks impact and is too formal and smooth. It does not reflect the band's rough and ready image.

HOW IS TEXTURE USED TO IMPROVE THE LOOK OF THE FINAL LAYOUT?

There is already texture in the main picture (sand and sea) and the designer makes use of this and its colours. The image has been square cropped to focus on the band. To support the 'indie' culture of the band, three additional textured backgrounds give the final layout a layered effect and a stained, informal feel that reflects the band's image. The stencil style title font adds another rough texture to the layout. The textures create a 'home-made' feel that supports the band's style and connects with their audience.

FINAL LAYOUT

EXAM PREP

The three small photographs are used effectively in the flyer.

Q1. Explain how the designer used the three small photographs to maximise; **contrast**, **emphasis** *and* **texture**.

Q2. Explain the purpose of the **neutral colours** *in the layout.*

Unity: *Agreement, harmony, unison. The combining or joining of separate things into one.*

Proximity: *Nearness, closeness in space or time.*

WHAT IS IT?

A layout comprises several items set out on a page or screen. Done badly, it can seem like the items are scattered randomly across the page or completely unconnected to each other. The skill of the designer in unifying (connecting) these items can make or break a layout. There are a number of ways to create unity in a layout.

DRAFT LAYOUT

The draft layout, above, has been set out in an organised way but each of the items occupies it's own space and, other than the guitars, there are no obvious connections between them.

HOW TO CREATE UNITY

There are several techniques to consider when setting out your page:

1. Physical unity is achieved by overlapping items using a layering effect.
2. Using text wrap or flow text to position text close to images is called proximity.
3. Colour matching helps to connect items visually.
4. Using accurate alignment creates an implied link between the items that are aligned.

MEETING THE CHALLENGE

The final layout, right, has been fine-tuned to produce a layout that has visual impact as well as a unified feel.

How has this been achieved?

Colour - the number of colours has been reduced. This creates a simpler more unified layout.

Colour - the blue guitars already colour match and now the red flashbar and lines have been colour matched to the controls on the guitar body.

Layering - tucking the flashbar and a line behind the guitar makes a physical connection between the items.

Text wrap - This creates a closeness between the text, the image and the quote, establishing connections and unity.

Flow text - This has been used to establish closeness and create a link between the product and the text.

Alignment - Accurate alignment down the right and left sides of the layout creates a visual connection between the items that are aligned.

The result is a unified layout in which each item is connected to other items. It works because of these connections.

FINAL LAYOUT

EXAM PREP

The final layout makes effective use of texture.

Q1. Explain why the textured background is so effective in this layout.

VALUE

WHAT IS IT?

Value is a term used to describe how reflective, bright, dark, intense or saturated a colour is. This is also known as colour tone and colour brightness. Some colours are brighter than others; yellow is brighter than maroon.

For our purposes, the brighter (more vivid the colour or paler the tone) the higher its value. Darker tones and deeper colours have a lower value.

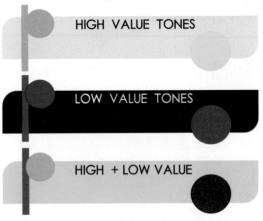

HIGH VALUE TONES

LOW VALUE TONES

HIGH + LOW VALUE

HOW DESIGNERS USE VALUE

Colours and tones both influence value. Designers tend not to refer to high and low value. Instead, they refer to bright (vivid colours and pale tones) and dark (deeper colours and darker tones).

Designers apply value by using it to create a mood; pastel shades are calming and relaxing while darker tones can be strong, vibrant, intense or dominant.

Dark and bright values together are used to create contrast or emphasis. Layouts without changes of value tend to be flat and lack visual impact.

CASE STUDY

The two smaller layouts, below, use tones that have little variation in value. The layouts are tonally flat and lack visual impact.

PALE TONES = HIGH VALUE

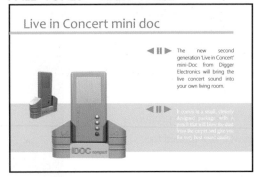

Compare the layout above with final layout 1 where the darker tones in the background contrast with the bright (pale) tones in the product. The result is much more eye-catching.

STRONG TONES = LOW VALUE

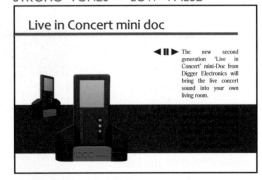

The layout, above, also lacks variation in value. Compare this with final layout 2 and you will find that the bright (pale) background colours throw the product images forward.

VARYING THE VALUES

When there are changes to tonal value or colour value in a layout, contrast is created and visual impact improves.

FINAL LAYOUT 1 - VARYING THE TONAL VALUES

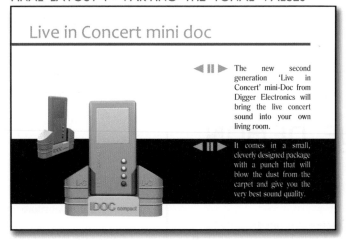

FINAL LAYOUT 2 - VARYING THE TONAL VALUES

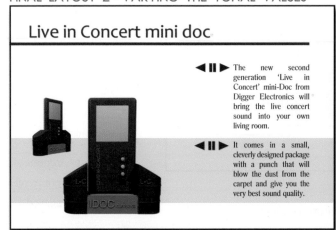

Value: *Importance, worth, significance, price, cost, rate.*

EXAM PREP

Layering has been used to good effect in the final layouts.

Q1. Explain how layering is used and how it benefits final layout 2.

There are several ways to create depth in a layout; layering is one method.

Q2 Describe another method the designer has used to create depth in final layout 2.

The body text in each of the layouts is justified.

Q3. Explain one advantage and one disadvantage of justified text.

WHITE SPACE

WHAT IS IT?

White space is an empty area on a page or screen that has two main functions in a layout.

1. It can create emphasis when an item is placed in the middle of or beside the white space; the item stands out more than if it was surrounded by clutter.

2. It allows the reader's eyes to rest, especially when it is used in a busy layout. It can be calming.

White space is built into most layouts; margins, gutters and header and footer spaces are all examples of white space. That type of white space is part of the layout structure. However, the designer can build white space into a layout deliberately to create emphasis or to allow the eye to rest.

Too little white space and a busy layout can become cluttered, confusing and difficult to read; see the draft layout (top).

White space should be considered whenever you are designing a layout and treated as an important 'item' integral to the layout.

TIP

White space does not have to be white. It's simply empty space in the layout.

CASE STUDY

The draft layout of the Danny Deever double-page article is busy and the only significant white space is wedged between the colour fill and the images. This is known as **'trapped white space'** and should be avoided. It creates a hole that draws the eye to the space itself and not the content.

Other problems with the draft layout are the small margins, small header and footer spaces and narrow gutter space between columns. There is no room for the layout to breath and it is daunting to look at and difficult to follow.

FINAL LAYOUT - HAS WHITE SPACE WORKED?

The final layout is vastly improved by the inclusion of white space.

- The left margin is much wider, emphasising the title; white space is often used around a title.
- The header space is much bigger and frames the article.
- There is room for the columns to sit comfortably without looking cluttered.
- The final layout appears less busy and looks much easier to read. It can breath and there is emphasis in the right areas.
- The white space has been distributed unevenly, emphasising the asymmetric balance and creating visual interest.

White space: *An area of a page or other printed surface where no text or pictures appear.*

DRAFT LAYOUT

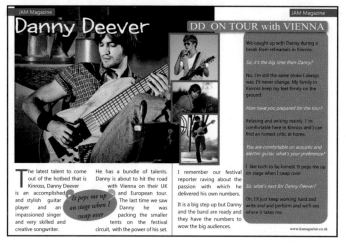

FINAL LAYOUT

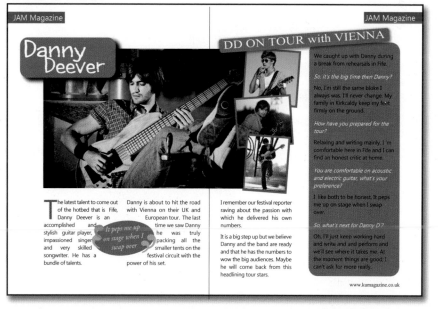

EXAM PREP

Both layouts include a pull quote

Q1. Explain the functions of a pull quote.

The final layout uses different methods of creating emphasis other than leaving white space.

Q2. Explain three other methods used to create emphasis in the final layout.

Go2 PROJECT

STAYING AHEAD OF THE CURVE...

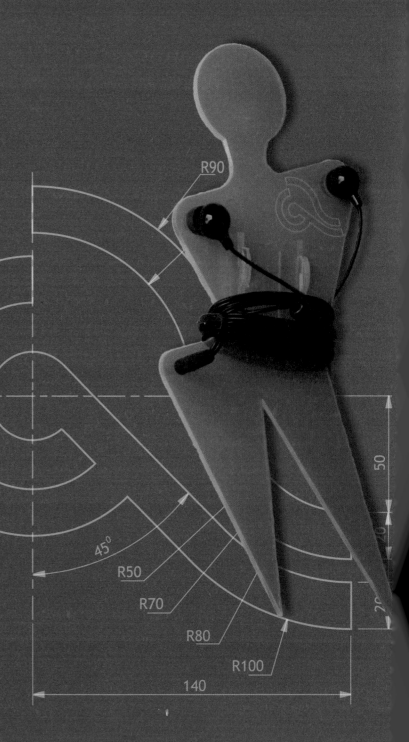

In this project you will use your tangency skills both on the drawing board and in computer-aided design to meet a challenging graphic brief. Go2 are a company specialising in modern product design that provides accessories to support their digital electronic range.

Along with the project brief, they have provided project data that you should study carefully. The exemplar in this section will give you a steer but you should make the most of the design opportunities to create an exciting and functional earphone winder storage product.

UNIT ASSESSMENT TASK

In this assessment task you will be able to show that you can produce creative and technically precise work. You will be using knowledge and demonstrating skills from across the 2D and the 3D Graphic Communication Units

BRIEF

Go2 are developing a series of stylised products to supplement their popular electronics range. You are asked to submit a design proposal for the Go2 Ear-bud Winder. Their initial concept is shown with a standard wall fixing bracket. Your challenge is to design an ear-bud winder that will appeal to a young target market.

SPECIFICATION

The Ear-bud Winder must:

- include smooth curves that make a tangent with straight lines and other curves.
- provide a suitable 'winding loop' for wrapping the cable.
- provide holes for locating the ear-buds and the jack plug.
- fit the standard wall bracket design.
- be made from 3mm thick acrylic.

THE STANDARD DESIGN

The design is simple and includes only a standard wall fixing bracket, a front panel and a screw. The wall fixing bracket will not change. It is your task to design the shape of the front panel that stores the ear bud cable and ear buds.

Go2 PROJECT- BRIEF

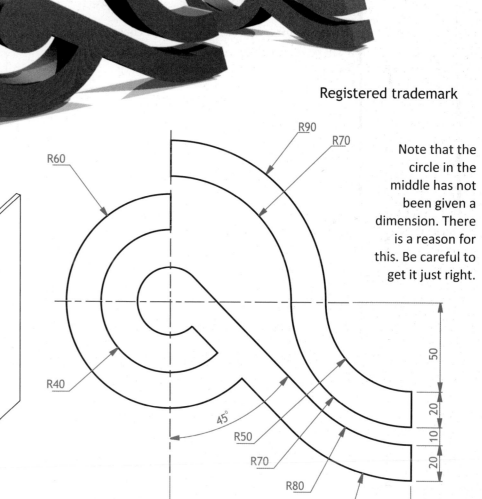

GO2 LOGO

Registered trademark

Note that the circle in the middle has not been given a dimension. There is a reason for this. Be careful to get it just right.

R90
R70
R60
R40
R50
R70
R80
R100
45°
50
20
10
20
140

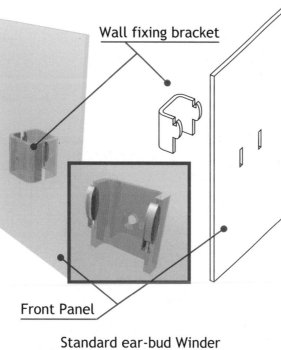

Wall fixing bracket

Front Panel

Standard ear-bud Winder

Go2 - PROJECT DATA

PROJECT DATA

The wall fixing bracket can be folded from a flat sheet to form the 'U' shape or built fully formed using a 3D printer (rapid prototyping). It screws to a wall and clips easily onto the front panel. The front panel is the part to be designed.

TASK

Model the *'Wall fixing bracket - Formed'* in CAD for use in assembly drawings.

Model the *'Wall fixing bracket - Flat'*. If you are using a CNC laser cutter and folding the bracket yourself, you will need to CAD model the bracket flat. The blank front panel is common to both methods. You will design this shape yourself.

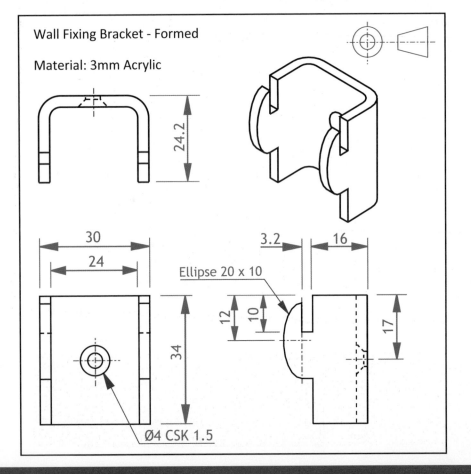

Wall Fixing Bracket - Formed

Material: 3mm Acrylic

24.2

30
24

Ellipse 20 x 10

3.2 16

12 10

34

17

Ø4 CSK 1.5

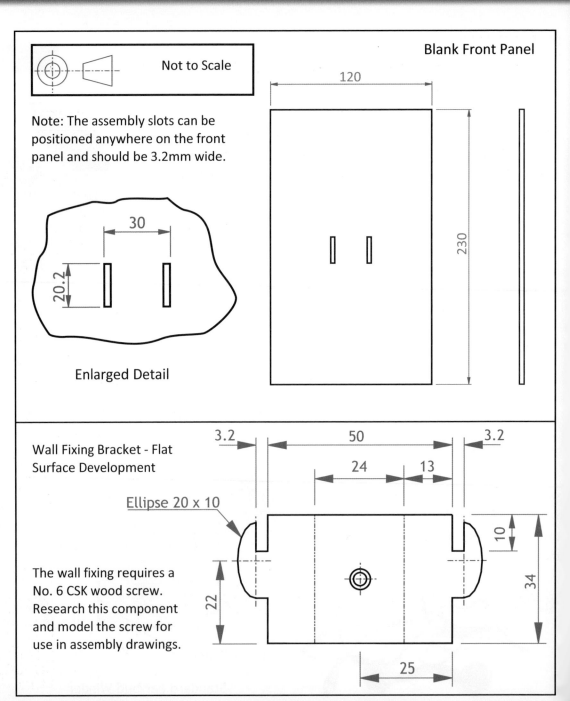

Not to Scale

Note: The assembly slots can be positioned anywhere on the front panel and should be 3.2mm wide.

Blank Front Panel

120

230

Enlarged Detail

30

20.2

Wall Fixing Bracket - Flat
Surface Development

Ellipse 20 x 10

The wall fixing requires a No. 6 CSK wood screw. Research this component and model the screw for use in assembly drawings.

3.2 50 3.2

24 13

10

34

22

25

DESIGN IDEAS

Sketch out your initial ideas for the front panel in 2D. Stick to simple, geometric shapes, don't over-complicate your designs.

Tip: Don't start your ideas by sketching curved shapes.
Begin by sketching straight lines before adding tangent curves to round off corners. While you shouldn't worry about sizes yet, it can be useful to sketch the two slots where you think they may go. This will help you to get a feel for the proportions of your design.

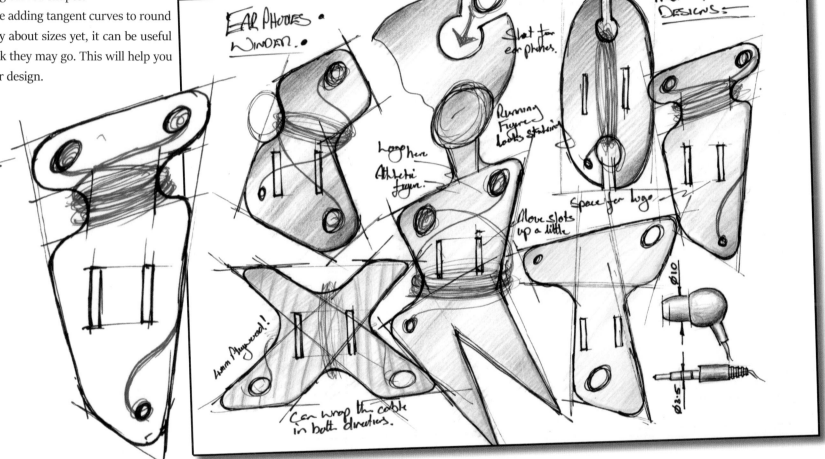

Sketch Straight edged shapes first

Then round the corners

Tip: Compiling a style sheet of images and ideas can help you to create modern, geometric or stylised shapes for the front panel.

This is good sketching practice. You should take every opportunity to improve your freehand sketching skills.

Go2 PROJECT - MANUAL DRAWINGS

TASK

You are asked to draw the Go2 logo and your own design for the front panel using 2D or 3D CAD. This can be tricky. One way of solving the problem and working out the best way to approach the CAD drawings is to draw them manually on paper first.

So, using a drawing board and instruments draw the Go2 logo to scale 1:1. The centre is an obvious starting point. Use this and work out the geometry of the logo.

The fully dimensioned detail drawing is available on page 171. You will need to make use of your problem solving skills to complete the logo. Do not make assumptions about sizes. Each line has a length, an angle or a radius and a location and each one should be drawn accurately. Remember, the task is to locate the centre of each arc and to draw the logo accurately. Now build the logo in your CAD package.

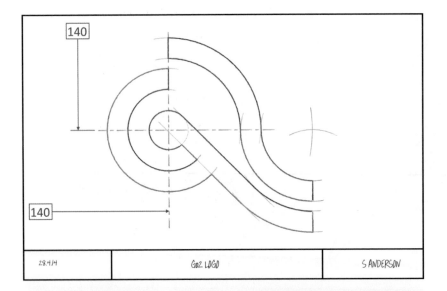

Note that the circle in the middle has not been given a dimension. There is a reason for this. Be careful to get it just right.

Accuracy is vital in tangency drawings so keep your pencil and compass lead sharp and set out measurements carefully.

MANUAL DRAWINGS - YOUR FRONT PANEL DESIGN

The process of drawing your design manually will help you understand how the drawing is constructed.

You will learn what to draw first and how to progress through the shape. It will help you plan the order in which you will tackle the CAD drawing.

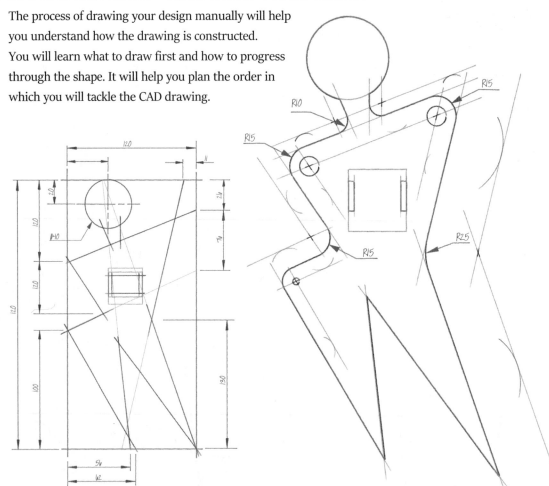

Choose one of your own designs and tackle the manual drawing in stages:

1. The only fixed size is the wall bracket; draw the two slots and the wall bracket first.

2. Draw your winder shape using straight lines only; circles are fine if you can position them easily.

3. Decide on the radius at each corner and plot the centre of each corner arc.

4. Draw each arc carefully, taking care to achieve accurate tangents.

5. Dimension your drawing fully.

CAD DRAWINGS

It can be more challenging to create a CAD model of your own design than one that has already been designed for you. Your manual preliminary drawings are vital. Have them beside you at the computer and check your dimensions carefully.

1. Constraints

It is important to construct the drawing carefully. Begin with a simple shape. In this case a rectangle is drawn and dimensioned. Two of the lines are locked or fixed in place. These constraints prevent the lines from being moved accidentally.

The design you have chosen should be drawn accurately, even if your design is a random abstract shape you should replicate it accurately with your CAD software. You can use either 2D or 3D CAD software to prepare CAD drawings.

2. Construction

More detailed construction is added.

Lines should be dimensioned to constrain them. Dimensions can be edited easily if you want to make changes.

Go2 PROJECT - CAD DRAWINGS

ABOUT CAD CONSTRAINTS

All CAD programs offer a variety of ways to constrain lines so that they can't be altered by accident. The constraints used in this project will include 'fixing' or 'locking' lines. This is shown here by the triangular symbols on the locked lines. Another important constraint is dimensioning. A dimension enables you to constrain a length and/or an angle that is easy to edit at a later stage.

3. Outlines

Once the construction is complete you can add outlines to define the shape of the front panel. Note that there are no curves at this stage. It's much easier to manage if you use straight lines.

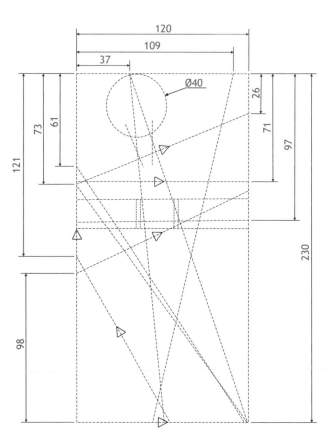

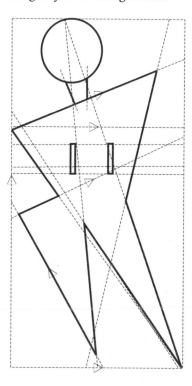

Go2 PROJECT - CAD DRAWINGS

If you use 2D CAD software to draw your winder it will enable you to cut the shape on a CNC Laser cutter. 3D CAD will allow this too but will also produce a 3D CAD model for use in production and promotional layouts.

The design here is drawn using 3D CAD and the drawing is exported to a 2D package to enable laser cutting. The 3D software will allow us to create a solid model and exploded views for use in the promotional instruction document.

Tip: Remember, you can cut your shape on a CNC laser cutter. You will learn how the line colour and thickness should be set so that the laser cutter can read your dxf file. It will be specific to the CAD software you are using.

NOTE: A **forming JIG** can be used to bend the wall bracket. You can download plans for a simple forming jig from our website.

4. Your CAD drawing will take shape quickly if you use straight lines to construct it.

5. Corner arcs can be added and dimensioned. Corners can be added either before or after a 3D model is built. Depending on your design you may make use of CAD features like tangency to create tangent curves.

6. Remember to add the Go2 logo to your design. This can be scaled to fit the space available.

7. Apply the correct line thickness and colours so that laser cutting and etching can be done.

8. Build the model by extruding the shape. The bracket, built in a similar way, can be assembled to it. Render them both in your illustration package.

9. The model can now be cut from acrylic or plywood. The bracket is folded and it is ready to assemble and use.

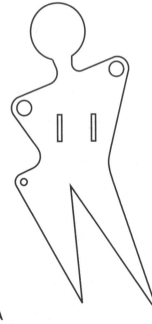
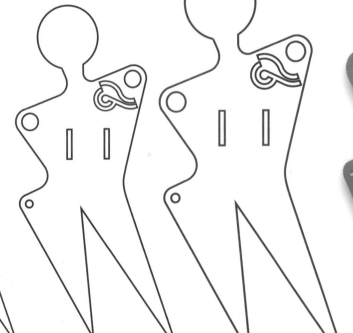

PROMOTIONAL BRIEF

Go2 require promotional packaging for the ear-bud winder.

The packaging format has already been designed.

Your task is to produce a promotional layout for the backing card that:

- Displays the product clearly
- Displays the product name
- Displays the Go2 company logo clearly
- Provides clear and graphical user instructions on the folded flap
- Includes a positive image of a user or users
- Appeals to a teenage target audience
- Conforms to printing restrictions of: full colour printing on one side of 180 micron card.

Note: The product and the wall bracket will be attached to the package through the two slots. The clear blister sleeve will slide onto the backing card, flexing over the product. The layout of the packaging need not be entirely visible until the product is removed.

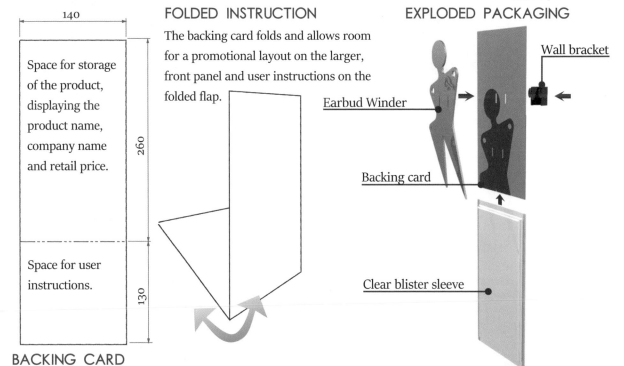

BACKING CARD

140

260

130

Space for storage of the product, displaying the product name, company name and retail price.

Space for user instructions.

FOLDED INSTRUCTION

The backing card folds and allows room for a promotional layout on the larger, front panel and user instructions on the folded flap.

EXPLODED PACKAGING

Wall bracket

Earbud Winder

Backing card

Clear blister sleeve

Go2 PROJECT- PROMOTIONAL BRIEF

TIPS

You have blank spaces to fill and a brief that specifies the content. But it is your own creativity that will make the layout work, promote the product effectively and connect with the young target audience.

Consider the options you have to create a focal point. You can use CAD illustrations, line drawings or, if you have made the ear-bud winder, photographs. Produce a selection of different images so that you can see what you have to work with and make the best choices for your layout.

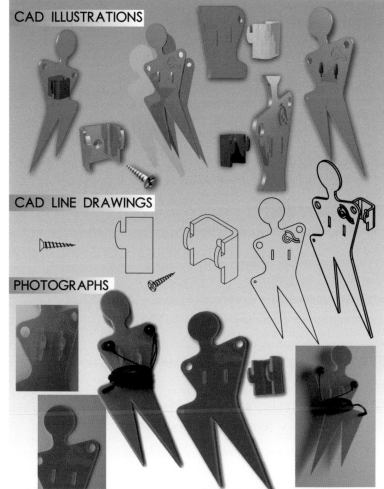

CAD ILLUSTRATIONS

CAD LINE DRAWINGS

PHOTOGRAPHS

Go2 PROJECT - THUMBNAILS AND DTP

Layout design can be done on the computer or on paper. In this example thumbnails are used. Be sure to annotate them to reference DTP features and how you intend to use Design Elements & Principles.

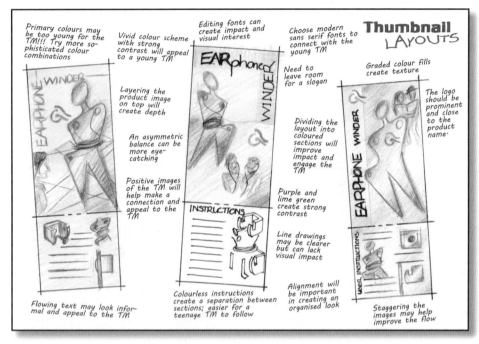

WHEN YOU CREATE YOUR LAYOUTS CONSIDER THE FOLLOWING:

What does the brief require?
In this case an unusual proportion is required to fit the packaging card.
Also, user instructions are requested on the folded flap.

What do you know about your target market?
The target audience is teenager and probably both genders.

What DTP features can you make use of?
Columns, Margins, Colour Fills, Typeface, Cropping, Text Wrap, Flow Text, Bleeds, Transparency, Drop Shadows are all available.

What design elements & principles can be used to make the layout sparkle?
Alignment, Balance, Contrast, Colour, Dominance, Depth, Unity and Line should all be tried.

FIRST DRAFT LAYOUT

Your first draft DTP layout should be based on one of your chosen thumbnail layouts.

On-going evaluation

Record notes to explain what you think works well and what can be improved upon. Refer to DTP features and Design Elements & Principles whenever you evaluate your promotional work.

Evaluation of Draft layout

The cropped photo creates an interesting shape. A drop shadow may create more depth.

Not sure about the small image, it clutters the layout.

The instruction flap looks untidy. I'll try stronger alignment.

The colour scheme is too conflicting. I'll try and improve it.

FINAL PRESENTATION LAYOUT

Modifications are easy to make using DTP. Try colour options and fine-tune the layout until it works. Check the brief and remember your target audience!

EXAM PREP

Task

Q1. Compare the ***first draft*** with the ***final presentation*** and explain how the designer's use of: **unity**, **dominance**, **alignment**, **rhythm** and **typeface** improved the layout.

PRODUCTION DRAWINGS

CAD production drawings can be created quickly and will provide you with two important benefits:

- You will achieve several more unit assessment standards
- It will provide you with valuable experience that will make the course assignment task easier to complete.

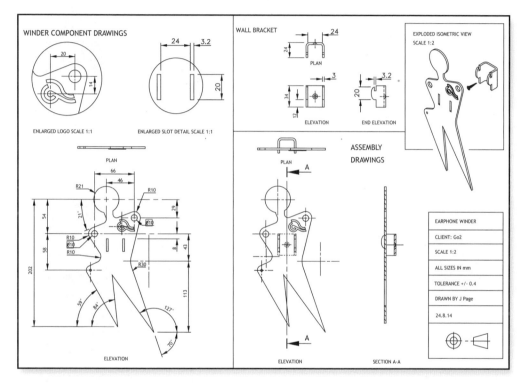

Orthographic Drawings

Include orthographic component drawings with dimensions. You will be surprised by the number of dimensions required to describe a product for manufacture. Indicate centres and show the radius of each arc.

Technical Detail

Exploded views, enlarged details and sections are all important for clarifying manufacturing information; try to include at least two examples of technical detail.

Pictorial Views

These can bring added clarity to assemblies. Show a pictorial assembly view, if possible an exploded pictorial view.

Go2 PROJECT - PRODUCTION DRAWINGS

EXAM PREP

Worksheet alert

You can download an A3 worksheet from our website to support you with this task.

TOLERANCING TASKS

The production drawings for the earphone winder only refer to tolerances on non-functional dimensions.

Q1. Explain what is meant by non-functional dimensions and where the tolerance for non-functional dimensions is found on production drawings.

Functional dimensions require specific tolerances.

Q2. Explain why functional dimensions require specific tolerances.

The features shown here (on the right) all require functional dimensions.

Q3. Work out suitable tolerances for each dimension shown on the right and add the tolerances to your own production drawings.

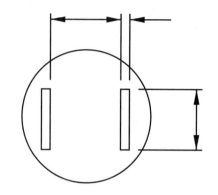

ENLARGED SLOT DETAIL

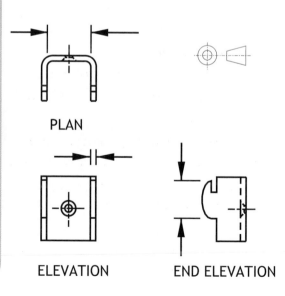

PLAN

ELEVATION   **END ELEVATION**

WALL BRACKET DETAIL

CREATING A MINI SCENE

SETTING THE SCENE

Placing your earphone winder in a suitable 3D CAD environment can enhance the appeal of the product. It will also give you the experience you need to create an outstanding environment in your course assignment.

Creating the models in the scene yourself will help improve your 3D modelling skills.

Tips:

- Think about the modelling techniques you have already used in the Go2 project and list the other modelling techniques that you know about.

- Try to use a variety of modelling techniques; extrusion along a path and revolved solids have been used in this scene.

- Look at the library of parts available, you can use a solid primitive or ready-made sketch to start a model. A hexagon was used here to model the pencils.

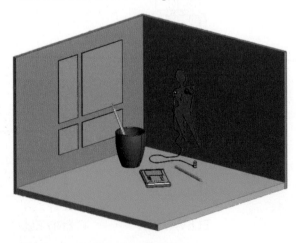

3D Scene before rendering

EARBUD winder scene

I used two light sources in my scene; room and day lighting. Attaching several materials to my models including: glass, plastics and textured granite helped me to create visual impact in the scene.

The materials and light sources I attached have created reflections and shadows to enhance the realistic 3D environment. Grouping the items closely helped to boost this effect.

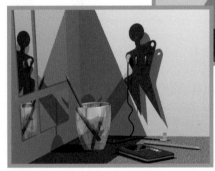

I took care to export high resolution images of my 3D models and the resulting scene is clear and sharp.

Materials

Choose your materials carefully. Shiny surfaces create reflections while natural materials (wood etc) create interesting textures and contrasts. Now is the time to experiment so that you are well prepared to 'wow the audience' with your course assignment.

Lighting

Your choice and positioning of lights will make a huge difference to the visual impact of your scene.

Composition

Grouping items closely can create interest and help to add reflections that bounce around the scene.

MINI ASSIGNMENT

GETTING READY FOR THE BIG ONE

Your final assignment task is a major piece of work; contributing 50% of your course mark. It is vital that you get it right. You will have most of the skills you need by now but completing this **mini-assignment** will help you consolidate those skills and put you in a much better position to excel in the final assignment.

What you gain by tackling the mini-assignment is experience and preparation. You will work in exactly the same way as you are going to in the final assignment and you will get the opportunity to deconstruct an existing product before creating production and promotional graphics. You will do all this using only five A3 sheets.

MINI ASSIGNMENT BRIEF

INTERIOR PRODUCT project BRIEF

Note:
This project is time-limited. You have 4 weeks (20 hours of class time) to complete it. The suggested time-scales for each of the 5 A3 sheets is shown. You will not generate your best work in this project but it will prepare you for the challenges of the course assignment. Refine your skills, improve your work speed and stick to the task. If you need more hours, do it in your own time.

Investigate products from the list below and record one or two graphically:

Product List

Stool / Leaflet dispenser / Wall storage product/ Desk Light / Floor lamp / Information display stand / In-Out Tray / Paper Storage rack / Wall-mounted flat screen / Seat/ Occasional table / Display rack.

Your task is to produce a 3D CAD model of a product from this list, create production drawings and promote it for sale. You should select a product that already exists but you may simplify or modify it if you wish.

Specification

The product should:
1. Be currently in use in a modern home, office or business environment.
2. Have a modern, stylish appearance.
3. Appeal to a young to middle aged (25 - 50 years old) target market.

Research:

Analyse the product:
- Analyse an existing example of the product, either a physical or graphical version.
- Identify the number of components used in the product and name them.
- Identify the materials used.
- Identify how the parts assemble.

Preliminary Sketches:

- Create preliminary sketches to describe how parts assemble.
- Prepare orthographic, dimensioned preliminary sketches.
- Create preliminary sketches to describe any moving or adjustable parts.

CAD Modelling & Production Drawings:

- Model and assemble each component 1:1 scale.
- Generate dimensioned production drawings.

Promotional Graphics:

- Render the model in an illustration package.
- Light the model to best effect.
- Position the model in a simple environment or on a surface.
- Prepare an effective, modern layout to promote the product.
- Create a simple but modern promotional DTP layout to appeal to the target market.

CHOOSING A SUITABLE PRODUCT

The purpose of the mini assignment is to prepare you for the course assignment. The success of the project depends on many factors one of which is the choice of product you will work from. Your teacher may choose a product for you, which will remove you from this decision. However, the danger, if you are selecting a product yourself, is that you choose a product that is either too complex or one that is too simple. Remember, there is a four week time constraint to this task so it's important that you tackle a project that allows you to complete the mini assignment over 5 pages and in just four weeks. The two products below demonstrate the limits of complexity that represents a suitable product for this task.

Check the products, below, before you select one for your mini assignment and select a product that sits somewhere between these two on the complexity scale. Remember to consider your own experience and abilities. This mini assignment should challenge you but must be achievable in the time available.

MAGAZINE TUBE - LOWER END OF THE COMPLEXITY SCALE

This product has:

4 different components, 2 webs, a screw thread, a ribbed bush, a fairly complex base.

It will allow a range of modelling features including:

Extrusion, revolve, extrusion along a path, shell, helix (on a screw thread), array, multiple, off-set workplanes and relatively simple draughting.

CHAIR - TOP END OF THE COMPLEXITY SCALE

This product has:

5 different components, multiple webs, a screw thread, a ribbed bush, 3 fairly complex parts.

It will allow a range of modelling features including:

Extrusion, revolve, extrusion along a path, loft, shell, helix, mirror, multiple offset workplanes and relatively complex draughting.

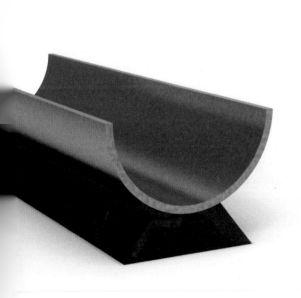
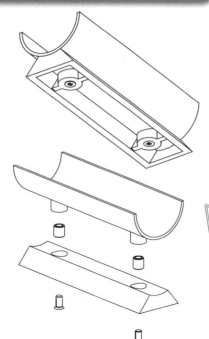
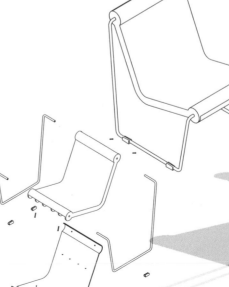

PRELIMINARY GRAPHICS 1

This mini-assignment will help you refine the skills you need in order to excel in the course assignment task.

It is however a time limited exercise. You will get no more than 4 weeks to do this work and you should stick rigidly to the time-scales indicated. You may have to settle for work that is unrefined or a little rough at the edges. Don't worry about this, it is the experience of working to tight deadlines, analysing a product and improving skills that you will focus on here.

Choose your product carefully. The best judge of your ability is you. You don't need to tackle a product as difficult as the chair shown in this example. If you are tackling a 'crash' course stick to a simpler product. You can learn the same skills using a simple product such as a lamp or a shelving rack. Both products shown here; the chair and the In/Out tray are sketched from physical products we have in school.

IMPORTANT TIPS

Make notes.

Record information that will help keep you on-track through the project:
The timescale - 4 weeks.
The main modelling techniques : Extrude/Revolve/Loft/Extrude along a path.
The main editing techniques: Shell/Add/Subtract/Array/Mirror.

Research and source suitable products.

Source products from magazines, brochures, the internet and real (physical) products.
You are looking for a product that is not too complex (remember your time limit). And you should try to analyse the product by working out the number of components it is likely to have. Investigate two or three products only.

Practice your sketching.

One of the key skills you need to develop here is freehand sketching. Make use of this opportunity. The example opposite features two existing products. They were both found in school. These have been sketched as assemblies in 2-point perspective. Establish good proportion and use the remote vanishing points carefully; develop your eye to recognise good perspective.

Explore the assembly details of each product.

How many components does each product have? What are the key features? How do they fit together? Are standard components used? Use sketches to explore these questions. Try to combine orthographic sketching with technical detail; sectional views, enlarged details and exploded views. Sketching skills are so important and now is the time to improve them.

Make best use of technical annotations.

Study the key features of each product and annotate your sketches to describe or clarify these features. Add notes to help you to understand how the product works or assembles or moves or looks. Get used to the process of annotating. A busy, well set out page that combines pictorial and orthographic sketching with neat, focused annotations is your target.

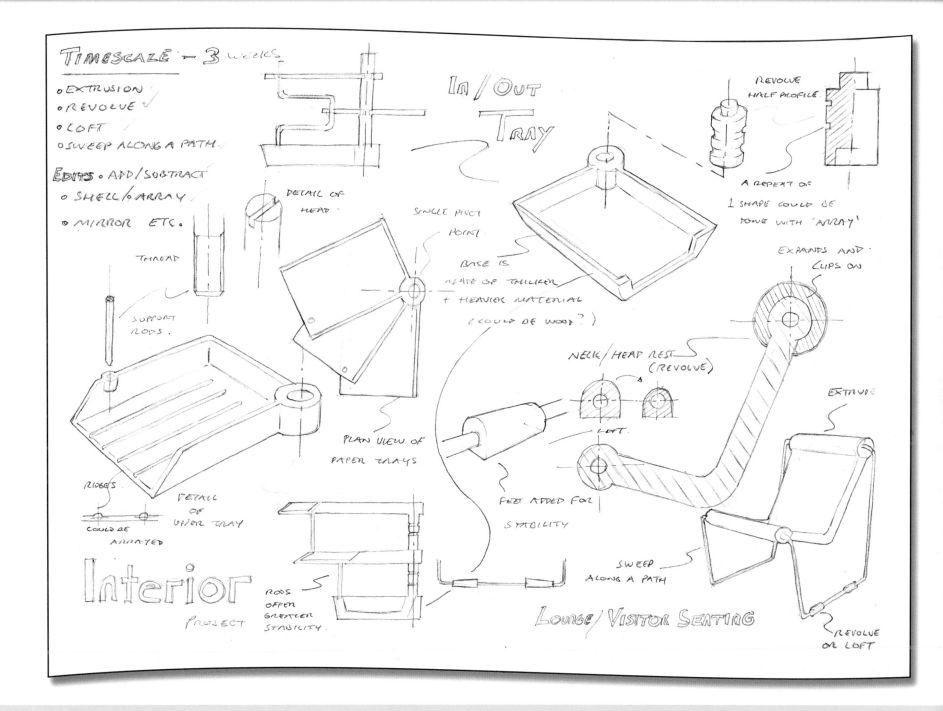

TIMESCALE - 3 WEEKS.

o EXTRUSION ✓
o REVOLVE ✓
o LOFT ✓
o SWEEP ALONG A PATH.

EDITS o ADD/SUBTRACT
o SHELL/ARRAY
o MIRROR ETC.

THREAD

SUPPORT RODS.

RIDGES

COULD BE ARRAYED

DETAIL OF UPPER TRAY.

Interior

PROJECT

DETAIL OF HEAD.

SINGLE PIVOT POINT.

PLAN VIEW OF PAPER TRAYS

RODS OFFER GREATER STABILITY.

In/Out Tray

BASE IS MADE OF THICKER + HEAVIER MATERIAL (COULD BE WOOD?)

NECK/HEAD REST (REVOLVE)

LOFT.

FEET ADDED FOR STABILITY

SWEEP ALONG A PATH

LOUNGE/VISITOR SEATING

REVOLVE HALF PROFILE.

A REPEAT OF 1 SHAPE COULD BE DONE WITH 'ARRAY'

EXPANDS AND CLIPS ON

EXTRUDE

REVOLVE OR LOFT

PRELIMINARY GRAPHICS 2

Sketch two orthographic views and a 2-point perspective view of the assembled product. Leave plenty of room for detailed component sketches.

Separate the product into components and sketch each one in turn. You should stick to orthographic sketches, these are easier to sketch and dimension. Dimension each component sketch.

Add a parts list and a simple title block. Oh, and remember to add view titles. Get into good habits now!

IMPORTANT TIPS

Plan how to use the space on the page.	It can be a good idea to quickly (roughly) sketch out where your main orthographic views and component sketches can be placed before you begin sketching for real. It will help you avoid running out of room on the page as you fill it.
Sketch each component orthographically.	Concentrate on proportion to ensure the sketches look realistic. Make sure you add important features like centre lines and hidden detail. Leave room around each view for dimensions. Remember, this can take up more than twice the area of the view itself. Keep things simple; it's OK to simplify components that are complex. Remember you have a deadline to meet.
Dimension the orthographic views.	Make sure your dimensioning is complete without getting too concerned over it. You are going to model each component so you need enough information to get you started. Use proper drawing standards when dimensioning. Get into good habits at this stage will make life much easier during the course assignment when it really counts.
Show technical detail.	Aim for two or three examples of technical detail. Create a sectional view an exploded view and possibly an enlarged detail. It can also be useful to show how any moving parts work or how adjustments can be made to the product when in use, e.g. the directional adjustments to a table lamp or the height adjustment on a swivel stool.
Annotations and titles.	Show a parts list. Give each part a name, number and, if you can, identify the material it is made from. Add a title block and don't forget the third-angle projection symbol.

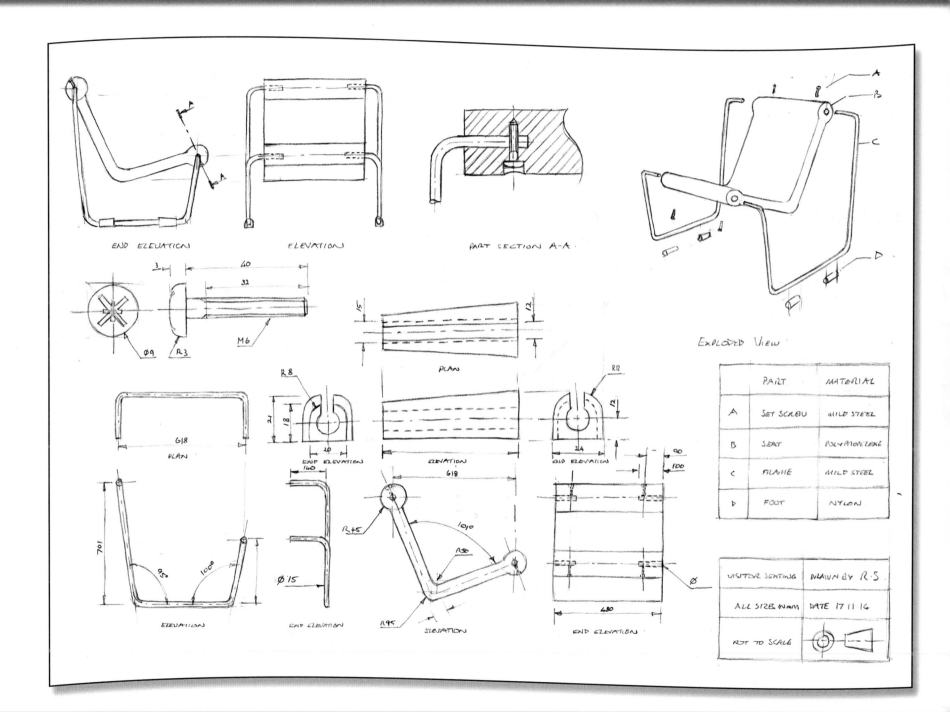

END ELEVATION

ELEVATION

PART SECTION A-A

EXPLODED VIEW

PLAN

M6

Ø9   R3

R8

END ELEVATION
140

PLAN

ELEVATION

R12

END ELEVATION

PLAN
618

618

701

95°   100°

Ø15

END ELEVATION

R45

R50

R95

ELEVATION

90
100

480

END ELEVATION

	PART	MATERIAL
A	SET SCREW	MILD STEEL
B	SEAT	POLYPROPELENE
C	FRAME	MILD STEEL
D	FOOT	NYLON

VISITOR SEATING	DRAWN BY R·S
ALL SIZES IN MM	DATE 17 11 14
NOT TO SCALE	

PRODUCTION DRAWINGS - COMPONENTS

Model each component separately. Build your main component first from scratch and work from this to top-down model the next component.

Analyse each component before you model it. Try to use a different CAD modelling technique for each one. This is the best way to get to grips with different modelling techniques. Remember, you will need to describe modelling techniques in the course exam; get used to all the modelling techniques now!

Once the models have been built and assembled, create production drawings and dimension them fully. Ensure you set the sheet out well. Leave plenty room for dimensions.

IMPORTANT TIPS

Plan to use all of the CAD modelling techniques.

Use your experience to work out which CAD modelling techniques are suited to each part. Test yourself by tackling modelling techniques that you are less comfortable with. You should always try to extend your experience of CAD modelling techniques by using, extrusion, revolving, lofting and sweep (extrusion) along a path. It would be good if you can also model a helix.

Use as many 3D CAD editing techniques as you can.

Applying a range of 3D CAD editing techniques can help you gather more marks in you assignment. You should practice this now; get used to identifying where an array or mirror, a shell, a round, a chamfer or a screw thread might be required. These editing techniques will help you pick up extra marks in the course assignment task. Get used to them now!

Project orthographic production drawings and dimension them.

As soon as you have modelled two components assemble them to ensure they fit together. Build your assembly by adding one part at a time. Create component production drawings leaving enough space around them to add dimensions.

Ensure your dimensioning and annotations are thorough.

You should apply a dimensioning checklist. Remember to include linear dimensions (lengths, breadths and heights). You should have diameters and radii. And you should dimension angles. Remember also to set the dimensions out neatly; use parallel dimensioning when you can and try to avoid crossing leader lines. The title block is important; remember to include the drawing scale and the scales of any drawings that differ from the drawing scale.

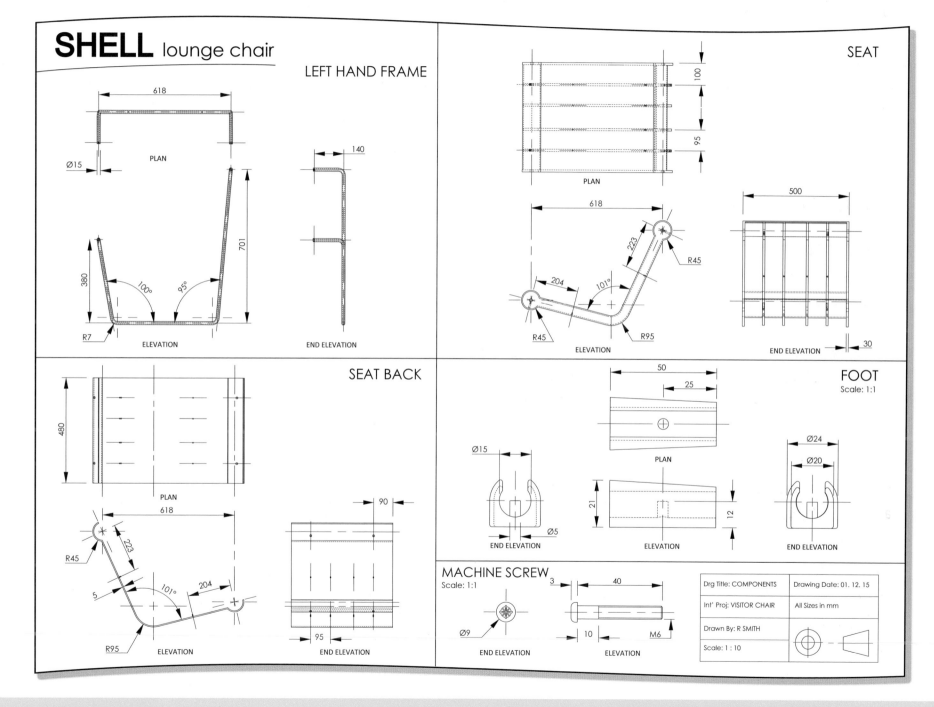

SHELL lounge chair

LEFT HAND FRAME

SEAT

SEAT BACK

FOOT
Scale: 1:1

MACHINE SCREW
Scale: 1:1

Drg Title: COMPONENTS	Drawing Date: 01. 12. 15
Int' Proj: VISITOR CHAIR	All Sizes in mm
Drawn By: R SMITH	
Scale: 1 : 10	

PRODUCTION DRAWINGS - ASSEMBLIES

Assembly drawings should include orthographic views and pictorial views. These must be set out correctly and convey technical information clearly and concisely.

Create orthographic views of your assembly. Scale them to suit the space available and leave space for other views and features.

Technical detail is important in production drawings. It provides information necessary for manufacture or assembly. Always include a pictorial or orthographic exploded view, a sectional view and an enlarged detail.

IMPORTANT TIPS

Ensure your assemblies are accurate and properly constrained.

Assemblies need to fit together accurately; components that are inaccurate and don't fit together correctly will show up in your assembly drawings and will cost you marks in your course assignment. Using a top-down modelling technique helps to ensure that each component fits correctly with the next one. Learn more about this in the 3D CAD section in this book, see page 83.

Create Orthographic and pictorial assembly drawings.

Orthographic assembly drawings are still a standard way of showing how a product looks. The orthographic views can show hidden detail. As long as the hidden detail does not clutter the drawing it is fine to show it. You should show at least three orthographic views and an isometric (or other) pictorial view.

Create Technical detail.

Technical detail is normally used when more information is required about the product. Manufacturers need **exploded views** and **sections** to support manufacture and assembly of the product. **Enlarged details** are useful when showing small details clearly. Try to incorporate at least three types of technical detail in your production drawings. There are extra marks to be gained in the course assignment so get used creating them here.

Layout and annotations.

A neat organised layout is important. The drawings need to convey information clearly and good spacing, accurate alignment and clear labelling are all vital. Annotations such as the title block and parts list contain valuable information and should be included on every production drawing.

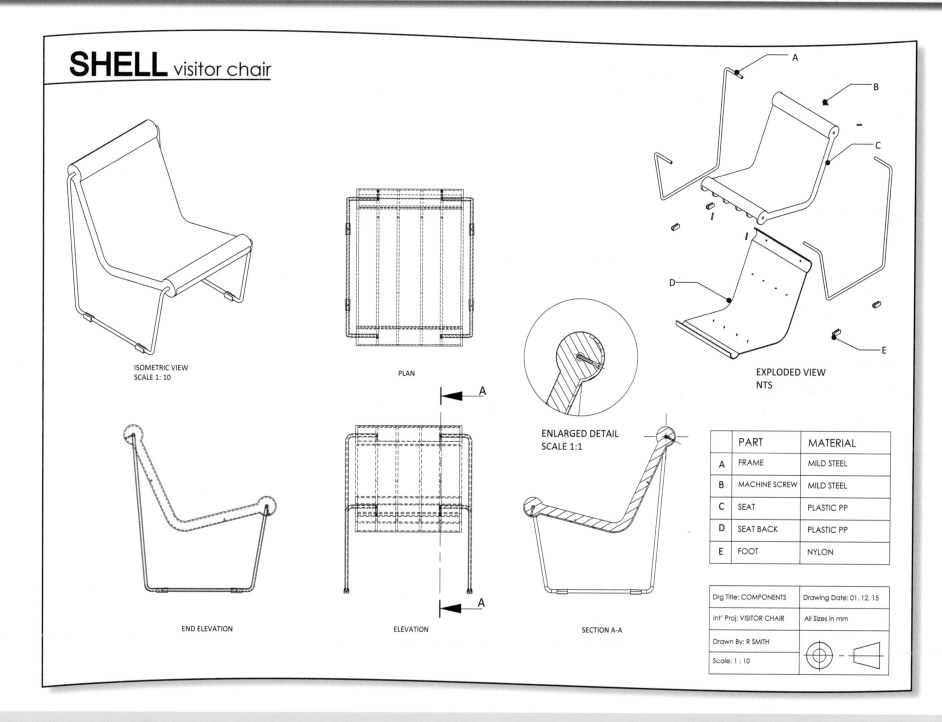

SHELL visitor chair

ISOMETRIC VIEW
SCALE 1: 10

PLAN

END ELEVATION

ELEVATION

ENLARGED DETAIL
SCALE 1:1

SECTION A-A

EXPLODED VIEW
NTS

A
B
C
D
E

	PART	MATERIAL
A	FRAME	MILD STEEL
B	MACHINE SCREW	MILD STEEL
C	SEAT	PLASTIC PP
D	SEAT BACK	PLASTIC PP
E	FOOT	NYLON

Drg Title: COMPONENTS	Drawing Date: 01. 12. 15
Int' Proj: VISITOR CHAIR	All Sizes in mm
Drawn By: R SMITH	
Scale: 1 : 10	

PROMOTIONAL GRAPHICS - ADVERTISING LAYOUT

To create stonking illustrations, ensure you blend carefully chosen colour combinations with crisp, sharp high resolution images. Remember, your image will be the focal point of your promotional layout; make sure it's the best it can be.

This is your chance to be creative and this is where you bring your creative layout skills together. Design or choose a background that compliments the product you are promoting.

How do you achieve visual impact? How do you make your layout speak to the target market? By understanding how to use **design elements and principles** to unify the layout, to bring dominance, to add contrast, to create unity, to create visual impact.
How do I do that? By applying DTP editing features like: drop shadows, bleeds, colour fills, colour matching, layering, transparencies, text wrap, typeface and reverse text.

IMPORTANT TIPS

Illustration work.

You have limited time but you must create illustrations that are sharp, well lit and well rendered with appropriate materials and colours. Use your rendering package creatively. Ask yourself: How can I position the product to best effect? Which colours and materials work best together? How can I ensure the images are crisp and sharp?

Creative layout design.

The brief asks for a modern layout. Don't make it overly busy. Keep it minimal and modern. Creating depth can be a challenge in a minimalist layout. Make best use of your illustration work by using more than one image. Having the large one in the foreground and the smaller one in the background gives the impression of distance and depth.

Select colours carefully.

Choice of colour can make or break a layout. Think of combinations of colours. This layout uses only two colours; a neutral grey and a mid-tone orange. The effect creates eye-catching contrast without cluttering the layout with too many colours. The orange acts as an accent colour and has been colour matched to create unity in the layout.

Ensure you meet the brief. What constitutes a 'modern' layout?

You need to understand the differences between 'formal' and 'informal' and 'traditional' and 'modern'. Modern features in the layout opposite are the **fonts**; sans serif with clean geometric lines, the **abstract colour fill** with subtle changes of tone, the **asymmetric balance** with **bleeds** and reduced **colour pallet** and the pale background with **multiple shadows** and **technical line drawings** ghosted in to emphasise the technical aspects of the product. Does it work? You decide...

PROMOTIONAL LAYOUT

Timescale 4hrs

SHELL

visitor's chair

modern | dynamic | unique   SHELL

STUDY CHECKLIST | GETTING READY FOR YOUR ASSIGNMENT AND EXAM

DRAWING TYPES AND STANDARDS

- I can describe tangency and calculate distance between centres.
- I can draw items using the principles of tangency.
- I can describe and draw auxiliary projection views.
- I can interperate items that interpenetrate and their surface developments.
- I can describe tolerances and calculate tolerances for components in an assembly.
- I can correctly apply British Standard symbols for engineering and construction drawings.
- I can analyse and create complex sectional views and apply cross-hatching correctly.
- I can interpret and draw forms of technical detail including sections, exploded views, enlarged details.
- I can create clear, accurate and detailed production drawings without assistance.
- I can describe the terms ASSY, PCD, scale, pitch, CSK, CHAMF, CBORE, M, Ø, SØ.

3D CAD AND ILLUSTRATION

- I can use and describe the extrude command to add or subtract material.
- I can use and describe the revolve command on a connected or offset axis.
- I can use and describe the helix command to make coils or springs forms.
- I can use and describe the loft command to create models that change from one shape to another.
- I can use and describe the extrude-along-path to create models that twist and flow.
- I can describe the terms: offset, workplane, axis, datum, sketch, feature, STEP and DXF.
- I can describe top-down and bottom-up modelling and create complex 3D CAD models with 5 parts.
- I can sketch, draw or explain modelling plans to describe 3D CAD modelling techniques.
- I can illustrate surfaces, materials and textures manually and using CAD illustration software.
- I can create scenes and contexts to place 3D models & create high res' renders of scenes & models.

DTP AND ELEMENTS AND PRINCIPLES

- I can use design elements & principles in my own work and evaluate their use in commercial layouts.
- I can use DTP software to create effective layouts in response to a plan or brief.
- I can describe and use pre-flight features in final copy layouts.
- I can create graphics, images and illustrations to suit the needs of a DTP layout.
- I can use DTP techniques and identify and describe DTP terms.
- I can analyse commercial layouts for DTP techniques and Es & Ps and suggest improvements.
- I can explain the terms; header, footer, gutter, margin, column, rule, sub-head and indent.
- I can describe RGB, CMYK, Spot-Colour, cropping, registration, bleed and explain colour theory.
- I can describe different printing technologies, their characteristics and their merits.
- I can describe the terms SVG, JPEG, PNG, PDF, DPI, PPI, resolution, vector, raster, OS and bleed area.

ASSIGNMENT YOUR CHANCE TO SHINE

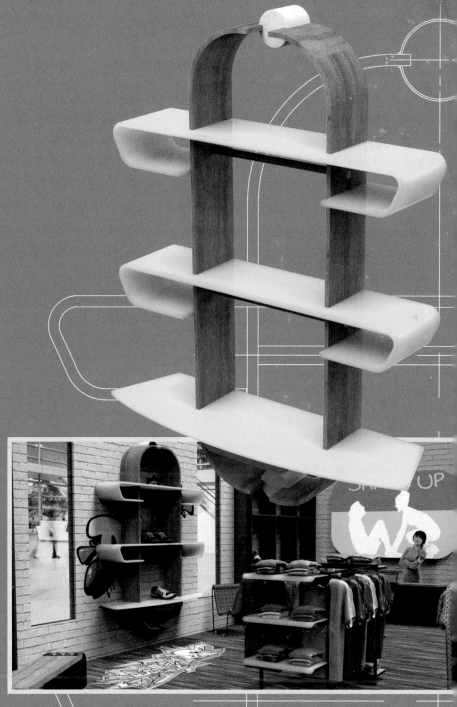

The assignment task is the first half of the course assessment; the other half is the course exam. Both assessments are worth 70 marks and each comprises 50% of the course mark. It's really worth doing well in the assignment task. Just think how much it will ease the pressure in the exam if you do well in the assignment.

The assignment gives you the opportunity to demonstrate your skills in the 3Ps: Preliminary, Production and Promotional graphics. It will take around 10 weeks and give you the chance to put the skills you have developed to good use. The resulting assignment folio can also make a big contribution to your personal portfolio.

THE BRIEF

WHAT IS A BRIEF?

The assignment brief is the document that kicks-off the assignment task. It will come with an introduction that assists you in planning your assignment and explains the marks available for each section. The brief is a statement that introduces the task. It is normally followed by a few pages of data and useful background information. The brief may also describe compulsory conditions and provide details of STEP files, fonts and colour schemes that should be included in your assignment.

HOW TO USE THE BRIEF

Your teacher will talk it through with you but you should read it carefully yourself more than once and make a short list of what you will need to find out more about. It is important that you refer to the data sheets as well as the brief. Your first task is to analyse the brief and carry out research.

OPTIONS

You have options when you analyse and research the brief. You can:

1. **Prepare a single page to record your analysis and research on.**

   Advantages: You will comfortably get the full analysis on a single A3 sheet and it keeps the analysis and research all together so it may be easier to manage. It gets this part over in one page. If you plan it carefully, you are likely to collect all 4 marks available for analysis and research.

   Disadvantages: This may take a full page in your assignment folio. You will have nine sheets left for your assignment task. It amounts to giving up 10% of your assignment space for only 4 marks.

2. **Build the analysis and research into the other pages in your assignment folio.**

   Advantages: It places the research where is is most useful. It doesn't give up a full page for only 4 marks of analysis and research.

   Disadvantages: It can be easy to lose track of the analysis and research and more difficult to work out whether you have done enough to secure all 4 marks.

   This book takes the second option; building the research into the assignment folio.

Introduction to the brief

Graphic Communication assignment: Sports fashion clothes retail shelving unit.

This assessment applies to the assignment for Higher Graphic Communication. This assignment is worth 70 marks out of the total of 140 marks. This is 50% of the overall marks for the Course assessment. The Course will be graded A–D.

Your assessor will let you know how the assessment will be carried out and any required conditions for doing it.

In this assessment, you will have to:

- produce a range of graphics in response to a brief

The assignment has four areas which receive marks, according to your ability to produce relevant:

- research and analysis (4 marks)
- preliminary graphics (15 marks)
- production drawing and CAD models (30 marks)
- promotional documents or a publication (21 marks)

You will be provided with:

- a graphic communication brief or situation
- some initial research information
- a 3D CAD model in STEP format
- data sheets containing critical information about the task

Notes on importing STEP files

STEP format files are included as part of this assignment assessment task. They are generic files and can be opened using any 3D modelling software. You may ask your assessor to confirm which method you should use to import these files.

STEP files are a common and generic file format that can be imported into 3D modelling platforms for further manipulation, if desired or required. There are three common methods for importing these file types which are: File, Import, or File, Insert, or by adding the STEP file as an assembly component in the assembly menu.

The Graphic Communication brief

An up-market **sports fashion shop** is being planned by the fashion retail company, **'Shape up'**.

'Shape up' is hoping to attract style conscious young people who make healthy lifestyle choices and purchase high quality sport and fitness fashion clothing. Initial market research has identified that people are looking for a shop that is **bright, functional but with modern styling and featuring geometric lines and shapes.**

'Shape up' considers the look of its shops to be very important and wants to create a focal point using a **purpose built display and shelving unit** in it's new shop. This shelving unit should reflect the market research data shown on this page and the next. The shelving unit may be free standing or wall mounted.

The new shop is planned for vacant premises in a busy shopping mall. The structure of the shop is fixed and the space set aside for the new shelving unit has been identified and is shown on the next page.

'Shape up' is accepting graphic proposals from young designers. Graphic proposals should contain a full range of preliminary, production and promotional graphics, including relevant research to justify the graphic proposals.

'Shape up' requires the following to be included in the graphic proposal:

- **Production drawings** to support the manufacture of the shelving unit.

- A **3D multi-sided, promotional display** with relevant **Desktop Published graphics** to advertise the store. It will be displayed both inside and outside the shop. A company logo; typeface and colours have been supplied. These may be altered to suit the promotional graphics.

- A **realistic illustrated scene** of the proposed shop layout containing the new shelving unit. It should show your shelving unit and promotional display item to best effect. Details of the space available in our new store are provided.

The **shelving unit** should include:

- a minimum of one shallow drawer to allow for storage of smaller items. The 3D CAD model of a standard shallow drawer has been provided. This 3D CAD model must be used within your design and must NOT be altered. You should show details of how you intend the drawer to slide open and close.

- a means of hanging items for display.
- Adequate shelving for folded sports and leisure clothes.

As part of your Course assessment task, you should consider:

- the range of drawings that may be required to fulfil the brief
- the technology and techniques you wish to use to create the graphics
- that 'Shape up' stores cater for an adult target market of both genders who want to look and feel good while training and relaxing. This will allow you to make judgements to support your design proposal.

You have been provided with data to assist you with the assignment. Read this data carefully and note any important factors that may influence the range of graphics that you will produce.

Your teacher will provide a planning and guidance sheet to help you progress through your assignment.

'Shape Up' wish you make a clear connection between the **promotional layouts** and the **target market**. They also want you to incorporate their **advertising slogan** and their **logo** in the promotional material.

Slogan:

"Serious about fitness, serious about style"

Logo:

Typeface: HEATHER BTN

Logo colours:

C - 22	R - 139
M - 0	G - 151
Y - 88	B - 151
K - 0	

C - 55	R - 220
M - 35	G - 223
Y - 38	B - 66
K - 4	

DATA SHEET

The standard shallow drawer is provided in a STEP file. The exact dimensions of the drawer are given below. The drawer is a single component made in moulded plastic. It is intended to be slid right out so that the contents (stop watches and heart rate monitors etc) can be viewed by the customers. You will need to determine how it can be slid in and out easily.

ACCESSORIES DRAWER

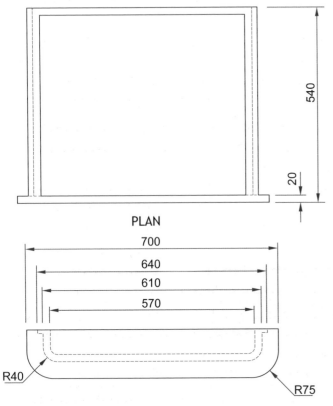

PLAN

ELEVATION

ACCESSORIES DRAWER

VIEW FROM FRONT

VIEW FROM REAR

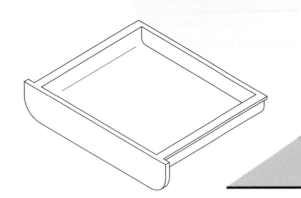

PICTORIAL VIEW

END ELEVATION

SHOP INTERIOR

Below is the external wall of the new 'Shape up' store. It has two long narrow windows centred on the wall. **The space between these windows is reserved for the new shelving unit**. The new shelving may be wall mounted or free-standing on the floor.

You may change the colour scheme and textures and you are free to include additional furniture, fittings and other items in your design proposal. You may add another wall to either side of the shop.

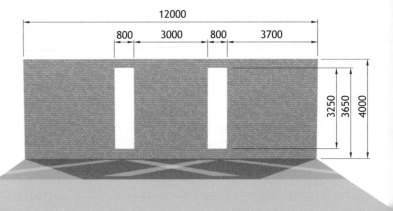

SHELVING

The clothes sold in the shop require that the shelving is a minimum of 450mm in depth.
The length of the shelving can vary.

ANALYSING AND RESEARCHING THE BRIEF

HOW TO PREPARE AN ANALYSIS

The assignment in this book will incorporate the analysis and research throughout the assignment pages, rather than containing it on a single page. However, it is still useful to do an analysis by making detailed notes.

The table opposite shows how the brief can be broken down into manageable parts that can each be researched one at a time. That is what an analysis achieves; breaking the brief down and studying each part in turn.

The research identified in the third column, can be carried out and included in the pages most closely linked to it.

Even if you only include some of the research you have identified in the assignment pages, you will pick up most or all of the 4 marks available for analysis and research.

Additionally, if you end up only using nine pages in your assignment, all of this analysis can be included in the form it appears here. So it is worth doing.

TASK

The research carried out and recorded later in this assignment that stems from the analysis on this page has been highlighted. This helps me keep track of the research I have done. You should do this with your assignment; it also makes it easy for your teacher to confirm your marks for the analysis.

ANALYSING THE BRIEF		
Brief information	**What do I understand from the information provided?**	**What research action can I take?**
Client: 'Shape-Up'	Shape-up' - A new sports fashion retailer, cares about image, aimed at young adult TM.	Download logo & typeface & check colour codes. Find out how I can get access to the typeface.
Target Market	Mainly young, trendy adults; logo & typeface appear to be aimed at this TM. Both male and female should be included in the promotional layouts.	Look at modern styling for the shelving and storage and shop fittings. What do existing sports shops look like? Research the styles the TM will respond to. Download images of suitable TM models. Try to include them in the promotional layouts.
Shelving	To display clothes and sports accessories. Storage of smaller items in a drawer. Allow surface space for display and serving. Study the space available.	Take account of drawer data provided. Research ergonomics re: shelf sizes and best drawer positions etc. Download and examine the drawer STEP file (work out the critical sizes). How can I assemble it in a shelving unit? How does it slide in and out? How will I join components together?
Hanging clothes	What kind of hanging device can I use; hook, rail, rod, rope, clip, strap, nets?	How much height do hanging sports clothes and spots items require? How can I incorporate a hanger into a shelving unit? How can I make a hanging device look stylish or discrete.
Shop interior	Should be welcoming, bright and reflect a healthy lifestyle. It has windows, how can I use the windows and walls effectively?	Research shop interiors, especially contents and furniture. What might be in a shop sales area? How do I make it bright and welcoming? What surface materials and textures are available in my rendering software?
3D Display	What type of display should I design? What could be included in the promotional layouts? Where will the logo go?	Could be wall mounted, hanging, standing etc it may need to be visible from a distance? Research existing display styles. Source and study promotional shop documents; brochures, posters, leaflets etc.
Aesthetics	The environment should be welcoming and bright. Textures, materials and colours will be important. Make the corporate colours in DTP and try other colours with them.	Explore materials and textures for the shelf and the environment: clean, hygienic, smooth, shiny surfaces. Or perhaps textured natural surfaces to suggest an outdoor feel. Try colours that compliment 'Shape Up's corporate colours; check out the logo carefully.
Ergonomics	Sales staff will likely be standing. Investigate standing heights and suitable shelf heights.	Display shelving may need to be high to be seen clearly? What are the max & min shelf widths for displaying clothes? The shelving unit can be free standing or wall mounted; what are the space restrictions?

PRELIMINARY GRAPHICS - INITIAL IDEAS

The focus of your assignment is the brief which will ask you to create a 3D model of an item, it can be an item of furniture or a smaller product. You have options when you tackle the assignment:

1. To copy and model an existing product.
2. To design your own product.

If you are designing your own item or product, the next four pages are recommended reading. This part of the process involves creating initial 2D design sketches that will help you get started on your preliminary graphics.

Don't get hung up about not being able to design. The earlier projects in this book each have a design focus. The assignment tasks at N5 also have a design option. You will have the necessary skills and experience to tackle the assignment task in the higher course. This stage of the assignment will **not be included in your assignment folio.** It is just to give you ideas and allow you to get your assignment off to a good start.

IMPORTANT TIPS

What if I can't think of ideas?	You can use catalogues or the internet as a starting point. You needn't just look at furniture. Buildings and architecture can provide starting points for design ideas. Use whatever source you think you need to inspire you and get you off to a good start.
Restrict your initial ideas to 2D shapes.	2D sketches are quick to produce and should give you enough of a starting point for you to develop them at the next stage. 2D sketching is also easier to do than pictorial sketching; leave that until later.
Make a few simple annotations.	Annotations will help you to record features that you like and help you to consider what you might improve on. Annotations will also help you to reference the brief. Your annotations should focus on the requirements of the brief.
Don't worry about the quality of design work.	These are initial design ideas which will not be assessed, so don't spend time enhancing them. They are simply intended to provide one promising idea that you can take forward and develop.
Don't over complicate the ideas.	At this initial stage you don't need to flesh out your idea, it will develop and change as you progress. Stick to 2D shapes and keep it simple. It is easier to add complexity later if you need to than it is to simplify an idea that is too complex.
Don't add too much detail.	You don't need to work out how many separate components the item will require, or how they will be assembled. That comes later. Your task now is to chose an idea or bits of several ideas to take to the block modelling stage.

ASSESSMENT SUMMARY

This page will not be included in your assignment folio and will not be assessed.

It will provide you with a starting point from which to develop your item or product.

Choose an idea or a combination of ideas to take forward to the block modelling stage.

This stage can also take the form of an image board downloaded or cut and pasted onto the sheet.

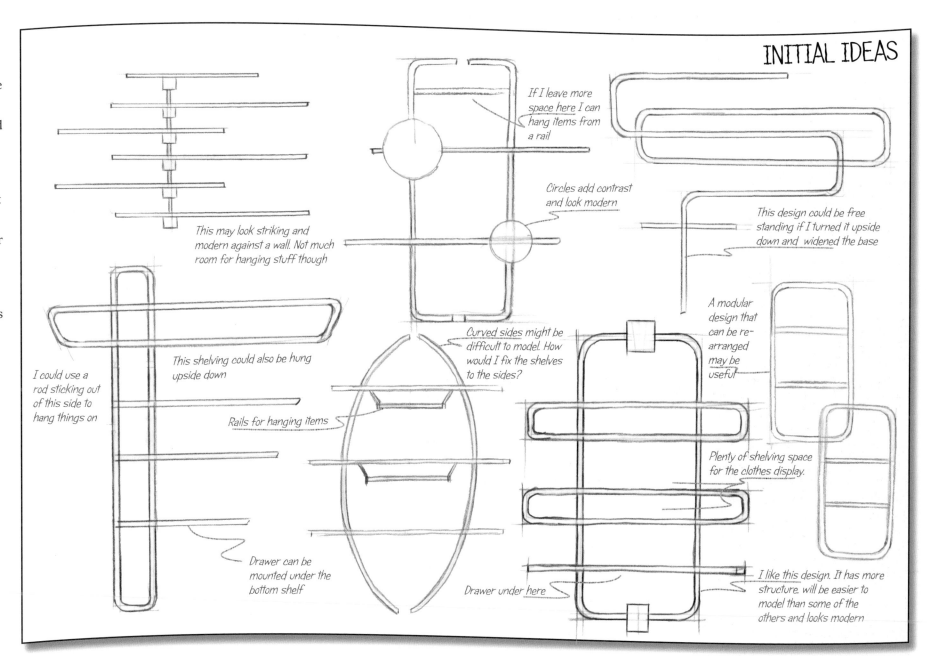

INITIAL IDEAS

If I leave more space here I can hang items from a rail

Circles add contrast and look modern

This design could be free standing if I turned it upside down and widened the base

This may look striking and modern against a wall. Not much room for hanging stuff though

A modular design that can be re-arranged may be useful

This shelving could also be hung upside down

I could use a rod sticking out of this side to hang things on

Curved sides might be difficult to model. How would I fix the shelves to the sides?

Rails for hanging items

Plenty of shelving space for the clothes display.

Drawer can be mounted under the bottom shelf

Drawer under here

I like this design. It has more structure. will be easier to model than some of the others and looks modern

PRELIMINARY GRAPHICS - BLOCK MODEL

It is useful at this stage to construct a 'block model' using 3D CAD. This block model will look like your initial design sketch but will only have one or two components. It's designed to help you establish the shape, form and proportions of the product as well as exploring features you may want to develop later.

The block model should come together quickly and need not appear in your final assignment folio. Though you can incorporate it into the preliminary graphics if you wish.

Remember, you don't have to design the item yourself. You can copy or modify an existing product or design one yourself from scratch. The choice is yours.

The shelving unit shown here has been designed from scratch. It was more fun than copying an original product but I did look closely at existing products to understand how they were constructed, assembled and fixed together. These details will be important when I develop this design in the preliminary graphics on the next three folio sheets.

IMPORTANT TIPS

Model the main part of your design idea or your chosen product.

Model the main part of your idea as close to actual size as possible. Check the space you have to work within; this may or may not be a restriction. Focus on ensuring that any dimensional restrictions are accurately drawn; how high, long or broad should it be? Ensure the proportions of your block model are realistic e.g. get the material thickness right.

Add additional design features.

There is no need at this stage to build separate components. Simply begin a new sketch and add new features to the main part. It's more important at this stage that you achieve a design that is likely to function well and that you are happy with. Remember, at this stage you are not modelling the fine detail of your design. Stick to the main features.

Evaluate your design and make modifications as you see fit.

As your block model takes shape you will see opportunities for adding features that will make the design function better or removing features that don't work as well as you thought they might. There will be an opportunity to modify your design at any stage of the assignment but the fundamental form and structure should take shape now.

Check the complexity of your design.

Ensure your design is not too complex, remember you will have to model it. Remember, also, if it is too simplistic you may not have the scope to pick up all the marks that are available. You teacher can advise you on the complexity of the design.

Check the design brief before you move on.

Don't move on until you have re-checked the brief. There may be important things that you have missed in your model. Now is the time to re-visit the brief, and your research, to double-check your design against these important parts of the assignment task.

PRELIMINARY GRAPHICS - BLOCK MODEL

Building a block model allows you to evaluate your design quickly before you spend too much time and effort on a design that is too simple or too complex or simply unsuitable.

Start with a simple solid block from which you can add or subtract to create your design.

This block was shelled....

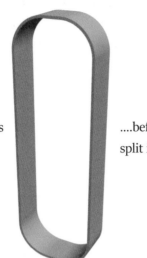

....before being split in two.

Shelves are added, not by assembling separate parts, but by adding another extrusion.

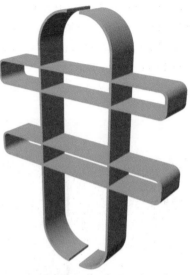

This was intended to be the final design but I felt that it wasn't complex enough. I felt that a hanger could be fixed underneath both shelves and will work as long as I leave enough room for hanging items.

The design I settled on has a cylinder at each end to help hold the two halves together. These may also be a way of fixing the unit to the wall. After checking the brief again I also remembered to add the drawer.

This is the design I am taking forward but, as you will see, it will change again before the end of the assignment task. So give yourself scope to make changes and be ready to problem solve your way through the build.

CHOSEN DESIGN

PRELIMINARY GRAPHICS - COMPONENT DETAILS

The following pages of preliminary graphics are all manually produced. However, they don't need to be manually produced, you can produce them using 3D CAD just as with the block model on the previous page.

It is worth remembering though that sketches and illustrations demonstrate your manual skills and you should make every effort to use them here in the assignment task.

The preliminary graphics demonstrated in this section have been split into three categories. This is to make it easier to identify suitable types of graphic. You can follow this method or mix up your graphics to suit your own preference.

The categories used here are:
1. Component details
2. Technical detail
3. Modelling plan

IMPORTANT TIPS

Use your block model as a starting point.
Import and print your block model to use as a starting point. Developing your design by making small improvements is normally done manually but can be done electronically. Try to make best use of your sketching and illustration skills in this section.

Sketch your design orthographically.
Sketch your chosen design in 2D orthographic views. Project features between views. Show the thickness of parts and focus on establishing good proportions. You can add the main dimensions too and check that they function and fit the space available.

Focus on the key components.
Concentrate on the main parts. Break the block model into separate components and sketch each one individually. Where you can, work out how the parts will assemble, use exploded views or sub-assemblies to explain how these parts fit together. You can ignore smaller components at this stage, concentrate on the main parts.

Identify and sketch separate components.
This is a challenging part of the assignment. Sketches can be a combination of 2D and pictorial. When producing pictorial sketches use 2-point perspective. Practice this skill to ensure the proportions are realistic and the lines of perspective are accurate.

Establish a connection between user and product.
You are creating a product that will be used by people. It's useful to show a simple figure (ergonome). Your teacher will have a wooden or plastic figure you can manipulate and sketch. Show the figure with the product. It can create a sense of scale and it will suggest how the product functions. It will also help you to work out the main dimensions of your product.

Use illustrations to communicate and clarify how the design works.
Use colour to identify separate components. Add texture and tonal scale to create realism. Light and shade close together create contrast and adding colour will create emphasis and impact. Don't overdo it though.

ASSESSMENT SUMMARY

Use of line, shape, form is of very good quality and proportion and demonstrates a clear purpose.

3 Marks

Adherence to drawing protocols and conventions is demonstrated in all of the work.

3 Marks

Communicating design features using light, shade, tone and texture demonstrating a very good skill and understanding in applying techniques.

3 Marks

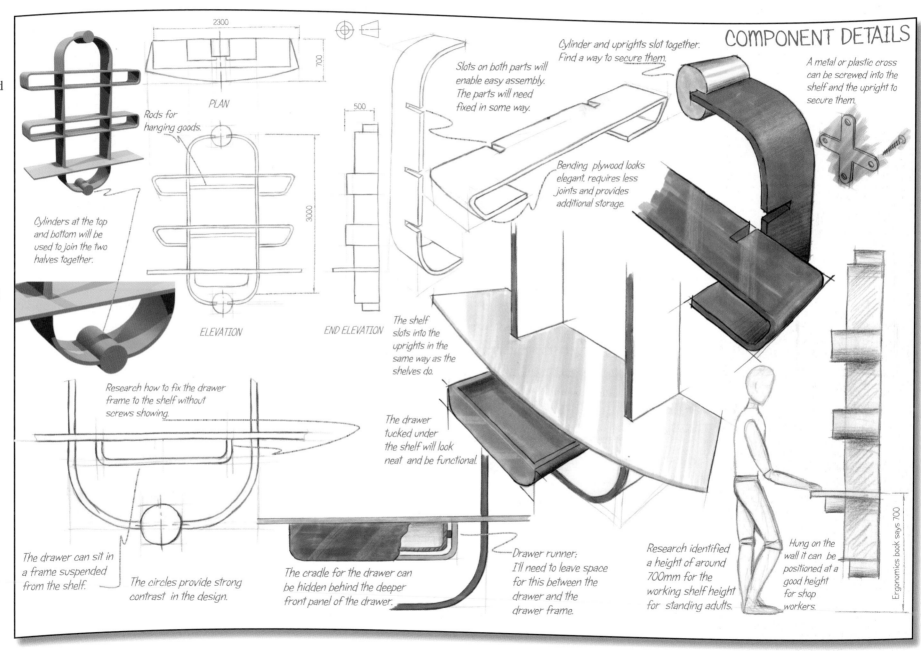

COMPONENT DETAILS

2300

700

PLAN

500

3000

ELEVATION

END ELEVATION

Rods for hanging goods.

Cylinders at the top and bottom will be used to join the two halves together.

Research how to fix the drawer frame to the shelf without screws showing.

The drawer can sit in a frame suspended from the shelf.

The circles provide strong contrast in the design.

The cradle for the drawer can be hidden behind the deeper front panel of the drawer.

Cylinder and uprights slot together. Find a way to secure them.

Slots on both parts will enable easy assembly. The parts will need fixed in some way.

Bending plywood looks elegant, requires less joints and provides additional storage.

A metal or plastic cross can be screwed into the shelf and the upright to secure them.

The shelf slots into the uprights in the same way as the shelves do.

The drawer tucked under the shelf will look neat and be functional.

Drawer runner: I'll need to leave space for this between the drawer and the drawer frame.

Research identified a height of around 700mm for the working shelf height for standing adults.

Hung on the wall it can be positioned at a good height for shop workers.

Ergonomics book says 700

PRELIMINARY GRAPHICS - TECHNICAL DETAIL

The aim of these three pages of preliminary graphics is to provide enough information so that the 3D model can be built. How you achieve this and where on the three pages the information is found is entirely up to you.

We have created an approach that you may find helpful when you tackle your own assignment. The technical detail page deals with the best ways to show how the parts assemble. If you are copying an existing product this might involve analytical sketches. If you have designed your own product it will include developing design ideas.

Creating technical detail requires that you understand the types of graphic that can explain how parts fit together. You should always try to include the following forms of technical detail in your assignment:

- Exploded views
- Sectional views
- Enlarged details
- How moving parts work

IMPORTANT TIPS

Use illustration skills.

You don't need to use marker pens in your illustrations, coloured pencils will be fine. However, marker pens are immediate and come in a vast range of colours and tones and provide a strong base colour that can bring visual impact to your preliminary work. See the section on manual illustration in this book. Colour, tone and texture can bring clarity and impact to your technical detail.

Identify and describe how components fit together.

Sketch exploded views (2D and pictorial). Use sectional views (full, part and removed sections where appropriate). Show how moving parts will work. Arrows can suggest movement. Create enlarged details to describe smaller features and components.

Use colour effectively.

Colour is not only used to create realism in illustrations, it can be used to distinguish separate parts. Check the colours used on these pages and how this helps to clarify the assembly details.

Make use of annotations.

Notes or annotations help explain features and details with more clarity. Look for ways to describe how parts fit together. Also, explain how you intend fixing parts to prevent them falling apart. Read the annotations on these pages to get a flavour of how you can develop your own annotation skills. Annotations can also help explain and record the research you have done.

Joining and assembly methods.

Whether you are designing your own product or working from an existing product you will need to investigate how parts can be joined together. Simple wood screws or machine screws may be sufficient but, equally, a variety of joining methods can be used. I looked up CAM bolts and nuts and assembled a simple joint in school to help me understand how they worked. This also allowed me to record some research in my preliminary graphics.

ASSESSMENT SUMMARY

Analysing a graphic brief and carrying out research activities. *(The marks for this are gathered throughout the assignment folio).*

4 Marks

Use of line, shape, form is of a very good quality and proportion and demonstrates a clear purpose.

3 Marks

Communicating design features using light, shade, tone and texture demonstrating very good skill and understanding in applying techniques.

3 Marks

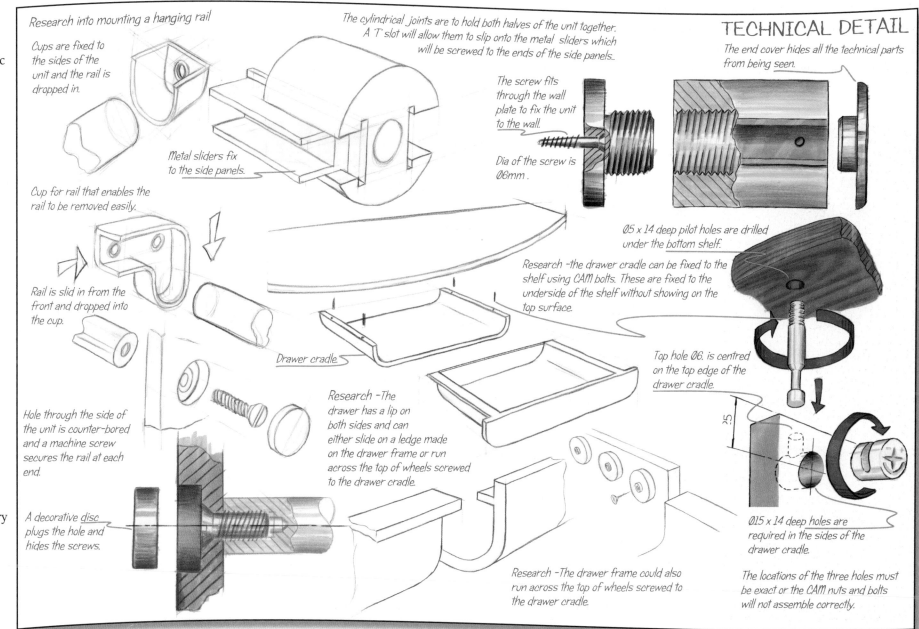

Research into mounting a hanging rail

Cups are fixed to the sides of the unit and the rail is dropped in.

The cylindrical joints are to hold both halves of the unit together. A 'T' slot will allow them to slip onto the metal sliders which will be screwed to the ends of the side panels.

Metal sliders fix to the side panels.

Cup for rail that enables the rail to be removed easily.

Rail is slid in from the front and dropped into the cup.

Hole through the side of the unit is counter-bored and a machine screw secures the rail at each end.

A decorative disc plugs the hole and hides the screws.

The screw fits through the wall plate to fix the unit to the wall.

Dia of the screw is Ø6mm.

TECHNICAL DETAIL

The end cover hides all the technical parts from being seen.

Ø5 x 14 deep pilot holes are drilled under the bottom shelf.

Research –the drawer cradle can be fixed to the shelf using CAM bolts. These are fixed to the underside of the shelf without showing on the top surface.

Drawer cradle.

Research –The drawer has a lip on both sides and can either slide on a ledge made on the drawer frame or run across the top of wheels screwed to the drawer cradle.

Top hole Ø6. is centred on the top edge of the drawer cradle.

25

Ø15 x 14 deep holes are required in the sides of the drawer cradle.

Research –The drawer frame could also run across the top of wheels screwed to the drawer cradle.

The locations of the three holes must be exact or the CAM nuts and bolts will not assemble correctly.

ASSIGNMENT

PRELIMINARY GRAPHICS - MODELLING PLAN

The modelling plan should be the last of your preliminary graphics. By this stage you should have firmed up your design and you should describe which modelling methods you will use to model each part.

Fitting an entire modelling plan onto a single page can be a challenge. It is a good idea to rough-out a modelling sequence for some of the parts and plan how best to use the space on the page.

The amount of detail you need will depend on how complex your design is. You will certainly need enough detail to enable you to sit with it at a computer and be guided through the main stages of your components. Don't worry too much if you can't plan everything in your design. The modelling plan here does not include the CAM bolt and barrel nut or the wood screws and I intend modelling them if I have time.

IMPORTANT TIPS

Plan for three different modelling techniques.

You will be awarded marks for using up to three different modelling techniques so try to build them into your modelling plan. The modelling plan for this shelving unit will use: solid extrusions, revolved surface models, revolved solids and extrusion along a path. I will revolve a helix for the screws and CAM bolts if I can.

Explain the modelling of the main components in simple stages.

Make each step clear using sketches and annotations. This is normally done using manual sketches, it's an excellent way to demonstrate your sketching ability as well as your CAD knowledge. However, it can also be tackled using 3D CAD and put together as you model each part. Be sure to save and record the stages as you go.

Ensure your dimensioning is thorough.

Dimensions have been identified on the previous two pages but it is here that you want to make sure your plan includes most of the dimensions required to construct the parts and build the model. Ensure you apply appropriate drawing standards and conventions when you add dimensions.

Should I plan how to model every part?

That depends on the complexity of your design (whether it's an existing product or your own design). Small items like screws, nuts and bolts can be downloaded to use, as long as you don't take credit for building them. On the other hand, if your design is relatively simple, modelling small parts yourself can help bring a greater level of complexity to your modelling.

ASSESSMENT SUMMARY

Contains most relevant technical details sufficient to inform building the CAD models and the development of production drawings and complex features.

3 Marks

Adherence to drawing protocols and conventions is demonstrated in all of the work.

3 Marks

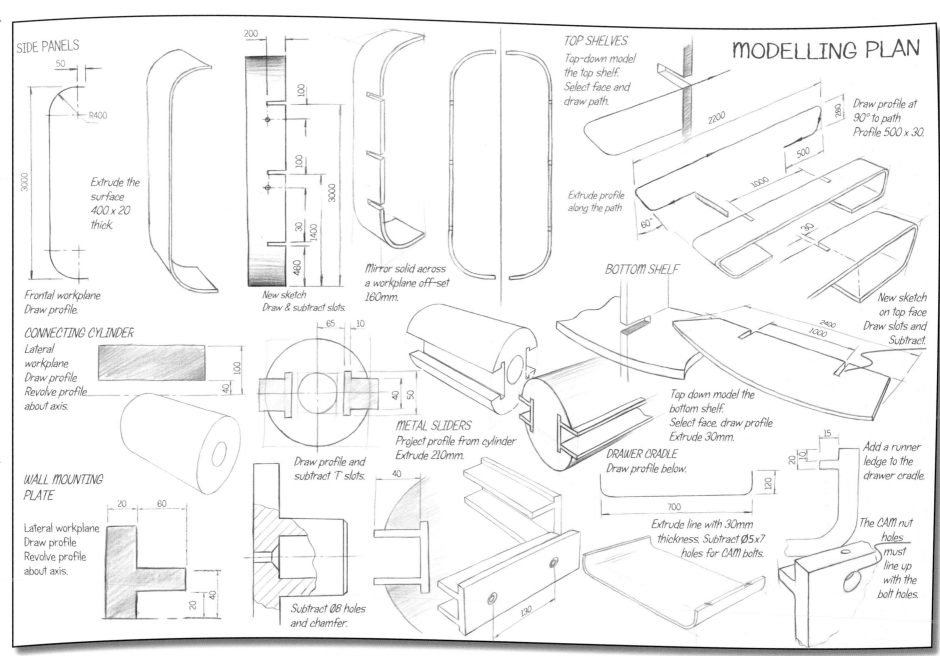

MODELLING PLAN

SIDE PANELS
50
R400
3000
Extrude the surface 400 x 20 thick.
Frontal workplane Draw profile.

200
100
100
30
1400
460
3000
New sketch Draw & subtract slots.

Mirror solid across a workplane off-set 160mm.

TOP SHELVES
Top-down model the top shelf. Select face and draw path.
2200
280
Draw profile at 90° to path Profile 500 x 30.
500
1000
Extrude profile along the path
60°
30

BOTTOM SHELF
New sketch on top face Draw slots and Subtract.
2400
1000

CONNECTING CYLINDER
Lateral workplane Draw profile Revolve profile about axis.
100
40

65 10
40
50
Draw profile and subtract 'T' slots.

METAL SLIDERS
Project profile from cylinder Extrude 210mm.

Top down model the bottom shelf. Select face. draw profile Extrude 30mm.

DRAWER CRADLE
Draw profile below.
120
700
40
Extrude line with 30mm thickness. Subtract Ø5x7 holes for CAM bolts.

15
20 10
Add a runner ledge to the drawer cradle.

The CAM nut holes must line up with the bolt holes.

WALL MOUNTING PLATE
Lateral workplane Draw profile Revolve profile about axis.
20 60
20 40
Subtract Ø8 holes and chamfer.

130

PRODUCTION DRAWINGS - COMPONENTS

Component drawings are required because each component will be manufactured separately before being assembled. The exception to this is when rapid prototyping (3D printing) is the method of manufacture, in which case the product is often built fully assembled and all-in-one printing process. This is not the case with the "ADANIA SHELVING".

Fitting all the dimensioned components onto a single page can be a challenge. You may need to use part of a second page. This is fine but will need careful setting out. Remember, how you present your production drawings is up to you. As long as they conform to accepted drawing standards. You will also have to settle on a scale for these drawings. This will depend on the size of the components and the size of the paper it will be printed on; in this case A3 paper.

Dimensioning takes up much more space than you imagine. Give each view plenty of room and leave room for a title block too. A product with lots of components requires lots of component drawings. This can lead to a challenges and confusion in the layout. On the next page the components each have a space of their own. The page has been split up using boxes. It is not essential that you do this but it can make the layout much clearer.

IMPORTANT TIPS

Establish a suitable scale but remember this can be easily changed if it doesn't work.

The scale used for the larger components here is 1:20. You will need to use a similar scale if you are drawing a large item such as a desk or household storage unit. Smaller products would require a scale of 1:10, 1:5, 1:4 or 1:2. You have a fixed (A3) space to fit all the components onto. Try the scale you think may work but change it quickly if it looks like the drawings won't fit on the page.

The scale should allow enough detail to be seen clearly.

Remember that you can change the scale of smaller parts to make details clearer. The scales used for smaller items here include 1:10, 1:2 and 1:1. You will determine the best scales to use to ensure clarity of detail. If you get the scales wrong and the detail can't be seen it can cost you marks.

Enlarged views and partial views will be very useful here; learn how to create them.

Drawing standards and features such as enlarged views, partial views and interrupted views are likely to crop up in the course exam, so get to grips with them now. Study the component drawings on the next page and identify the enlarged, partial and interrupted views. There are also views that are both enlarged and partial views. Work out how and why these have been created.

Annotations and the content of the title block are important.

Annotations are used to describe features that are difficult to show using dimensions alone. They are an important feature of production information. The title block also includes more formal annotations such as scale and tolerance etc.

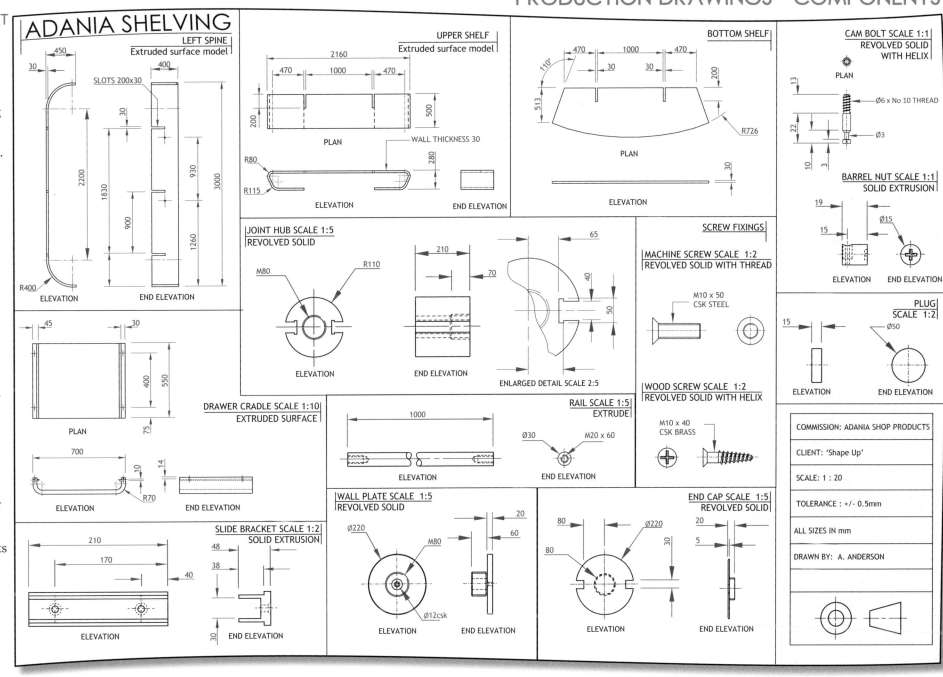

ADANIA SHELVING

LEFT SPINE
Extruded surface model

ASSESSMENT SUMMARY

A minimum of three different CAD modelling techniques should be used.

3 Marks

For full CAD modelling marks all components must demonstrate very good skill in draughting and modelling.

6 Marks

Models demonstrate a broad range of complex CAD modelling edits and features.

3 Marks

UPPER SHELF
Extruded surface model

BOTTOM SHELF

CAM BOLT SCALE 1:1
REVOLVED SOLID WITH HELIX

BARREL NUT SCALE 1:1
SOLID EXTRUSION

JOINT HUB SCALE 1:5
REVOLVED SOLID

SCREW FIXINGS

MACHINE SCREW SCALE 1:2
REVOLVED SOLID WITH THREAD

ENLARGED DETAIL SCALE 2:5

WOOD SCREW SCALE 1:2
REVOLVED SOLID WITH HELIX

PLUG
SCALE 1:2

DRAWER CRADLE SCALE 1:10
EXTRUDED SURFACE

RAIL SCALE 1:5
EXTRUDE

SLIDE BRACKET SCALE 1:2
SOLID EXTRUSION

WALL PLATE SCALE 1:5
REVOLVED SOLID

END CAP SCALE 1:5
REVOLVED SOLID

COMMISSION: ADANIA SHOP PRODUCTS
CLIENT: 'Shape Up'
SCALE: 1 : 20
TOLERANCE : +/- 0.5mm
ALL SIZES IN mm
DRAWN BY: A. ANDERSON

PRODUCTION DRAWINGS - ASSEMBLY

Assemblies are a key feature of production drawings. An assembly shows the components in place and gives the manufacturer a clear picture of what the assembled product will look like.

Dimensioning is not normally a feature of assemblies. Only the main dimensions are shown and this is to indicate the overall size of the assembled product.

Assembly drawings are shown in both orthographic and pictorial forms. You should show both. It is fine to use rendered pictorials here as long as clarity is not reduced.

IMPORTANT TIPS

How big should my assembly drawings be?

Assembly drawings will normally include both large and small components so it is vital that you scale them as big as is practicable on an A3 page. Clarity of detail is the key and drawings that are too small will not show detail clearly. Pictorial assemblies are a useful way of communicating form and proportion. Always indicate the scale of the pictorial line drawing if it is different from the main orthographic drawings.

How do I ensure the smaller details are clear?

You will likely include a sectional view on this page. There may be details on the section that need enlarged for clarity. Choose your enlarged details carefully; it is not enough to show an enlarged detail of just any part. Choose joints and features that show vital assembly information. Always add the scale of the enlarged view. Enlarged views can also be used to add clarity to component drawings. A small detail that requires dimensions can be enlarged prior to dimensioning.

How much hidden detail do I show?

Hidden detail is important but if it is too small or if it clutters the drawing then leave it out. There will be scope to include hidden detail in the component drawings.

What annotations should I use?

View titles, scales and a fully complete title block are essential. Add other annotations as required in order to improve understanding of the drawings.

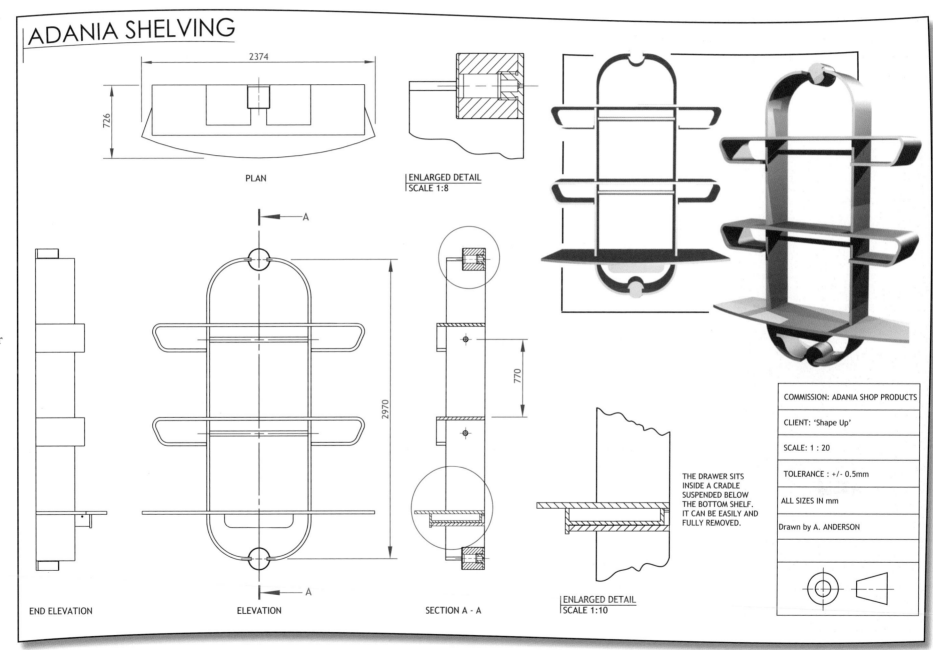

ADANIA SHELVING

2374

726

PLAN

ENLARGED DETAIL
SCALE 1:8

A

2970

770

END ELEVATION

ELEVATION

SECTION A - A

THE DRAWER SITS
INSIDE A CRADLE
SUSPENDED BELOW
THE BOTTOM SHELF.
IT CAN BE EASILY AND
FULLY REMOVED.

ENLARGED DETAIL
SCALE 1:10

| COMMISSION: ADANIA SHOP PRODUCTS |
| CLIENT: 'Shape Up' |
| SCALE: 1 : 20 |
| TOLERANCE : +/- 0.5mm |
| ALL SIZES IN mm |
| Drawn by A. ANDERSON |

PRODUCTION DRAWINGS - TECHNICAL DETAIL

The technical detail page describes how the component parts assemble or work together. The types of drawing you use should be chosen to suit the product and the information you need to communicate. The previous page already includes sectional views and enlarged detail. These are both forms of technical detail.

There are several different types of technical detail you can use. Choose 3 or 4 from the following:

- Exploded views (orthographic or pictorial)
- Sectional views (through, half, stepped, part, removed and revolved sections)
- Enlarged details
- How moving parts work
- Sub-assemblies

Annotations are important in the technical detail page. You should include a parts list, allocating a name and number to each part.

IMPORTANT TIPS

How many types of technical detail do I need?

You will need 3 different types to secure all the marks for technical detail. The most common types are: sectional views, enlarged details and pictorial exploded views. Others, such as, stepped sections, part sections and revolved sections and details of moving parts are all valid. Use what you feel is necessary to describe the feature.

Do I need to show every component in an exploded view?

If you are exploding a large product you will not be expected to show all the small components. Fixings and standard components like screws and CAM bolts etc are often too small to show on a large exploded view.
You should include a parts list with a name for each part.

Small fixings are important, so how, and when, should I show them?

Smaller features and parts can be shown as enlarged details. Remember to include the scale of the enlarged details. These details can either be line drawings or rendered illustrations as long as they are clear and readily understood.

Should sub-assemblies be shown as assembled or exploded?

Both if you can fit them in. The more information you can give about assembly will help the manufacturer plan the assembly of the real product during manufacture. It can also help the consumer if it is a flat-packed, self- assembly product. Assembly details can be used in the assembly instructions for the consumer.

ADANIA SHELVING

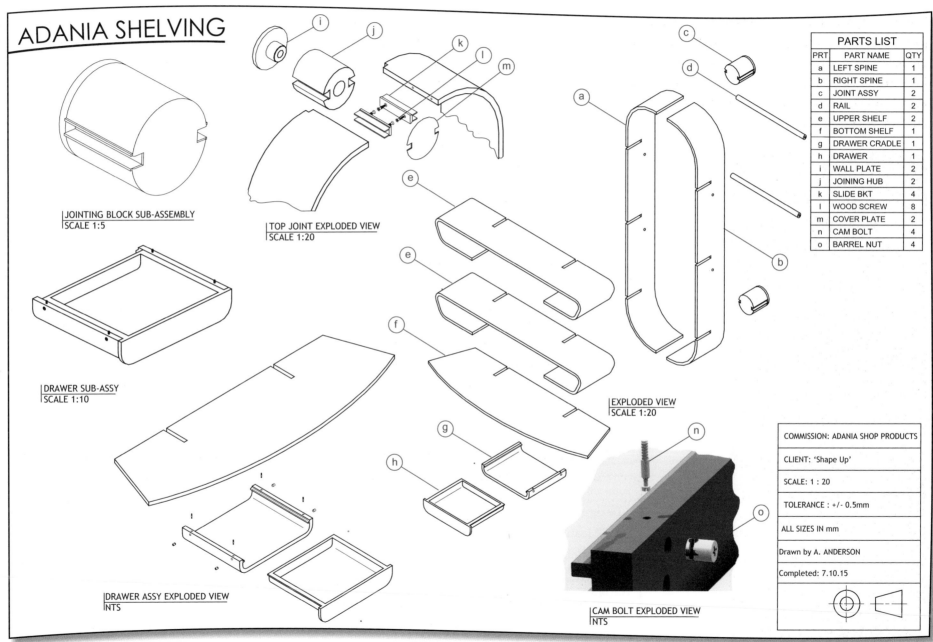

JOINTING BLOCK SUB-ASSEMBLY
SCALE 1:5

DRAWER SUB-ASSY
SCALE 1:10

TOP JOINT EXPLODED VIEW
SCALE 1:20

EXPLODED VIEW
SCALE 1:20

DRAWER ASSY EXPLODED VIEW
NTS

CAM BOLT EXPLODED VIEW
NTS

PARTS LIST		
PRT	PART NAME	QTY
a	LEFT SPINE	1
b	RIGHT SPINE	1
c	JOINT ASSY	2
d	RAIL	2
e	UPPER SHELF	2
f	BOTTOM SHELF	1
g	DRAWER CRADLE	1
h	DRAWER	1
i	WALL PLATE	2
j	JOINING HUB	2
k	SLIDE BKT	4
l	WOOD SCREW	8
m	COVER PLATE	2
n	CAM BOLT	4
o	BARREL NUT	4

COMMISSION: ADANIA SHOP PRODUCTS	
CLIENT: 'Shape Up'	
SCALE: 1 : 20	
TOLERANCE : +/- 0.5mm	
ALL SIZES IN mm	
Drawn by A. ANDERSON	
Completed: 7.10.15	

PRELIMINARY GRAPHICS - THUMBNAIL LAYOUTS

The promotional layouts are your chance to pull your creative talents together and to take your assignment to a new level. You have already assembled a 3D model that your layouts will be displayed on. It is important that your promotional layouts fit the 3D model and can be displayed to good effect in the environment.

Analysis of the brief

You will design at least two layouts because the brief asks for a multi-page or multi-sided layout. Check the brief carefully to make sure you know exactly what your constraints and options are. In this case the brief ask that the promotional layouts are aimed at young people who make healthy lifestyle choices and like sports fashion clothes. I have downloaded examples of the target market and other images that may help.

Your thumbnail designs can be drawn or sketched manually or take the form of early electronic layouts. Use the method that best suits you. You will probably be near the end of your assignment by now and will be running short of time. Check how much time you have left and plan how you will use it. What graphics still need to be produced? Allocate a portion of the time left to each one. You may choose to create a 3D CAD model to display your layouts. This need not be complex.

IMPORTANT TIPS

Prepare an A3 sheet with templates in good proportion.

> The templates should be of the same proportions as your **3D display model.** This can be done manually or using DTP. The example here is a combination of both. The **slogan**, **body text (write your own), logo** and **images** you have downloaded can be pasted onto the sheet before you begin creating thumbnails. It gives you immediate reference to the possible content. Leave ample space for annotations and for the first electronic draft of your layout which can be printed and glued onto your thumbnails.

Create thumbnails with the templates in position.

> The thumbnail layouts here are side-by-side. This is because the promotional layouts will be viewed side-by-side on the 3D display. The layouts should work together and need to be designed together.

Ensure you show how your layouts develop.

> Your layouts should show a range of ideas and demonstrate the development of one idea, showing how it improves. This may show significant changes from thumbnail to final layout or take the shape of some fine-tuning; small but noticeable improvements. Space was set aside for the DTP version. It shows the first-draft development of one idea but includes features from other ideas. It has been glued in place. Use annotations to evaluate your ideas and justify your improvements; these will be important in your assessment.

Focus your annotations on 3 areas.

> Your annotations should concentrate on three areas;
> 1. **Design elements & principles**: Alignment, balance, colour, contrast, depth, dominance and unity should certainly feature.
> 2. **DTP features:** Fonts, columns, headers & footers, text wrap, cropping, drop shadows, transparency and bleeds are all important.
> 3. **The brief:** Your annotations should explain how you are meeting the brief.

Check the brief and make sure you have answered it.

> The brief states that the 3D promotional display should promote the shop and include the slogan. It leaves plenty of scope for layout options. Try to make use of the logo and try to show an example of the target market (a figure). Downloading a selection of suitable images and recording text ideas helps to make the process of designing a little easier.

ASSESSMENT SUMMARY

The brief is analysed in detail and specific information on the requirements for graphics that meet a market purpose, content and style is gathered.

Research is relevant and confirms the graphic requirements comprehensively.

4 Marks

Planning activities are thorough and demonstrate an effective range of layout variations. Justification of design elements, principles and DTP features relaQtes specifically to the brief and demonstrate a good understanding of the impact of layout.

3 Marks

Company name: 'Shape up'

Body text

'Shape up' outlets stock only the very best unisex sportswear. You will find a colour range and style to suit you whatever your sport. Almost half our regular stock has been reduced in the run-up to summer. Check out our bargains online and in store today.

Men's items for sale: Vests, Joggers, Shorts Tops, Trainers, Trunks, Monitors, Watches.
Women's items for sale: Vests, Joggers, Shorts, Tops Running shoes, Swimsuits, Monitors, Watches.

Slogan

Serious about fitness,
Serious about style.

Colour scheme is bright but a bit too sporty and not sophisticated enough for the target audience.

I like the textured background though. I might use it.

Splitting the logo across both layouts is interesting but doesn't work as well as I hoped. The red colour fills top and bottom create unity and emphasise the slogan.

Research

The colour scheme has to compliment the company colours. I'll try out both harmonising and contrasting colours. Primary and secondary colours won't attract trendy, upmarket customers. I will try to use more sophisticated combinations to create a vibrant but sophisticated colour scheme. I will try neutral colours in the scheme.

Images

The brief asks for images of the target market. I've sourced some suitable images

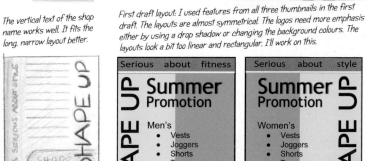

Serious looking figures will work best and tie in with the serious emphasis of the slogan. Splitting the background colours creates a strong backdrop. Overlapping the background creates dominant items.

The colours used in the logo will emphasise the shop's colours and create unity when displayed in the store. They also create a cultured and up-market look.

Using an asymmetric layout across the two panels creates contrast and visual interest.

The vertical text of the shop name works well. It fits the long, narrow layout better.

Logo

Images

Wrapping text around the figure creates a connection between the figure and the text. Bleeding the figure off the page saves space and looks modern.

Placing the figure on the top layer with the logo behind suggests depth and the action pose looks more dynamic. The figures represent the target market and is aspirational.

THUMBNAILS

First draft layout: I used features from all three thumbnails in the first draft. The layouts are almost symmetrical. The logos need more emphasis either by using a drop shadow or changing the background colours. The layouts look a bit too linear and rectangular. I'll work on this.

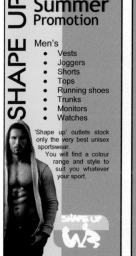

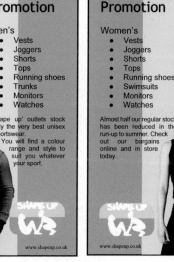

Serious about fitness	Serious about style

SHAPE UP — **Summer Promotion**

Men's
- Vests
- Joggers
- Shorts
- Tops
- Running shoes
- Trunks
- Monitors
- Watches

'Shape up' outlets stock only the very best unisex sportswear. You will find a colour range and style to suit you whatever your sport.

www.shapeup.co.uk

SHAPE UP — **Summer Promotion**

Women's
- Vests
- Joggers
- Shorts
- Tops
- Running shoes
- Swimsuits
- Monitors
- Watches

Almost half our regular stock has been reduced in the run-up to summer. Check out our bargains online and in store today.

www.shapeup.co.uk

PROMOTIONAL GRAPHICS - RENDERS AND LAYOUTS

By this stage you have selected layouts that fit your display and promote the new brand effectively and you may already have created a first draft using DTP.

You have a fixed space to fill and it is important that you use the DTP features to try out different layout positions and sizes.

Check the brief against your first draft. Do your layouts meet the brief? Is your message clear? Can you organise the layouts better? Can you create more visual impact?

IMPORTANT TIPS

Establish the structure of the layout first.

Use the grids and guidelines on your DTP software to establish the structure of the layouts. Create header and footer spaces, equal margins and a column structure. Then you can populate the main space.

Experiment with sizing, layers and positioning.

Sizing and layering effects can be used to create a dynamic layout. Larger items are more dominant and items on the top layer appear closer to the viewer. The first draft lacked depth. Look at the final layouts opposite; there is depth, dominance, alignment and unity. Try to work out how these effects were achieved and try them in your own layouts.

Experiment with colours.

Your colour scheme should be eye-catching but also work with the company colours. The initial colour scheme, from the thumbnails, is only a guide and you should use the colour swatches on your DTP software to explore the colour options including tints and shades. It is so easy to change colours. Use the colour picker tool to match colours and to make accents colours that create unity in your layouts.

Consider full cropping to create visual impact.

Full cropping saves space by removing the background. It creates visual interest by introducing a different shape to the layout and it allows different backgrounds to be tried out. It also gives the figures emphasis and impact in the layouts.

Make use of bleeds, colour fills, text wrap and reverse text.

DTP features are immediate and can have a huge impact on your layout. Experiment by making small adjustments until all the features work together to best effect. Questions to get you thinking: *What are the most dominant items in the layouts opposite?* The layouts incorporate both full and square cropping; *What impact do these techniques have on the layouts? What effect does colour matching have on the layouts?*

ASSESSMENT SUMMARY

The promotional layouts respond to all the requirements of the brief. They incorporate DTP features, applied with a high level of skill. The layouts make very good use of design principles and elements and have significant visual impact.

9 Marks

Note: The 3D display model, on the far right, was designed and built earlier. This one is a simple, single component model but you can make it more elaborate if you feel you need to pick up more marks for 3D modelling.

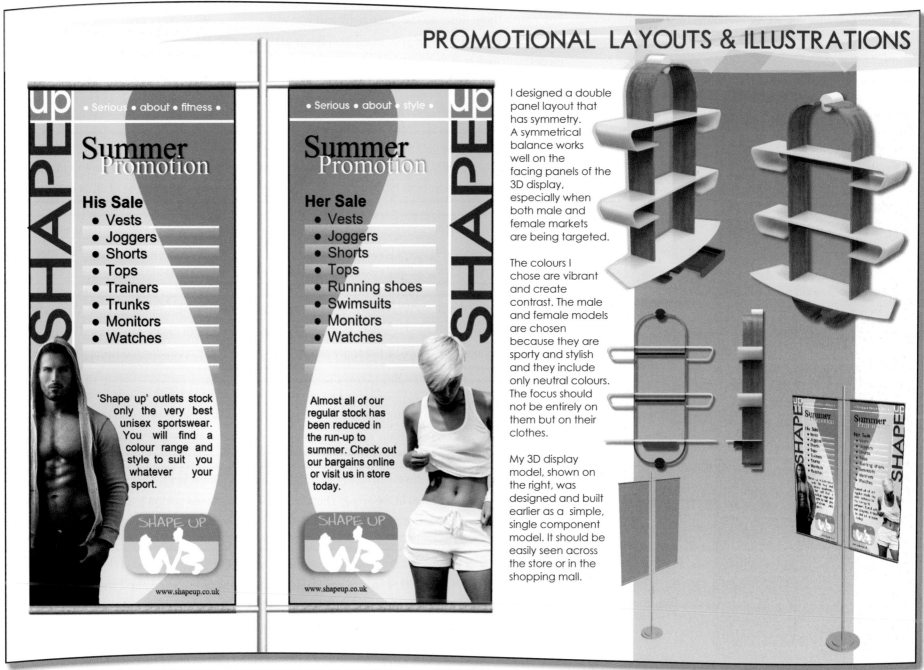

PROMOTIONAL LAYOUTS & ILLUSTRATIONS

I designed a double panel layout that has symmetry. A symmetrical balance works well on the facing panels of the 3D display, especially when both male and female markets are being targeted.

The colours I chose are vibrant and create contrast. The male and female models are chosen because they are sporty and stylish and they include only neutral colours. The focus should not be entirely on them but on their clothes.

My 3D display model, shown on the right, was designed and built earlier as a simple, single component model. It should be easily seen across the store or in the shopping mall.

PROMOTIONAL GRAPHICS - CREATING AND POPULATING A SCENE

It is important that you set aside enough time for setting up your scene. Doing a good job will take some thought and several hours.

You have a three-dimensional space to fill and you will already have decided where your main item (your 3D model) will look best and fit best. You must ensure that all parts of the scene are scaled (sized) correctly.

What other items can you model to compliment your interior space and your main 3D model? Try not to overpower these main items. Ensure the scene is visually balanced in content, colours and textures.

IMPORTANT TIPS

Ensure your scene is correctly assembled.

> Just like the assembly of your main model, the scene has to be accurately assembled. You must use constraints correctly and ensure the positioning of items is carefully done. You will lose marks if you have models that appear to project through walls or the floor. Scaling items correctly is also important. It can be very obvious to your assessor if the scaling of an item is out of proportion.

Consider all of the 3D modelling techniques.

> There are marks available for demonstrating three modelling techniques in your assignment. You have, extrusion, revolving, lofting, helix and extrusion along a path to choose from. If you have not included at least three of these in your main model, now is your opportunity to work them in. Check out any restrictions (and opportunities) built into the brief.

Source ready-made, free to use, 3D models.

> Free sites such as 'Grab CAD' and '3D Warehouse' offer two opportunities: 1. To download and use 3D models from their site and 2. To upload and showcase your own 3D models. Remember, models you did not create can be used in the scene and credit will be gained when they contribute to assembling the scene as long as you don't take credit for modelling the downloads; which is

Set up a remote external plane for the external image.

> Your scene will have windows and you should consider what may be on the other side of the windows. Is it likely to be an indoor or outdoor area? Source images to use through the windows. You should create a surface to apply the decal to and off-set it on the outside of the scene. This can create a subtle 'extra dimension' to your scene and help you pick up valuable marks.

Consider where your decals will go and create surfaces for them.

> You will need to create a suitable 3D display to satisfy the promotional part of the brief. This will be positioned so that it can be viewed clearly. You may also want to use a logo in the scene. Think about where it should go and the size and space you need. Adding graphics and simple text in a scene can give it real impact. A graphic also provides opportunity to use colours to create unity.

Construct your scene to maximise the effect.

> Your scene will be busy, you may have a dozen or more items to organise. Use combinations that work well together so that you can view them in the same shot. Position items so they can be viewed together. You should also consider surface textures. Reflective materials like mirrors, windows and shiny surfaces can be placed beside items which will bounce reflections around. These effects can be dynamic and create strong visual impact. This will demonstrate to your assessor that you know how to manipulate items in a scene effectively. Try to work out how this was done in the scene opposite.

ASSESSMENT SUMMARY

The environment is assembled with the main model and other supplementary models, appropriately scaled and placed in context.

3 Marks

SETTING UP THE SCENE

3D DISPLAY SCREENS

The double-sided 3D display I created for the scene can display two promotional posters on either side. It has a weighted base for stability.

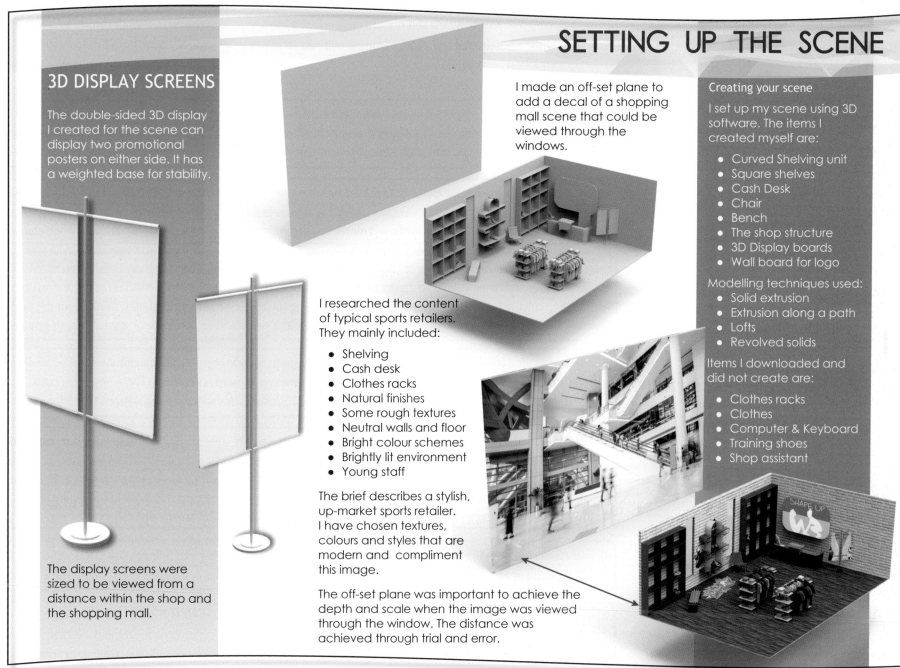

I made an off-set plane to add a decal of a shopping mall scene that could be viewed through the windows.

Creating your scene

I set up my scene using 3D software. The items I created myself are:

- Curved Shelving unit
- Square shelves
- Cash Desk
- Chair
- Bench
- The shop structure
- 3D Display boards
- Wall board for logo

Modelling techniques used:
- Solid extrusion
- Extrusion along a path
- Lofts
- Revolved solids

Items I downloaded and did not create are:
- Clothes racks
- Clothes
- Computer & Keyboard
- Training shoes
- Shop assistant

I researched the content of typical sports retailers. They mainly included:

- Shelving
- Cash desk
- Clothes racks
- Natural finishes
- Some rough textures
- Neutral walls and floor
- Bright colour schemes
- Brightly lit environment
- Young staff

The brief describes a stylish, up-market sports retailer. I have chosen textures, colours and styles that are modern and compliment this image.

The off-set plane was important to achieve the depth and scale when the image was viewed through the window. The distance was achieved through trial and error.

The display screens were sized to be viewed from a distance within the shop and the shopping mall.

PROMOTIONAL GRAPHICS - RENDERING YOUR SCENE

A good scene render will bring your 3D environment to life. Carefully chosen colours will create contrast or harmony and unity.

Well selected materials and textures will give it a life-like, three-dimensional feel. Skilful lighting will cast shadows that suggest depth and solidity.

This is your opportunity to create impressive visual impact by using all the rendering features available in your rendering package.

IMPORTANT TIPS

Apply materials to surfaces as well as parts (models).

The surface materials you apply are raster. They mould to the surface of an object and give it the impression of solidity. Careful selection of materials can make an object look solid and heavy or light and fragile. The function of the models in your scene will suggest suitable materials but you should experiment with materials from the pallet, you may be surprised by what works best in your scene.

Adding Decals.

Decals are similar to material textures but without repeating patterns (tessellations). They are designed to simulate posters, stickers or images. 3 marks are available for positioning, orienting and scaling high quality promotional layouts into your scene. One mark can be gained for adding the logo alone, while full marks require effective use of your promotional DTP layouts and the logo.

Colours.

Colour can have the most immediate impact on the viewer. Colour needs to be used skilfully but is often used badly. Many materials enable you to change their colour, so experiment. It is not about choosing the most appropriate colour for an object but has more to do with finding colours that work well together. You are playing the role of an interior designer, think about the mood you want to create. Should it be bright and lively or calming and subdued? Should it be masculine, feminine or appeal to both genders?

Textures.

Textures are a vital component of your scene. You should aim to include objects that are shiny and reflective and others that have a matt finish. Other objects may be flexible and soft, while some can be hard and robust. These opposites create contrast in your scene and contribute to the realism and impact of it. As with colours, take time experimenting with combinations of textures.

Lighting.

Lighting is often where the real impact of a scene is created. You will be able to adjust the intensity, direction and focus of lighting in your scene. Think carefully about where you need highlights and where you want to emphasise colours or textures. Lighting will enable you to achieve this. Think about the moods your lighting can create. Do you need the scene to be lit in a bright, lively way or toned down and relaxing? Do you want lots of strong tonal contrast or a more even balance of highlights and shadows? It can also be badly used; avoid too many dark shadows and avoid creating light sources from unrealistic directions, e.g. from the floor.

Depth of field.

If your rendering software allows you to create depth of field, try this. In the example opposite, the scene with the clothes rack in the foreground is out of focus. This helps emphasise the depth in the scene. It suggests the viewer's eye is focusing on other items.

Selecting the best viewing angles.

You need to capture a variety of views that show the content of the scene to best effect. You must avoid catching the 'edges' of your scene. Try viewing the scene from different elevations (heights) as well as different angles. Look for combinations of items that work well when viewed together; the main shelf works well with the yellow clothes rack and the wooden items create unity when viewed in the same scene.

ASSESSMENT SUMMARY

Illustration techniques used are fully relevant to the environment and demonstrate very good skills in application.

The environment should be illustrated by techniques that demonstrate light on form, such as: fills, highlights, shadows and textures (appropriately scaled), to enhance and contextualise the model.

6 Marks

Illustrations are used creatively throughout to enhance the environment and fully support the requirements of the brief.

3 Marks

SHAPE-UP Sports Retailer
Interior design proposal

HIGHLIGHTS & SHADOWS
I have been careful to create crisp highlights and contrast these against dark shadows. The shadows are not too dark; they still reveal detail, colours and textures.

COLOUR
My combinations of colours provide a bright but slightly sophisticated scheme. I have avoided pure primary colours often found in sports shops in favour of contrasting yellow and blue tones. There is still a brightness in the scene but it is more upmarket in its softness of tone.

Adding images of people helps confirm the scale of other items in the scene.

LIGHTING
I used a variety of lighting effects and light sources to create a bright, realistic interior for the shop. The out of focus clothes rack in the foreground creates depth of field and adds to the realism of my scene.

MATERIALS & TEXTURES
My scene was rendered in a CAD illustration package. I used many textures on the floor, the walls and the furniture and fittings to give the scene a realistic and solid look.

WITH THANKS TO...

BRIGHT RED PUBLISHING LTD
Cover image © Caleb Rutherford - eidetic; Bright Red Publishing Ltd

Acknowledgements

Every effort has been made to seek all copyright holders. If any have been overlooked, then Bright Red Publishing will be delighted to make the necessary arrangements. Permission has been sought from all relevant copyright holders and Bright Red Publishing are grateful for the use of the following:

Scott Hunter & Peter Linton/graphics throughout. P3 - titov dmitriy/Shutterstock.com; Monkey Business Images/Shutterstock.com; FERNANDO BLANCO CALZADA/Shutterstock.com; Albachiaraa/Shutterstock.com; dotshock's /Shutterstock.com; Solis Images /Shutterstock.com; Alexander Raths /Shutterstock.com; Ragma Images /Shutterstock.com. P5-28 With thanks to the British Standards Institute. P33 - Sebastian Kaulitzki/Shutterstock.com; Peter Sobolev/Shutterstock.com; B Brown/Shutterstock.com; karamysh/Shutterstock.com; PlusONE/Shutterstock.com. P59-65 - With thanks to the British Standards Institute. P76 - CssAndDesign/Shutterstock.com; Adverta; Africa Studio/Shutterstock.com; StockLite/Shutterstock.com; GTS/Shutterstock.com; 3d Brained/Shutterstock.com; Oleksiy Mark/Shutterstock.com. P77 - Ollyy/Shutterstock.com; Julia Nikitina/Shutterstock.com; Marc Nicke/Shutterstock.com; 3d brained/Shutterstock.com; ProfyArt/Shutterstock.com. P78 - Becky Stares/Shutterstock.com;Nickylarson974/Shutterstock.com; Becky Stares/Shutterstock.com; alice-photo/Shutterstock.com; yayha/Shutterstock.com; AlinaMD/Shutterstock.com; Babii Nadiia/Shutterstock.com; GraphEGO/Shutterstock.com; nav/Shutterstock.com; Marius Pirvu/Shutterstock.com; ramcreations/Shutterstock.com; Oleksiy Mark/Shutterstock.com. P79 - With thanks to Marks and Spencer; Alexander Kalina/Shutterstock.com; PhotoStock10/Shutterstock.com; smartape/Shutterstock.com; Moreno Soppelsa/Shutterstock.com; Professional photography/Shutterstock.com; april70/Shutterstock.com; oriontrail/Shutterstock.com; Ikonoklast Fotografie/Shutterstock.com; zhu difeng/Shutterstock.com; Rehan Qureshi/Shutterstock.com; P80 - Marine/Shutterstock.com; Africa Studio/Shutterstock.com. P81 - Gts/Shutterstock.com; Ivan Vukovic/Shutterstock.com; Gts/Shutterstock.com; Gts/Shutterstock.com; Gts/Shutterstock.com; Pincasso/Shutterstock.com; Danicek/Shutterstock.com; CssAndDesign/Shutterstock.com; Antun Hirsman/Shutterstock.com; Brian A Jackson/Shutterstock.com. CAD - P83 KPG_Payless/Shutterstock.com; P84 RAGMA IMAGES/Shutterstock.com; Solis Images/Shutterstock.com; Alexander Raths/Shutterstock.com. P85 Vaniato/shutterstock.com; Roger Costa Morera/shutterstock.com; Julia Nikitina/shutterstock.com; Jibon/shutterstock.com. P94 With thanks to Derek Sneddon. P98 With thanks to Callum Buchanan. P102 With thanks to Amy Broadhurst. P103; P103 Frank Fielder/Shutterstock.com; P103 nikkytok/Shutterstock.com. P104 - Monkey Business Images/Shutterstock.com; Sergi Lopez Roig/Shutterstock.com; Dmitry Kalinovsky/Shutterstock.com; whiteMocca/Shutterstock.com. P108 Billion Photos/shutterstock.com. P117 Adam Gregor/shutterstock.com; Chiyacat/shutterstock.com; stuart.ford/shutterstock.com; Billion Photos/shutterstock.com; Andrei Mayatnik/shutterstock.com. P118 Africa Studio/shutterstock.com; Tzubasa/shutterstock.com; Antlio/shutterstock.com; jaroslava V/shutterstock.com; Zoommer/shutterstock.com; Jorg Hackemann/shutterstock.com. P121 - Bruce Rolff/Shutterstock.com; firek1/Shutterstock.com. P122 - firek1/Shutterstock.com; Kit8.net/Shutterstock.com; Rihardzz/Shutterstock.com; Oleksiy Mark/Shutterstock.com. P123 - With thanks to serif: Serif, the Serif logo, PagePlus and all other Serif product names are trademarks or registered trademarks of Serif (Europe) Ltd; Ljupco Smokovski/Shutterstock.com; Stefan Schurr/Shutterstock.com. P127 - elxeneize/Shutterstock.com; ostill/Shutterstock.com; ostill/Shutterstock.com; ostill/Shutterstock.com; dotshock/Shutterstock.com. P128 - Anna Moskvina/Shutterstock.com; Philip Date/Shutterstock.com; Skylines/Shutterstock.com; nevodka/Shutterstock.com; wavebreakmedia/Shutterstock.com; Evgeniya Moroz/Shutterstock.com. P129 - Maria Evseyeva/Shutterstock.com; DigitalHand Studio/Shutterstock.com; domnitsky/Shutterstock.com; Philip Date/Shutterstock.com; Zai Aragon/Shutterstock.com; VGstockstudio/Shutterstock.com; AlexProkop/Shutterstock.com. P130 - 4 Original images based of serif; With thanks to serif: Serif, the Serif logo, PagePlus and all other Serif product names are trademarks or registered trademarks of Serif (Europe) Ltd. P131 - ostill/Shutterstock.com; EpicStockMedia/Shutterstock.com. 132 - Stefan Schurr/Shutterstock.com; Tetiana Dziubanovska /Shutterstock.com; szefei/Shutterstock.com. P136 - R.Iegosyn/Shutterstock.com; YanLev/Shutterstock.com; Sergey Nivens/Shutterstock.com. P137 - BONNINSTUDIO/Shutterstock.com; oover/Shutterstock.com; Syda Productions/Shutterstock.com; Ollyy/Shutterstock.com; Marcin Balcerzak/Shutterstock.com; lenaer/Shutterstock.com. P138 - Petrafler/Shutterstock.com; IM_photo/Shutterstock.com; Bruce Rolff/Shutterstock.com; Africa Studio/Shutterstock.com. P139 - Alliance/Shutterstock.com; R. Gino Santa Maria/Shutterstock.com; Tetiana Dziubanovska/Shutterstock.com; Pressmaster/Shutterstock.com; LOVEgraphic/Shutterstock.com; EDHAR/Shutterstock.com; Monkey Business Images/Shutterstock.com. P140 - Kiselev Andrey Valerevich/Shutterstock.com. P141 - Kiselev Andrey Valerevich/Shutterstock.com. P142 - Kiselev Andrey Valerevich/Shutterstock.com; Pixotico/Shutterstock.com. P143 - Kiselev Andrey Valerevich/Shutterstock.com; georgemphotoValerevich/Shutterstock.com; tkemot/Shutterstock.com; Keith Publicover/Shutterstock.com; Allies Interactive/Shutterstock.com; Zoom Team/Shutterstock.com; Jason Stitt/Shutterstock.com; StockLite/Shutterstock.com. P144 - Kiselev Andrey Valerevich/Shutterstock.com; Pixotico/Shutterstock.com; georgemphotoValerevich/Shutterstock.com; tkemot/Shutterstock.com; Keith Publicover/Shutterstock.com; Allies Interactive/Shutterstock.com; Zoom Team/Shutterstock.com; Jason Stitt/Shutterstock.com; StockLite/Shutterstock.com. P146 - With thanks to serif: Serif, the Serif logo, PagePlus and all other Serif product names are trademarks or registered trademarks of Serif (Europe) Ltd. P148 - Kiselev Andrey Valerevich/Shutterstock.com; Pixotico/Shutterstock.com; georgemphotoValerevich/Shutterstock.com; tkemot/Shutterstock.com; Keith Publicover/Shutterstock.com; Allies Interactive/Shutterstock.com; Zoom Team/Shutterstock.com; Jason Stitt/Shutterstock.com; StockLite/Shutterstock.com. P149 - Stock image/Shutterstock.com; Iakov Filimonov/Shutterstock.com; Jesus Cervantes/Shutterstock.com. P150 - Tiplyashina Evgeniya/Shutterstock.com; concept w/Shutterstock.com; iamshutter/Shutterstock.com; 3dmask/Shutterstock.com; Oleksiy Mark/Shutterstock.com; Rafa Irusta/Shutterstock.com. P156 - elenabo/Shutterstock.com; ekler/Shutterstock.com. P159 - Alex West/Shutterstock. P160 - With thanks to Daniel Lockhart. P162 - Velychko/Shutterstock.com. P166 - With thanks to Archie MacFarlane Photography www.archiemacfarlane.com; Andrey Armyagov/Shutterstock.com; dwphotos/Shutterstock.com; donatas/Shutterstock.com; alex west/Shutterstock.com; TADDEUS/Shutterstock.com; graphixmania/Shutterstock.com. P167 - llaszlo/Shutterstock.com. P169 - coka/Shutterstock.com; Milles Studio/Shutterstock.com; coka/Shutterstock.com; coka/Shutterstock.com. P171 - JIANG HONGYAN/Shutterstock.com. P178 victorsaboya/Shutterstock.com. P181 - P193 With thanks to Richard Smith. P195 - Ostill/Shutterstock.com; P195 - Jason Salmon(assistant)/Shutterstock.com; P197 - ostill/Shutterstock.com. P217 - Ysbrand Cosijn/Shutterstock.com; lithian/Shutterstock.com; CURAphotography/Shutterstock.com; Undrey/Shutterstock.com; CURAphotography/Shutterstock.com; Cara-Foto/Shutterstock.com; CURAphotography/Shutterstock.com; Evgeniya Porechenskaya/Shutterstock.com; mimagephotography/Shutterstock.com; GaudiLab/Shutterstock.com; ostill/Shutterstock.com; R.Iegosyn/Shutterstock.com; FeyginFoto/Shutterstock.com; ostill/Shutterstock.com. P219 - CURAphotography/Shutterstock.com; Evgeniya Porechenskaya/Shutterstock.com; ostill/Shutterstock.com. P221 - Evgeniya Porechenskaya/Shutterstock.com; CURAphotography/Shutterstock.com; ostill/Shutterstock.com; WMIX/Thinkstock.com; Jason Salmon/Shutterstock.com Evgeniya Porechenskaya/Shutterstock.com; CURAphotography/Shutterstock.com; ostill/Shutterstock.com; Jason Salmon/Shutterstock.com; Elnur/Shutterstock.com. Viorel Sima/Shutterstock.com; WMIX/Thinkstock.com with extra special thanks to Richard Smith for his creative genius and to Mary Linton and Bryony Hunter for putting up with this project for far, far too long...

First published in 2016 by:
Bright Red Publishing Ltd
1 Torphichen Street
Edinburgh
EH3 8HX

Copyright © Bright Red Publishing Ltd 2016
Cover image © Caleb Rutherford

The rights of Peter Linton and Scott Hunter to be identified as the author of this work have been asserted by them in accordance with Sections 77 and 78 of the Copyright, Designs and Patents Act 1988.

A CIP record for this book is available from the British Library.

ISBN 978-1-906736-92-7

Printed and bound in the UK by Charlesworth Press.

To access the worksheets and discover more about Graphic Communication and a range of design, engineering and technology subjects, visit www.DesignClass.co.uk